Approaches to Teaching the Novels of Samuel Richardson

Approaches to Teaching
World Literature

Joseph Gibaldi, series editor

For a complete listing of titles,
see the last pages of this book.

Approaches to Teaching the Novels of Samuel Richardson

Edited by

Lisa Zunshine

and

Jocelyn Harris

The Modern Language Association of America
New York   2006

For information about obtaining permission to reprint material from MLA book
publications, send your request by mail (see address below), e-mail
(permissions@mla.org), or fax (646-458-0030).

Library of Congress Cataloging-in-Publication Data

Approaches to teaching the novels of Samuel Richardson/
edited by Lisa Zunshine and Jocelyn Harris
p. cm. — (Approaches to teaching word literature ; 87)
Includes bibliographical references and index.
ISBN-13: 978-0-87352-922-8 (alk. paper)
ISBN-10: 0-87352-922-7 (alk. paper)
ISBN-13: 978-0-87352-923-5 (pbk. : alk. paper)
ISBN-10: 0-87352-923-5 (pbk. : alk. paper)
1. Richardson Samuel, 1689–1761—Study and teaching.
2. Epistolary fiction, English—Study and teaching.
I. Zunshine, Lisa. II. Harris, Jocelyn. III. Series.
PR3667.A67 2005
823'.5—dc22   2005026832
ISSN 1059-1133

Cover illustration of the paperback edition:
Mr. Richardson Reading the MS History of Sir. Cha. Grandison at North End, by Susanna
Highmore Duncombe. 1751. The Pierpont Morgan Library, New York. MA 1024.

Published by The Modern Language Association of America
26 Broadway, New York, New York 10004-1789
www.mla.org

CONTENTS

PREFACE TO THE SERIES

In *The Art of Teaching* Gilbert Highet wrote, "Bad teaching wastes a great deal of effort, and spoils many lives which might have been full of energy and happiness." All too many teachers have failed in their work, Highet argued, simply "because they have not thought about it." We hope that the Approaches to Teaching World Literature series, sponsored by the Modern Language Association's Publications Committee, will not only improve the craft—as well as the art—of teaching but also encourage serious and continuing discussion of the aims and methods of teaching literature.

The principal objective of the series is to collect within each volume different points of view on teaching a specific literary work, a literary tradition, or a writer widely taught at the undergraduate level. The preparation of each volume begins with a wide-ranging survey of instructors, thus enabling us to include in the volume the philosophies and approaches, thoughts and methods of scores of experienced teachers. The result is a sourcebook of material, information, and ideas on teaching the subject of the volume to undergraduates.

The series is intended to serve nonspecialists as well as specialists, inexperienced as well as experienced teachers, graduate students who wish to learn effective ways of teaching as well as senior professors who wish to compare their own approaches with the approaches of colleagues in other schools. Of course, no volume in the series can ever substitute for erudition, intelligence, creativity, and sensitivity in teaching. We hope merely that each book will point readers in useful directions; at most each will offer only a first step in the long journey to successful teaching.

Joseph Gibaldi
Series Editor

PREFACE TO THE VOLUME

"Students of Richardson have all been fortunate in their instruction," writes Carol Houlihan Flynn (xiii–xiv), reflecting on Richardson's ability to enthrall and exasperate anew each generation of literary scholars and on the richness of the teaching tradition engendered by critical readings of his work. The goal of this volume is to capture the best of this tradition and to reintroduce Richardson into the undergraduate curriculum as one of the most exciting and pedagogically rewarding of English writers.

The steadily growing critical engagement with his "troubling fables" (Rivero, Preface vii) confirms that Richardson warrants such a reintroduction. Writing in 1989, Margaret Anne Doody and Peter Sabor pointed out that since the late 1960s, Richardson had moved to the foreground of literary criticism, becoming a subject of "some thirty full-length studies, together with hundreds of articles, chapters in books, doctoral dissertations, and master's theses" (Introduction 4). Today, scholarly interest in his work is far from abating. The period 1990 through 2000 saw publication of more than forty monographs that either focus exclusively on Richardson or consider his novels at length, bearing out Pat Rogers's assertion that "however we look at the matter, Richardson is at the centre of eighteenth-century writing" (222).

Recent critical trends have proved beneficial for Richardson. Albert J. Rivero notes that because of the

> apparent duplicities of his fictional representations, Richardson has appealed to deconstructionists and reader-response critics, and because of his concerns with issues of class and gender, he has attracted Marxist and feminist critics. Indeed, feminist criticism . . . has transformed Richardson into the preeminent eighteenth-century British novelist, whose "feminism" has been hotly debated. (Preface vii)

As Siobhan Kilfeather points out, many critics, including William B. Warner, Terry Castle, and Terry Eagleton, have found "that writing about Richardson is such a gripping and partisan activity that one is provoked into battle with other critics" (254). Richardson might well have delighted in having caused such battles, since he confessed that he wrote precisely to provoke his readers into passionate debates about his characters' behavior, debates in which he could participate, draw his friends out, and instruct them in "correct" readings of his novels. That Richardson continues to vex and polarize his readers today provides the best testimony to his literary and cultural vitality.

Despite the thriving state of Richardson studies, a discrepancy exists between the wealth of scholarly inquiry into his work and the scarcity of publications about the teaching of his novels. Sadly, Richardson appears to be a case in point for Robert Markley's observation that "given the development of eighteenth-century studies over the last two decades, there is still comparatively little attention paid to the time and effort that most of us devote to teaching the literature of the period" (665). Among numerous articles on Richardson that have appeared since the 1970s, only a few address pedagogical issues. In those that do, Richardson's prospects in the classroom appear far from rosy. *Clarissa* is pronounced difficult and too long and *Sir Charles Grandison* plainly unfit for the undergraduate curriculum—views implicitly confirmed, until 2001, by the out-of-print status of the authoritative Oxford University Press edition of *Grandison* from 1972. *Pamela* does not fare much better. It is typically referred to as a novel that must be taught for its crucial role in English literary history but that consistently fails to engage students because of its outmoded obsession with female chastity.

Such dismissive remarks fail to reflect what is actually happening in the classroom. As Florian Stuber brilliantly demonstrated in his account of teaching *Pamela* at the Fashion Institute of Technology, Richardson's first novel can and does have a powerful effect on undergraduates. The so-called unteachable *Grandison* (the Oxford edition, reproduced under license by Otago University Print) is also taught successfully, both in its full length and in substantial excerpts, in institutions ranging from small liberal arts colleges to state universities. Finally, *Clarissa*, Richardson's masterpiece, has been going through a pedagogical renaissance. It is regularly assigned, unabridged, as the main text in a variety of undergraduate and graduate courses, offering students a powerful lens through which they can consider "still prevalent psychological, sexual, social, economic, and of course literary paradigms at the catastrophic moment of their formation" (Lewis, in this volume).

In developing a volume on Richardson in the MLA Approaches to Teaching series, the editors thus aimed to encourage more instructors to teach the novels that are rumored to be too difficult or too long for undergraduates, such as *Clarissa* and *Grandison*; to rediscover the stirring classroom potential of *Pamela*; and to show how advanced critical discussion of Richardson lends itself to creative pedagogical practices. We asked the volume's contributors to be realistic about the feelings that the prospect of reading a 1,500-page epistolary novel may provoke in even the most dedicated English major and to be specific in describing strategies that they use to make Richardson exciting for students.

This volume reflects the demographic and theoretical diversity of eighteenth-century studies, for contributors include both seasoned Richardsonians and their younger colleagues and represent a broad range of critical and pedagogical approaches. Topics include feminist, historicist, anthropological, and cultural studies approaches; strategies for making *Clarissa* and *Grandison* a focal point of a course versus incorporating these novels into an eighteenth-century survey course, a genre course (such as Studies in the Novel), or a special-topics course; teaching Richardson's longer novels to different student populations (for example, in state schools and in private colleges) as well as in different calendar systems (for example, the quarter, the semester, and the year-long system); and the use of Internet resources.

The "Materials" part of the volume lists currently available editions of *Pamela*, *Clarissa*, and *Grandison*; discusses background publications, such as responses to Richardson's novels by his contemporaries; and enumerates critical works figuring prominently in the survey of scholars carried out before the publication of this volume. This part also tackles issues raised by the survey and provides a short catalog of online resources.

The "Approaches" part is divided into five sections. The introductory section explains how the essays in this volume can help the instructor deal with issues that, as the survey shows, recur in a Richardsonian classroom. Such issues include both the challenges (e.g., the difficulties posed by the length of Richardson's novels, the problem of students' skepticism, the subject of Clarissa's and Pamela's intense religiosity) and the topics that remain at the forefront of Richardson criticism and lend themselves to productive classroom discussions (e.g., Richardson's feminism and the aesthetic value of his revisions). The second section, "Backgrounds," features three essays that address such overarching themes as the textual instability of *Pamela* and *Clarissa*, the significance of Richardson's printing career for the study of his fiction, and the pedagogical uses and current availability of his private correspondence. The remaining three parts focus on *Pamela*, *Clarissa*, and *Sir Charles Grandison*, a division primarily of convenience and one that should not prevent an instructor from cross-applying approaches from sections dedicated to different novels.

Essays in this volume, unless otherwise noted, quote from Thomas Keymer and Alice Wakely's edition of *Pamela*; Angus Ross's edition of *Clarissa*; and Jocelyn Harris's edition of *Sir Charles Grandison*; citing Harris's part numbers, not Richardson's volume numbers.

The editors are deeply grateful to the participants of the survey, whose names appear at the end of the volume, for their generous and detailed responses; to Sonia Kane, MLA acquisitions editor, for her careful guidance of this project from its inception; to Angela Gibson, MLA assistant editor, for her thorough copyediting of the manuscript; and to the anonymous reviewers of the volume for their helpful and positive feedback.

LZ

Part One

MATERIALS

Primary Works

Editions of *Pamela* currently available to instructors are those prepared by Thomas Keymer and Alice Wakely; by Peter Sabor; by William M. Sale, Jr.; by T. C. Duncan Eaves and Ben D. Kimpel; as well as by S. Field, who has brought together under one cover *Pamela* and *Shamela*. For a comparative analysis of different editions of *Pamela*, see Keymer's essay in this volume. Essays by Janet Aikins Yount and Patricia Brückmann in this volume touch briefly on the topic.

Currently available editions of *Clarissa* are Angus Ross's *Clarissa; or The History of a Young Lady*, based on Richardson's first edition of the novel (1747–48), and George Sherburn's abridged *Clarissa*. A facsimile copy of Richardson's third, revised edition (1751), prepared by Florian Stuber for The *Clarissa* Project, is now out of print, although survey participants report using excerpts from privately owned or library copies to supplement the more regularly assigned Ross and Sherburn editions. For example, survey participants often add to Ross's edition Lovelace's letter about his plot to kidnap Anna and Mrs. Howe, from Richardson's third, revised edition. The surveyed instructors were unanimous in considering Sherburn's edition inferior to the point of being detrimental to students' appreciation of Richardson, although some of them pointed out that unless one has the time and energy to put together one's own abridgment, Sherburn remains the only feasible choice for those not ready to teach the unabridged book. A new abridgment of the novel, based on Richardson's third, revised edition, is being prepared for Broadview Press by Toni Bowers and John Richetti.

Ross's edition works well in the classroom, with two minor caveats. First, the surveyed instructors find less than helpful the absence of any volume breaks in it. They observe that students feel intimidated by what appears to be a continuous 1,500-page block of text. This problem can be solved, however, by asking them to mark the original volume boundaries, as Jayne Lewis suggests in her essay for this book. Second, survey participants regretted that the plot is given away on the back cover, though they also observed that students often do not even notice that tell-tale blurb. If they do, their dismay can be redirected into a discussion of what it means not to read *Clarissa* for the plot. Moreover, perhaps in response to these concerns, Penguin has recently come up with a new cover for Ross's edition. It features Allan Ramsay's *Sir Edmund and Lady Turner* on the front (instead of Joseph Highmore's *The Harlowe Family*) and different back cover copy. Whereas the Highmore cover informs its readers outright that Clarissa "falls prey to Lovelace, is raped and dies," the more circumspect Ramsay cover tells us that Lovelace "proves himself to be an untrustworthy rake whose vague promises of marriage are accompanied by unwelcome and increasingly brutal sexual advances."

The History of Sir Charles Grandison, edited by Jocelyn Harris for Oxford University Press and first published in 1972, has been reproduced under license from Oxford and may be ordered from Otago University Print: contact Steve Williams at steve.williams@stonebow.otago.ac.nz. This valuable edition had been out of print for more than twenty years. Whether it will stay in print and regain its place in the curriculum as one of the most influential books of the eighteenth century is now up to instructors. We certainly hope that this Approaches volume's essays on teaching *Grandison* will inspire more Richardsonians to introduce their students to this entertaining and many-layered novel.

Other works by Richardson, such as *The Apprentice's Vade Mecum; or, Young Man's Pocket Companion* (1734), *The Familiar Letters on Important Occasions* (1741), and *Pamela II* (1741; see *Pamela's Conduct in High Life*), are currently out of print and available only through libraries and online used-book retailers. The full text of Richardson's fourth, revised edition of *The Familiar Letters* (1750) is, however, accessible through Chadwyck's *Literature Online* database (*LION*), as are Richardson's first and third, revised editions of *Clarissa*; his first and sixth, revised editions of *Pamela*; and the first edition of *Grandison*. New and fully annotated editions of the complete works and all the correspondence are currently being prepared as *The Cambridge Edition of the Works and Correspondence of Samuel Richardson*, in twenty-five volumes. The general editors are Keymer and Sabor, the textual editor is Alex Pettit, and the volume editors make up a large international team. The first volumes should appear in about 2009.

Background Materials

Richardson's letters appear in a wide variety of sources, ranging from the six volumes of *The Correspondence of Samuel Richardson*, edited by Anna Laetitia Barbauld, to *Selected Letters of Samuel Richardson*, edited by John Carroll (see Sabor in this volume).

Instructors will find invaluable two ambitious collections of background materials for *Clarissa* and *Pamela*: the three volumes of *Samuel Richardson's Published Commentary on* Clarissa, *1747–1765* and the six volumes of *The* Pamela *Controversy: Criticisms and Adaptations of Samuel Richardson's* Pamela, *1740–1750* (Keymer and Sabor). The *Published Commentary* includes all that Richardson himself published on *Clarissa* and material by such eighteenth-century authors as William Warburton, Albrecht von Haller, and Aaron Hill, together with the wealth of Richardson's prefatory materials and responses to his critics. It also includes *Letters and Passages Restored from the Original Manuscripts of the History of* Clarissa (1751) and *A Collection of Moral and Instructive Senti-*

ments, *Maxims, Cautions and Reflections Contained in the Histories of* Pamela, Clarissa *and* Sir Charles Grandison (1755).

The Pamela *Controversy* features prefatory and closing essays from different editions of *Pamela* as well as numerous parodies, spin-offs, and unauthorized revisions of the original novel, such as Henry Fielding's *Shamela* (1741); Josiah Relph's "Wrote after Reading *Pamela*" (1747); notorious anonymous publications such as "Pamela the Second" (1742) and *Pamela Censured* (1741); J. W.'s *Pamela; or, The Fair Impostor* (1743); Charles Povey's *The Virgin in Eden* (1741); Eliza Haywood's *Anti-Pamela* (1741); and John Kelly's *Pamela's Conduct in High Life* (1741). Included are dramatic and operatic versions of Richardson's bestseller, such as Henry Giffard's *Pamela: A Comedy* (1741); Joseph Dorman's *Pamela; or, Virtue Rewarded, An Opera* (1742); and Carlo Goldoni's *Pamela, A Comedy* (1750). Also collected are visual representations, such as John Carwitham's engravings from *The Life of Pamela* (1741), Hubert François Gravelot and Francis Hayman's engravings from the octavo edition (1742), Hayman's "Pamela Fleeing from Lady Davers" (c. 1741–42), Gravelot's "Pamela and the Fortune-Teller" (c. 1740), and Joseph Highmore's engravings of scenes from *Pamela* (1745). Both collections are accompanied by introductory and explanatory notes by prominent of the eighteenth century scholar.

Richardson Criticism

The following biographies of Richardson have been published to date: Brian W. Downs's *Richardson* (1928); Alan D. McKillop's *Samuel Richardson, Printer and Novelist* (1936); William Merritt Sale, Jr.'s *Samuel Richardson: Master Printer* (1950); and T. C. Duncan Eaves and Ben D. Kimpel's *Samuel Richardson: A Biography* (1971). Tom Keymer is writing a new biography for Blackwell.

Richardson is a subject of seven wide-ranging collections of essays: Carroll's *Samuel Richardson: A Collection of Critical Essay*; Valerie Grosvenor Myer's *Samuel Richardson: Passion and Prudence*; Margaret Anne Doody and Peter Sabor's *Samuel Richardson: Tercentenary Essays*; Albert J. Rivero's *New Essays on Samuel Richardson*; Carol Houlihan Flynn and Edward Copeland's edited volume, *Clarissa and Her Readers: New Essays for the* Clarissa *Project*; David Blewett's *Passion and Virtue: Essays on the Novels of Samuel Richardson* and the special issue of *Studies in the Literary Imagination*, edited by Murray L. Brown and entitled *Refiguring Richardson's* Clarissa.

Given the burgeoning state of Richardson scholarship, it is impossible to list here all pertinent monographs and uncollected essays. For that, instructors should turn to individual essays in this volume that discuss critical materials

relevant to their methodology. In compiling the following list, the editors have
relied primarily on the materials of the survey.

Important book-length studies of Richardson include Cynthia Griffin Wolff's
Samuel Richardson and the Eighteenth-Century Puritan Character; Mark
Kinkead-Weekes's *Samuel Richardson: Dramatic Novelist*; Doody's *A Natural Passion: A Study of the Novels of Samuel Richardson*; William B. Warner's
Reading Clarissa: *The Struggles of Interpretation* and its polemical rejoinders,
Terry Castle's *Clarissa's Ciphers: Meaning and Disruption in Richardson's* Clarissa and Terry Eagleton's *The Rape of Clarissa*; Flynn's *Samuel Richardson: A
Man of Letters*; Christina Marsden Gillis's *The Paradox of Privacy: Epistolary
Form in* Clarissa; Sylvia Kasey Marks's Sir Charles Grandison: *The Compleat
Conduct Book*; Jocelyn Harris's *Samuel Richardson*; Thomas Beebee's *Clarissa
on the Continent: Translation and Seduction*; Tassie Gwilliam's *Samuel Richardson's Fictions of Gender*; Keymer's *Richardson's* Clarissa *and the Eighteenth-
Century Reader*; Lois E. Bueler's Clarissa's *Plots*; Donnalee Frega's *Speaking
in Hunger: Gender, Discourse, and Consumption in* Clarissa; Janine Barchas's
The Annotations in Lady Bradshaigh's Copy of Clarissa; Ewha Chung's *Samuel Richardson's New Nation: Paragons of the Domestic Sphere and "Native"
Virtue*; and Keith Maslen's *Samuel Richardson of London, Printer: A Study of
His Printing Based on Ornament Use and Business Accounts*. The books by
Kinkead-Weekes, Doody (*Natural Passion*), and Harris (*Samuel Richardson*)
were recommended by several survey participants as particularly valuable for
instructors teaching Richardson for the first time.

Many of the useful background studies dealing with eighteenth-century literature devote one chapter or several to Richardson's fiction. Listed in order of
publication, they include Dorothy Van Ghent's *The English Novel: Form and
Function*; Ian Watt's *The Rise of the Novel*; Robert F. Brissenden's *Virtue in
Distress: Studies in the Novel of Sentiment from Richardson to Sade*; Nancy K.
Miller's *The Heroine's Text: Readings in the French and English Novel, 1722–
1782*; Lennard Davis's *Factual Fictions: The Origins of the English Novel*; Leopold Damrosch, Jr.'s *God's Plots and Man's Stories*; Robert A. Erickson's, *Mother
Midnight: Birth, Sex, and Fate in Eighteenth-Century Fiction (Defoe, Richardson, and Sterne)*; Linda Kaufmann's *Discourses of Desire: Gender, Genre, and
Epistolary Fictions*; Michael McKeon's *The Origins of the English Novel 1600–
1740*; Nancy Armstrong's *Desire and Domestic Fiction: A Political History of
the Novel*; John Bender's *Imagining the Penitentiary: Fiction and the Architecture of Mind in Eighteenth-Century England*; Terry Lovell's *Consuming Fiction*; Carol Kay's *Political Constructions: Defoe, Richardson, and Sterne in Relation to Hobbes, Hume, and Burke*; John Mullan's *Sentiment and Sociability: The
Language of Feeling in the Eighteenth Century*; Patricia Meyer Spacks's *Desire
and Truth: Functions of Plot in Eighteenth-Century English Novels*; Madeleine
Kahn's *Narrative Transvestism: Rhetoric and Gender in the Eighteenth-Century
English Novel*; G. J. Barker-Benfield's *The Culture of Sensibility: Sex and Soci-*

ety in Eighteenth-Century Britain; John P. Zomchick's *Family and the Law in Eighteenth-Century Fiction: The Public Conscience in the Private Sphere*; Ann Jessie Van Sant's *Eighteenth-Century Sensibility and the Novel: The Senses in Social Context*; Jonathan Lamb's *The Rhetoric of Suffering: Reading the Book of Job in the Eighteenth Century*; Robert A. Erickson's *The Language of the Heart, 1600–1750*; *The Cambridge Companion to the Eighteenth-Century Novel*, edited by John Richetti; Elizabeth Heckendorn Cook's *Epistolary Bodies: Gender and Genre in the Eighteenth-Century Republic of Letters*; Everett Zimmerman's *The Boundaries of Fiction: History and the Eighteenth-Century British Novel*; Margaret Anne Doody's *The True Story of the Novel*; William B. Warner's *Licensing Entertainment: The Elevation of Novel Reading in Britain, 1684–1750*; April London's *Women and Property in the Eighteenth-Century English Novel*; Helene Moglen's *The Trauma of Gender: A Feminist Theory of the English Novel*; and Janine Barchas's *Graphic Design, Print Culture, and the Eighteenth-Century Novel*.

The following essays have been listed by the survey participants as particularly helpful in their classroom discussions of Richardson: Christopher Hill's "Clarissa Harlowe and Her Times"; Judith Wilt's "He Could Go No Farther: A Modest Proposal about Lovelace and Clarissa"; John Traugott's "*Clarissa*'s Richardson: An Essay to Find the Reader"; Sue Warrick Doederlein's "*Clarissa* in the Hands of the Critics"; John A. Dussinger's "Love and Consanguinity in Richardson's Novels"; Margaret Anne Doody's "Saying 'No' Saying 'Yes': The Novels of Samuel Richardson"; Anthony E. Simpson's "'The Blackmail Myth' and the Prosecution of Rape and Its Attempt in 18th-Century London"; Frances Ferguson's "Rape and the Rise of the Novel"; Kristina Straub's "Reconstructing the Gaze: Voyeurism in Richardson's *Pamela*"; Christopher Flint's "The Anxiety of Affluence: Family and Class (Dis)order in *Pamela; or, Virtue Rewarded*"; Ann Louise Kibbie's "Sentimental Properties: *Pamela* and *Memoirs of a Woman of Pleasure*"; Lois A. Chaber's "A 'Fatal Attraction'? The BBC and *Clarissa*" and "'This Affecting Subject': An 'Interested' Reading of Childbearing in Two Novels by Samuel Richardson"; Liz Bellamy's "Private Virtues, Public Vices: Commercial Morality in the Novels of Samuel Richardson"; Mary Vermillion's "*Clarissa* and the Marriage Act"; Hilary Schor's "Notes of a Libertine Daughter: *Clarissa*, Feminism, and the Rise of the Novel"; Patricia Brückmann's "Desdemona's Strawberries and Clementina's Ark: Text, Textiles, and Scripture in *Sir Charles Grandison*"; and Cynthia Wall's "The Spaces of *Clarissa* in Text and Film."

Survey Issues

Richardson's novels, because of their popularity and their influential role in the rise of the novel of subjectivity, sit comfortably in a wide variety of courses, whether novel courses; period courses; cultural studies courses; or theme courses on gender, sexuality, and narrative innovation. Both *Clarissa* and *Pamela* are regularly taught in eighteenth-century novel courses, in eighteenth-century survey courses, and in upper-division and graduate special-topic seminars, such as Historicizing Gender and Sexuality in English Literature, 1660–1750; Women's Narratives; Eighteenth-Century England and the Colonies; Biography and Autobiography; Richardson's *Clarissa* and the Theory of the Novel; Sensibility, Enlightenment, and Literary History; and Richardson and Fielding. Instructors typically allot two weeks for teaching *Pamela* and from two to three weeks for the abridged *Clarissa*. The unabridged *Clarissa* takes anywhere from four weeks, in a particularly cooperative graduate seminar, to half a term, the whole term, or even the whole year for both undergraduate and graduate courses.

Grandison is taught in courses on the eighteenth-century novel and in special-topics courses, such as Sentimentalism, The Poetics of Space, The Comedy of Manners, and Richardson's *Sir Charles Grandison*. The time allotted ranges from one week (when only excerpts from the novel are taught) to two weeks (when only part 1 from Harris's tripartite edition is taught), six weeks, or the whole semester (when the entire novel is on the syllabus). Several survey participants have taught courses combining *Pamela* and *Clarissa*, and two of them have taught all three novels in graduate courses focusing on Richardson.

Pamela II is taught predominantly in excerpts and in conjunction with *Pamela*. For example, one survey participant made a group of students responsible for reading passages from *Pamela II* and contemporary responses to it, then for presenting their findings to their classmates. The ensuing discussion focused on such issues as critical and popular reception of the text; Richardson's response to the text's reception; the concept of the sequel, particularly as considered in the context of the early modern novel; and the effects of sequels on original texts in the eighteenth century and today.

The Apprentice's Vade Mecum and *Familiar Letters* serve as background materials in a broad variety of courses featuring any of the three main novels. For example, one instructor begins her discussion of Richardson with a short selection from *Familiar Letters* containing the preface and a few businesslike form letters (two letters of recommendation [letters 31 and 32] and a series of letters requesting a balance of accounts [letters 42–44]). When teaching *Pamela*, this instructor ends the unit with letters that gave rise to *Pamela* (138 and 139); when teaching *Clarissa*, she focuses on the letter describing a young woman's close call in a brothel (letter 62).

To keep students up to date in their weekly readings of the longer novels, many instructors require them to compose journal entries after each reading installment. One instructor alerts her undergraduates early on to Warner's argument that *Clarissa* is a compilation of warring viewpoints and ideological agendas and that Clarissa's letters to Anna can be read as part of a project of glorious self-vindication ultimately embodied in the book Clarissa regards as her (*Reading* Clarissa). The instructor therefore tells her students to entitle their journals "Clarissa's 'True' Diary," asking them to react to each of their reading assignments with a first-person entry. By taking this point of view, students can presumably express Clarissa's "true" feelings, unmarred by her need to "perform" herself—ostensibly for Anna, but, in the long run, for a general reader. This journal writing has both advantages and liabilities. It allows the instructor to monitor students' progress because they can neither rewrite nor respond to the character's sentiments in a meaningful way unless they have done the required reading and thought through it. Students also use the ideas developed in their journals as starting points both for their classroom discussions and longer papers. What makes this journal exercise challenging is the sheer emotional difficulty of sustaining a "suspicious" reading of Clarissa's letters to Anna. Inevitably, students begin to elaborate on Clarissa's feelings in her "true" diary rather than reveal the events purportedly glossed over in her official accounts of what is going on. At the same time, however, although it seems easier to resist Lovelace's version of events than Clarissa's, the challenge of resisting both versions can lead the class into productive conversations about emotional identification with the protagonist as a constitutive feature of any novel and about the development of the literary tradition of the unreliable narrator.

Another helpful strategy for keeping up with *Clarissa* is self-timed reading. Although this method was suggested by a survey participant who has taught the abridged version, it can also work for the unabridged novel. As the instructor reported, *Clarissa* was scheduled toward the end of the course, between Alexander Pope's "Eloisa to Abelard" and *The Rape of the Lock* and Samuel Johnson's *Rasselas*. Students were expected to have read the book before they began discussing it in class. To encourage prompt reading, the instructor asked students during the first week of class to time themselves reading the first ten pages of the novel. As part of an in-class exercise, she then had each student multiply the number of minutes by fifty (10 multiplied by 50 equals, roughly, 500 pages). They divided that number by ten to get to the approximate number of minutes they would have to schedule each week during the ten weeks before they began discussing *Clarissa*. Reading notes were required for all texts assigned in the course, and, as the semester progressed, the instructor periodically checked progress on the *Clarissa* notes.

On the whole, the survey participants observed that although students can be initially intimidated by the length of Richardson's novels, especially *Sir Charles Grandison* and the unabridged *Clarissa*, some time into the semester their anxiety often gives way to a feeling of accomplishment. Instructors speak of students' brandishing Ross's tome (the 1985 edition) in front of their incredulous and impressed peers, proud about having read and understood a 1,500-page-long eighteenth-century novel. Similarly, in the case of *Grandison*, David Hensley tells about a student writing in the course evaluation: "I do feel somewhat proud to have completed the most infamously boring novel in English letters (of course, all of us who have read it know this judgment to be false!)."

Other pedagogical challenges involved in teaching Richardson include students' skepticism about his "perfect" heroines, their difficulty in grasping the significance of religion for Pamela and Clarissa (both issues are addressed in the introduction to the "Approaches" part), their resistance to the slow development of the plot or what they perceive as a downright lack of plot, and the trouble they have keeping up with the opposing narrative perspectives in *Clarissa*.

Not surprisingly, many of these challenges turn out to be ultimately rewarding. For instance, survey participants report that encouraging students to articulate their skepticism about the perfection of Pamela and Clarissa can lead to stirring debates about Richardson's "feminism." Similarly, conversations may begin by trying to understand why modern readers, despite their living in a culture permeated by electronic letter writing and cinematic experimentation with narrative point of view, still feel alienated by epistolary narrative in general and *Clarissa's* multiple perspectives in particular. Such conversations offer effective pathways into a discussion of the novel as genre: its much debated cultural history, its special status among other representational forms, and its construction of a responsive reader.

One survey participant suggests responding to students' complaints about the passivity of Richardson's most wronged heroine by introducing them early to Warner's *Reading* Clarissa, which forestalls such responses. She reports that one of her graduate students, who initially disliked Clarissa for "doing nothing" except writing and complaining, began to appreciate Clarissa as an active shaper of her own story after she read Warner's chapter "Building a Book into an Empire of Meaning." Assigning Warner alongside the first volumes of *Clarissa* thus encourages students to pay more attention to the style of narrative, and especially to textual details enhancing Clarissa's authorial agency—even if doing so gives away parts of the plot.

The assignments characterized as effective by survey participants explored the meaning of eighteenth-century concepts like duty, obedience to parents and masters, improvement, gentleman, lady, virtue, prudence, fortitude, industry, civility, decorum, and punctilio. Another successful assignment focused students' attention on specific details, asking them, for example, to figure out how long it takes after the death of Mr. B.'s mother before Mr. B. makes his first pass and why the amount of time goes so easily unnoticed. Yet another called for students to map the movements of Pamela and Clarissa in order to emphasize Richardson's use of symbolic geography, an endeavor that can draw on such studies as Edward Copeland's "Remapping London: *Clarissa* and the Woman in the Window" and on Franco Moretti's *Atlas of the European Novel, 1800–1900* (a book that does not deal with Richardson, but whose analysis of the patterns of mapping the urban space in novels can be profitably applied to *Clarissa*).

Some instructors reported that writing letters in the voices of Richardson's characters works well for diverse populations of students. *Grandison* is particularly rewarding in this respect because of its easy, engaging style and the appealing spunk of both Harriet (especially in the early volumes) and Charlotte. *Pamela*'s complexities are also fruitful. By asking students to write a letter in Pamela's voice after they have finished reading the novel, instructors make them poignantly aware of her shift of tone once her virtue is "rewarded." Students acknowledge the challenge faced by Richardson at that narrative juncture; they realize that, in order to write convincing letters, either they have to invent more struggles and afflictions for Pamela, for example, showing her jealous of her husband's attentions to another woman at a party (a useful prefigurement of *Pamela II*), or they have to effusively comment on her ever-increasing happiness expressed in a style that slides into self-congratulatory smugness. A discussion-provoking variation on the letter-writing assignment in a course featuring several eighteenth-century novels is to ask students to write a letter from Moll Flanders to Clarissa or from Emma to Pamela. This task throws into stark relief the importance of class affiliations for the eighteenth-century narrative voice.

Survey participants strongly recommended introducing students to the works of William Hogarth and Highmore to give them a sense of the material world of eighteenth-century England. They differed, however, about the role that the BBC *Clarissa* should play in the classroom. Whereas most agreed that it helped students visualize everyday eighteenth-century life, several instructors were concerned about its hint at incestuous attraction between James Harlowe and Arabella Harlowe, which is introduced to provide a motivation for James's violent and seemingly inexplicable hostility to Clarissa. At the same time, survey respondents admit that the contrast between the simplified adaptation and Richardson's complex original prompts lively discussions, especially if students watch the movie after they have read the book and some critical accounts of it, having become, so to speak, experts on *Clarissa*. Chaber's essay, "A 'Fatal Attraction'? The BBC and *Clarissa*," provides a helpful framework for such discussions.

One survey participant felt strongly that Stephen Frears's *Dangerous Liaisons* represents a better alternative to the BBC *Clarissa* because it captures more of the spirit of Richardson's novel. Another suggested having students watch the BBC *Tom Jones* along with reading *Clarissa* to make them aware of the delicate line between the comic and tragic potential of the eighteenth-century plot about a young woman who runs away from her family to avoid marrying a man whom she finds repulsive.

All survey participants sounded enthusiastic about their experience teaching Richardson. Many commented on their surprise in discovering, on first undertaking *Clarissa* or *Sir Charles Grandison*, how effective these novels can be in drawing students into heated and even personally revealing debates about the "perfect" heroes and heroines, the relationship between parents and children, standards of honesty in men and women, the relation between the individual and society, as well as about the permutations of literary taste both in the eighteenth century and today.

Online Resources

For a full version of *Pamela, Clarissa, Sir Charles Grandison*, and *Familiar Letters*, see the section entitled *Eighteenth-Century Fiction (1700–1780)* at the *Literature Online* site (http://lion.chadwyck.com).

For an extensive collection of eighteenth-century resources, with links to Richardson sites that include John A. Dussinger's "Selected Bibliography: Samuel Richardson," see *Eighteenth Century Resources*, maintained by Jack Lynch (http://www.c18.rutgers.edu/biblio/richardson/html).

For a description of the BBC version of *Clarissa*, with Saskia Wickham as Clarissa and Sean Bean as Lovelace, see www.compleatseanbean.com/clari.html. A videocassette or DVD of the movie is available through online shopping sites.

For sites that complement selected essays that appear in this volume, see

> www.unh.edu/english/faculty/yount/pamela_illustrations.html. This site, Janet Aikins Yount's home page, features twenty-nine original illustrations to the sixth edition of *Pamela*, with facing pages of text.
>
> www.radcliffe.edu/gcws/courses/syllabi/NGf95.html. This site provides the syllabus for the course Narratives of Kinship in Industrializing Societies: Literary and Ethnographic Approaches, described in Ruth Perry's essay.
>
> www.jimandellen.org/showclarydates.html. This site contains Ellen Moody's record of the 1995 online discussion "Reading *Clarissa* in Real Time" discussed in Judith Moore's essay.
>
> http://library.marist.edu/faculty-web-pages/morreale/Eighteenth-Century/18c-F02-home.htm. The site features "Clarissa Web Project," an assignment described in Mark James Morreale's essay.

Part Two

APPROACHES

Introduction

Here we provide not so much an overview of each essay in the volume as a navigational grid for answers to questions that crop up frequently in the Richardsonian classroom. Our grouping of the essays reflects their engagement with such questions, even though their methodologies and approaches differ widely.

Dealing with the Problem of Length

An important trend in teaching the unabridged *Clarissa* is to spread it over the whole semester or a large part of the semester, so that students read an average of 150 pages a week. Some instructors opt for heavier reading loads in the beginning of the term to speed their students toward the arguably more exciting central part of the novel. They may then assign other readings, either interrupting the students' work on *Clarissa* for one or several class meetings or adding to it; see, for instance, Judith Moore's strategy of reading *Clarissa* and *Cecilia* simultaneously. Reading *Clarissa* over the whole term instead of trying to fit it into two or three weeks resolves concern about the prohibitive length of Richardson's novel. As Ruth Perry observes, "to fully appreciate Richardson's masterpiece, one has to live with *Clarissa* for a long time."

Clarissa is, in fact, suitable for a term-long reading project. A layering strategy of assigning other primary texts along with it not only approximates the real conditions in which it was first read, when other novels, plays, poems, letters, and pamphlets competed for its audience's attention, but also adds an important structural element to the learning environment. Commenting on her class's weekly practice of analyzing randomly selected passages from *Clarissa*, Janine Barchas notes that she was "surprised to find that many of the issues that [she] had tagged for that week, whether narrative reliability, heroism, or conduct literature, might still be reached by means of a passage chosen at random." It seems that no matter which text students are reading or which sociocultural or literary-historical feature of eighteenth-century life they are discussing, using *Clarissa* as an ever-present backdrop means that they can always turn to it to reground and nuance their arguments. Because of what Jayne Lewis calls its intricate engagement with an "array of cultural institutions, literary practices, and socioeconomic arrangements," *Clarissa* may constitute the best primary as well as the best secondary reading for an undergraduate course in eighteenth-century literature.

Lewis's experience of devoting a ten-week senior seminar to *Clarissa* has demonstrated that, given enough time, undergraduates do succeed in making Richardson's novel their own in ways that often surprise the instructor. Her essay is helpful for teachers wishing to undertake for the first time a term-long exploration of *Clarissa*, because she describes in detail each class meeting dedicated to the novel—its pedagogical goals, specific classroom activities, and the background and critical readings assigned for it.

A creative variation on the strategy of living with *Clarissa* is discussed in Barchas's essay. In a course that also featured *Pamela*, her graduate students read *Clarissa* for the whole academic year, which in New Zealand begins in February and runs to November—roughly approximating the "calendar year that organizes the novel." Such an experiment is possible because of the particularities of the academic year in the Southern Hemisphere, but it could be adapted to the Northern Hemisphere.

Teaching *Clarissa* in a thirteen-week semester, Jocelyn Harris structures her course so that the students also have time to read "re-visionings" of the novel. They choose from a list that ranges from Lady Echlin's alternative ending to *Clarissa* and Choderlos de Laclos's *Les liaisons dangereuses* to Virginia Woolf's *Mrs. Dalloway* and Ian McEwan's *Atonement*. One remarkable pedagogical bonus of orienting the course "post-*Clarissa*" is that, to understand why and how other writers disagreed with Richardson's original text and its tragic ending in particular, students have to look back to ancient, medieval, and Renaissance literary traditions, all of which provided crucial grounding for Richardson's conceptualization of his themes and characters.

The strategy of making one novel a focal point for the whole course also works for *Pamela*. As Florian Stuber demonstrates, turning *Pamela* into a "semester project" fosters unprecedented emotional engagement with the main heroine and heightened attention to textual detail (11). Similarly, several contributors to this volume have successfully taught undergraduate and graduate courses focusing on *Grandison*. In Cynthia Wall's graduate seminar, which used works by Alexander Pope, Mary Leapor, John Bunyan, Eliza Haywood, Walter Scott, and others to explore the eighteenth-century poetics of space, *Grandison* became the central text, exemplifying the mid-century shift from treating physical spaces as paraliterary to bringing them "visibly inside the house, inside the novel," and inside the characters' gendered subjectivity. In Teri Ann Doerksen's undergraduate seminar, students discussed *Grandison* "almost daily," making it a "lens" through which they examined eighteenth-century texts ranging from Daniel Defoe's *Moll Flanders* to Matthew Lewis's *The Monk*. Her class even evolved its own spatial metaphor when students referred to their classroom as their "cedar-parlor," described in *Grandison* as the room in Harriet's childhood home, a place where they "felt comfortable analyzing and extending the conversations that they had read in Richardson's text." David Hensley has taught several graduate seminars focusing on *Grandison*, in which at least half of the meetings were spent almost entirely on the novel, with the other half "leading up" to it through a series of extensive readings in its philosophical and literary contexts. The novel was "always on the table, and participants constantly [referred] to it from the start" of the semester, seeking to bring out the "often underestimated dialogism of [*Grandison's*] conceptual and affective alternatives."

Dealing with Student Skepticism

Survey participants commented on the challenge of making *Pamela* and *Clarissa* real for undergraduates and of sustaining students' interest in the too slowly unfolding adventures of Richardson's perfect and seemingly passive heroines. Robert Markley's essay discusses his students' persistent disagreement with Richardson's identification of "female psychological interiority—a woman's 'integrity'—with masculinist notions of chastity, virtue, and daughterly obedience." He suggests turning the resistance to Richardson's ideology into a teaching tool by encouraging students to see the novels at their most dynamic precisely where they fail the author's "didactic aims" of teaching "good [girls]" how to "repress [themselves]." Felicity Nussbaum offers a literary-historical background for what Markley characterizes as Richardson's didactic endeavor to "excite and then repress the ghosts of female desire" when she situates *Pamela* in the context of two seemingly disparate discourses of its time: on the one hand, eighteenth-century conduct books and sermons prescribing how young women should behave in compromising situations and, on the other, pornographic romances, such as *Fanny Hill*. When students consider Richardson's *Pamela* in relation to both these discourses, they begin to understand how his ambition simultaneously to instruct (moralize) and delight (titillate) fueled the numerous eighteenth-century parodies of *Pamela*.

Acknowledging the force of students' skeptical reaction to the explicit pedagogical agenda of *Pamela* as well as to the overall "sincerity of Richardson's ethical purpose," Michael McKeon proposes a framework that situates *Pamela's* ambitious challenge to the period's socioethical status quo in the history of the English domestic novel. In McKeon's course, undergraduates who read *Pamela* after Aphra Behn's *Love-Letters between a Nobleman and His Sister* begin to uncover the complex political meaning as well as the formal generic consequences of Behn's strategy of luring her readers "into reading a private plot as a mere romance only to insinuate its actual status as a signifying stand-in for public affairs of great importance." They then compare her strategy with Richardson's insistence on valorizing Pamela's "private" experience on its own terms. Students reconsider *Pamela's* didacticism, which they might have initially perceived as self-congratulatory, when they see it in the context of Richardson's innovative attention to processes by which "common people" internalize "the social ethics that obtain, for those of elevated social and political status, in the premodern world."

Kristina Straub responds to student frustration over Pamela's seemingly self-imposed immobility—Why does she keep writing instead of leaving at once?!—by drawing on eighteenth-century debates over the "servant problem." She reminds her students that the "morally uncompromising right of a domestic worker to sell her labor to her own best advantage is not a universal or ahistorical assumption." As Pamela struggles to maintain her integrity under cultural conditions that pointedly conflate the domestic servant-woman's economic agency with her sexual agency, she turns to letter writing as the only respectable form "her moral agency can take." Complementing Straub's historical perspective on Pamela's seemingly puzzling loyalty to the "good job gone bad" is Nicky Didicher's strategy of making Pamela's situation seem more real to the average North American undergraduate. Didicher's students consider the behavior of Pamela's employer and her response to his advances in the light of various discourses of sexual harassment in Western society today. The assumption underlying this approach to *Pamela* is that although "the term *sexual harassment* and its current legal boundaries are a product of our culture, not Richardson's," the behavior described by the term as well as psychological reactions of the harasser and his or her victim are to a certain extent universal. While cognizant of the sensitivity of this potentially "very personal or emotionally stressful subject," Didicher makes a case for using it to engage the students who find Richardson's first novel "romantic and therefore unbelievable."

The "Intense Religiosity" of Richardson's Novels and the Classroom

Instructors wishing to initiate discussion about the meaning of religion for Richardson's protagonists will find useful Elizabeth Kraft's essay on *Pamela*. Kraft draws on Luce Irigaray's definition of ethical erotic love as a relationship based on the recognition by both parties of their "essential alterity." She encourages her students to see how Pamela's Christian beliefs allow her to express her right to be loved as a complex, autonomous human being rather than to be simply appropriated by another, as Mr. B. attempts to do in the beginning of the story. Pamela's deep faith thus signals the possibility of a personal and even public social reform, because through faith the heroine evolves an ethically compelling alternative to the view that by seducing "his Mother's Waiting-Maid," Mr. B. commits no crime, since he "hurts no Family by it" (134).

Jocelyn Harris's essay explores the possibility that *Clarissa*'s somber rearticulation of the biblical stories of Job and Christ precipitated something close to a religious crisis in many of its first readers. As Harris puts it, "when these professed Christians begged that [Clarissa] should live, they denied a basic tenet of their faith, the existence of an afterlife superior to this one. Under the sway of Richardson's persuasive and affective realism, they essentially declared themselves unbelievers." Kraft's and Harris's arguments chart a productive space for considering *Pamela* and *Clarissa* as deeply implicated in their period's "intense religiosity" (Kraft) and at the same time as relentlessly testing the interpretive boundaries of the religious idiom.

Grandison, with what Doerksen calls its "delicate negotiations between the Protestant and the Catholic," accomplishes yet something different in its discussion of religion. By exploring the relation between national and religious identities, Richardson's last novel anticipates gothic narratives. It also offers students a useful perspective on the engagement of eighteenth-century belles lettres with categories of public and private. As Doerksen's experience of teaching *Grandison* to undergraduates suggests, "any student who understands the intricacies of Sir Charles's and Clementina's varied rationales for marrying or not marrying will understand cultural expectations of gender, political ramifications of religious identity, and eighteenth-century moral impulses."

The daunting goodness of Sir Charles, which prompted one of Hensley's students to speak of the novel's protagonist as "the good man we love to hate," can be profitably considered in the context of Richardson's reaction to the Miltonic worldview, in which evil can be dangerously attractive. Hensley encourages his students to contrast Richardson's "good man" to such would-be rakes as John Greville, Sir Hargrave Pollexfen, and Sir Thomas Grandison, who could have strutted proudly on the Restoration stage but who by Richardson's time are diminished both in "power and authority." Hensley's discussion connects with Jeremy Webster's rethinking of the figure of the Restoration rake in *Pamela* as well as with Harris's analysis of Lovelace as a tragic successor to both the legendary Earl of Rochester and Milton's Satan. Students who have had some previous exposure to Milton may find thought provoking the exploration of what Hensley calls the "intellectual vulnerability" of Richardson's "secular sentimental rewriting of Milton's Christian epic."

Debating Richardson's Feminism

Although the question of whether or not Richardson was a feminist may remain, as Lewis puts it, "truly unanswerable," debates about Richardson's feminism or his patriarchal ideology continue to constitute a rewarding pedagogical strategy. This volume offers several ways of initiating and developing such debates, ranging from the exploration of *Pamela* and *Clarissa* as "paternal fantas[ies]" (Markley) and noting *Grandison*'s "preoccupation with [women's] excesses" (Hensley) to considering Richardson as having an identification with women that was "unusually strong" (Perry). Markley's essay reminds us that in our position as parents and mentors it may come more naturally to us than to our students to espouse Richardson's perspective on what makes a "good girl" (an approach further nuanced by Moore's observation that as "exemplary" as Clarissa is, her "merits are insufficient to ensure [her] triumph"). Lisa Zunshine's essay on teaching *Grandison* considers its creed that, left alone and unpressured by her family, a good girl will choose the right man. This potentially empowering sentiment is compromised by the realization that Harriet is never really alone, since she is expected to report her every move in a big city in long, grammatically impeccable letters to "her Lucy" (*Grandison* 69). Students, many of whom have themselves just left home for the first time to go to college, find this detail particularly pertinent.

Thus lovingly but surely circumscribed, Harriet at least seems to be safe from the novel's tireless exposé of women who think, feel, and travel too much. As Hensley points out, whether "excessively rational . . . or excessively emotional . . . or even more dangerously transgressive . . . , all the women except Harriet typically lack balance, measure, and harmony." To help students contextualize the novel's somewhat embarrassed reading of acceptable female behavior, Hensley introduces them to a series of protofeminist publications "contemporary with the writing and publication of *Grandison*."

Complicating further Richardson's position on female agency and sexuality are suggestive readings of Mrs. Jewkes offered by Jeremy Webster and Patricia Brückmann. Webster uses Alexander Smith's 1716 story "Madam Clark, Mistress to the Earl of Rochester," featuring the grandmother–turned–procuress whose conniving irrevocably ruins her innocent granddaughter, to introduce Mrs. Jewkes as a throwback to the dark figure of the Restoration bawd. Brückmann, by contrast, focuses on the "richly obscene" vegetative allusions of *Pamela* to offer a surprisingly "lively and humane" interpretation of Richardson's "bawdy nurse." Spurred by Brückmann's close attention to textual details, her students begin to recognize how Mrs. Jewkes and "the landscape in which she functions" reorient both the narrative and the heroine toward the issues of "production and reproduction"—a crucial reorientation if Mr. B. and Pamela are ever to come to a mutually satisfying agreement.

Moore's essay considers questions reported by survey participants as coming up repeatedly in students' discussions of Richardson: What are the ideological and aesthetic implications of a "male novelist telling a woman's story from multiple points of view, including her own?" What cultural conditions make such cross-gendered ventriloquism particularly appealing or particularly problematic? Moore discusses her experience of teaching *Clarissa* alongside Frances Burney's *Cecilia* in a course on women's narratives that encouraged students to explore the complex assumptions behind their belief "that women's stories can be told only by women or that only women will find them compelling."

Perry, who taught with an anthropologist an interdisciplinary graduate seminar where texts from nineteenth-century Tonga and twentieth-century Africa were juxtaposed with *Clarissa*, demonstrates that reading a 250-year-old novel written by a man can affect one's understanding of the socioeconomic challenges faced by women in modern industrializing economies. She reports that her anthropological exploration of the politics of kinship and property in *Clarissa* inspired a South African member of the seminar to develop a set of "policy recommendations for distributing land among rural women" in her own country. *Clarissa's* focus on distortions of the traditional "cognatic, bilateral kinship system such as had always been practiced in English society" and the negative effects of those distortions on the situation of women helped the students "understand how existing land redistribution policies might not protect rural African women in the new economy."

Richardson as a Printer: New Pedagogical Approaches

In the 1990s, the renewal of critical interest in Richardson's career as a printer represented a salubrious break with the earlier tendency to "wonder," as Keith Maslen puts it, "that a London tradesman could escape the 'sordid views' of his class to write with art and passion of the workings of the female heart, setting his realistic narratives in a social domain from which he was by birth and occupation excluded." An effective way to convince students of the surprising resilience of that old sentiment is to direct them to the back cover of the Ross's *Clarissa* (the one featuring Highmore's *The Harlowe Family*), which informs them that in *Clarissa*, "one of the greatest European novels and its author's triumph, Samuel Richardson *had luck or prescience to hit upon the story* that became a myth to his own age, and remains so now" (emphasis mine), and ask them to substitute "Richardson" with "Shakespeare." The condescending nature of the back cover's compliment becomes apparent once students realize that they are not often encouraged to think of Shakespeare as having luckily hit on the story of Hamlet or King Lear. Harris's "Richardson: Original or Learned Genius?" furnishes rich material to challenge the myth of Richardson's middle-class benightedness occasionally pierced by strokes of creative luck.

The essays by Maslen and Barchas vigorously reengage the meaning of what Barchas describes as Richardson's unique position as "printer, author, and publisher." Maslen has uncovered the real extent of Richardson's printing output, which radically challenges the traditional concept of Richardson's political and aesthetic horizons and destabilizes the comfortable division between Richardson as "a poetic writer and a prosaic tradesman." Maslen's essay encourages teachers to direct students first to compare Richardson's practice of "printing to the moment" with his famous "writing to the moment" and then to inquire into the use of printer's ornaments in *Clarissa*. Responding, as it were, to Maslen's concluding question, "Why did Richardson use so many printer's ornaments?" Barchas shows that such ornaments bear directly on the meaning of each episode in which they were used. The author of *Clarissa* deployed "graphic design and layout" not only "to augment the passing of time in the letters as well as among them" but also to "mark hesitations imposed by the letter writer that reflect unease." It is crucial, therefore, that students are exposed to the original physical appearance of *Clarissa*, and Barchas's essay discusses resources and strategies available to the instructor committed to exploring Richardson's peculiar identity as a printer-writer.

Teaching Richardson's Revisions

An instructor choosing between existing editions of *Pamela* and *Clarissa* may wish to consider more than just technical aspects such as price, font size, and accompanying scholarly commentary. Richardson's project of revising his novels started before publication, continued until his death, and was then taken up by his daughters. This resulted, as Tom Keymer argues, in there being no unquestionably authoritative version of *Pamela* and *Clarissa*, for "no criteria can establish that any Richardson novel survives in its definitive or perfect state." But because different editions of *Pamela* and *Clarissa* produce somewhat different versions of these novels, such textual instability presents the teacher with a valuable pedagogical opportunity to explore both "the pressures of conservative tastes on innovative texts"—for Richardson revised most heavily in response to his contemporaries' complaints about the impropriety of his novels—and the "conditions of literary production in the eighteenth-century marketplace for print" (Keymer).

Keymer's overview of the different editions and his analysis of the vexed concepts of original and final texts provide an excellent starting point for the broad range of classroom approaches explored by this volume. First, his argument links suggestively with Brückmann's close reading of "wicked" gardening references in *Pamela*, since the 1801 edition, prepared by Richardson's daughters, eliminated unbecoming jests involving cucumbers and beans. Second, it dovetails with Markley's strategy of drawing students' attention to the failures of Richardson's didactic project. For example, Keymer notes that a "swarm of detailed adjustments" often pulls the text away from its main ideological drift, opening up suggestive fissures in the novel's intended moral message. Third, the overview Keymer provides works well with Barchas's observation that Richardson used printer's ornaments to mark the passing of time in *Clarissa*: as she demonstrates, the 1751 edition of the novel "allows for a sustained association between graphic symbol and letter writer."

Peter Sabor's essay highlights the feedback mechanism behind Richardson's "compulsive rewriting," specifically in the writer's correspondence with readers whose advice he eagerly sought and whose "often conservative and conventional tastes" he tried, at significant emotional expense, to accommodate. Richardson's remarkable epistolary oeuvre of some 1,650 letters will become available in full as part of the Cambridge University Press twenty-five volume edition of his work and correspondence. In the meantime Sabor's essay provides a detailed overview of the currently available sources for Richardson's correspondence and discusses its pedagogical applications. For example, teachers faced with students' incredulity at the sheer volume of letter writing, letter copying, and letter forwarding in his novels will find helpful Sabor's analysis of Richardson's own epistolary practices.

The "unstable nature of [Richardson's] novelistic imagining" is rich with opportunities for close reading, as John Richetti demonstrates in his comparative analysis of the first and third editions' versions of a scene between Lovelace and Clarissa in St. Albans. One sentence in the first edition is transformed into a lengthy dramatic dialogue in the third, a revision that can lead to a productive classroom discussion of the complex generic affiliations of Richardson's novel and of the aesthetic value of his obsessive corrections. Online editions of *Clarissa* make possible a variety of classroom exercises based on comparing the same letter in different versions of the novel.

The illustrations that Richardson commissioned for his books complicate further his "continual dialogue first with readers of his manuscript and then with the wider audiences for his printed texts" (Richetti). Janet Aikins Yount even suggests that Richardson might have undertaken yet another series of textual revisions because he was inspired by illustrations prepared by Francis Hayman and Hubert François Gravelot for the sixth edition of his *Pamela* (1742). The collection of twenty-nine illustrations, available for the first time at Yount's home page, is an important pedagogical tool. Her essay in this volume discusses strategies for using these images (four of which are reproduced with the essay) to help students fully grasp the interactive mode of Richardson's narrative.

For instructors whose students want to create their own interactive versions of Richardson's novels, Mark James Morreale describes the project of making a "collaborative academic Web site that annotates and illuminates a small portion of *Clarissa*." With what Morreale calls its "frequent use of cross-referencing, its allusive character, and its weblike structure," *Clarissa* represents an inviting text for such a project. Given the growing availability of Richardson resources on the World Wide Web, the collaboration described by Morreale could also be profitably undertaken by students wishing to annotate parts of *Pamela* and *Grandison*. Although the technology available for creating a collaborative Web site will inevitably change in the coming years, the pedagogical value of such an enterprise will endure.

BACKGROUNDS

Assorted Versions of Assaulted Virgins; or, Textual Instability and Teaching

Tom Keymer

As a printer, Richardson dealt extensively in stabilization: in the fixing of meaning, or at least text, to the page. As printer of his own fiction, however, he indulged in opportunities for ongoing revision that leave the texts of his novels almost uniquely unstable. If there is any adequate analogy in literature of the extended period, it is perhaps with poems by Samuel Taylor Coleridge such as "The Rime of the Ancient Mariner" and "Dejection," which survive in multiple revised versions spanning several decades. If there is anything close to an analogy in fiction, we might perhaps liken the multiple states of a Richardson novel to the hand-marbled pages inserted by Laurence Sterne in *Tristram Shandy*: stable traces of a liquid original, snapshots of a medium in permanent flux, each image unlike the last. Typically, a Richardson novel was tested before publication on sample readers in a manuscript version that no longer survives and then published in several lifetime editions, each revised in a way that casts its predecessor as provisional or transitional only; it was under revision again near the end of Richardson's life, and republished decades later in an edition claiming to incorporate his last alterations.

There is no room here to detail one possibility thrown up by this complex textual situation, which would be to include Richardson in a course exploring issues in textual theory through three or four key eighteenth-century works that survive in different states. Alexander Pope's *Dunciad* (in the original, Variorum, and four-book versions) and Jonathan Swift's *Gulliver's Travels* (in the Motte and Faulkner editions) offer complementary cases made all the more stimulating by the different determining factors in play each time. In combination with *Pamela*, works like these open up questions not only of authorial reseeing but also of the impact on the texts we inherit of contingencies from the time(s) of publication including censorship, topicality, and reception. I return below to the option of making the revision of Richardson's fiction an object of study in itself. My basic purpose, however, is to address the practical question that arises in whatever context we now teach one or more of the novels: which version to select?

Sir Charles Grandison is the simplest case. First published in 1753–54, with a simultaneous second edition in larger format, it went almost immediately into a third edition, but no other followed in Richardson's lifetime except in the case of the closing volume, which was reprinted in 1756 with a few revised sheets. In the second edition, 928 textual changes are introduced (Pierson 164); 932 more in the third (166); 448 more in the posthumous fourth edition of 1762 (174); and 605 more when "a new edition, with last corrections by the author" appeared in 1810 (180, 178). Most of these revisions are local and slight, though of discernible cumulative impact. Distributed as they are across a work of such encyclopedic bulk, they make *Grandison* by far the most lightly revised of Richardson's novels. Nor, in any case, is there any practical and available alternative to the first-edition text, which Jocelyn Harris chose to follow in her Oxford English Novels / World's Classics edition of 1972 after exhaustive study of the motivations and effects of Richardson's revisions, which revealed a pattern of retrospective acquiescence in conventional standards and conservative tastes as brought to bear by the reading public. "To the extent that he allowed outside pressure to influence his work," Harris writes, "each edition is progressively less his own, further removed from the original conception, and often destructive of the spontaneity or colloquial tone of the first edition" (1: xxviii).

Pamela is more problematic. Having published the novel in 1740, Richardson consistently underestimated demand for his best-selling work, which was in its sixth authorized edition within eighteen months, with further editions to follow in 1746 and 1754. A further revision of *Pamela* begun as *Grandison* entered publication in 1753 was apparently completed in 1758, but Richardson was revising it again in his last few months before death, in ways no doubt reflected in the posthumous edition of 1801, the fourteenth, which had been publicly anticipated as early as 1786 as "the new edition, in which much was altered, and the whole new-modelled" (qtd. in Eaves and Kimpel, "Revisions" 73). With over 8,400 substantive changes, ranging in size from substitutions of single words to whole pages cut or added, the 1801 edition brings to its belated climax a process of revision in which each published version differs markedly from the last, and often extensively so, even when separated from its predecessor by just a few weeks. There are 841 textual changes in the second edition; 950 in the fifth; 633 in the octavo sixth, including large additions.

But it is with *Clarissa* that the collation statistics become truly eye-watering. Having circulated for years in manuscript versions that can only conjecturally be reconstructed, the novel was serially published in 1747–48, with textual revision still ongoing even as publication was in train. In 1749 the first four volumes (to page 761 in Ross's edition) reappeared in a second edition, which, with over a thousand substantive changes per volume, not only constitutes a thorough stylistic overhaul of the novel but also interpolates hundreds of additional passages and makes significant cuts. Among the many thousands of further changes introduced in the third edition of 1751, 739 run to more than a printed line, and 127 of the largest additions (some newly rewritten, others retrieved and revised from the prepublication manuscripts) were enough to make up an entire volume of *Letters and Passages Restored*.[1] Nor did Richardson then settle for Samuel Johnson's friendly advice—the advice of a true professional, as Richardson never was as an author—that this was the edition "by which I suppose Posterity is to abide" (Johnson 1: 48, letter of 9 March 1751). Even when extracting passages from *Clarissa* for *A Collection of Moral and Instructive Sentiments* (1755), Richardson compulsively revised them, and at about this time he told Mary Watts of keeping open a revision in progress of all three novels, with changes to be entered "as my friends, or my own reperusal, have suggested" (Richardson, *Selected Letters* 225).[2] At the end of the year he claimed to have given his "last Hand" to *Clarissa* (in Richardson, *Richardson-Stinstra* 97), and the fourth edition of 1759 enters only a few substantive changes. But the revising impulse kicked in again thereafter, and when only months from death Richardson requested from his closest literary confidante, Lady Bradshaigh, her annotated copies of *Pamela* and *Clarissa* as sources for a further rewrite. Like the consumptive Tristram at the end of Sterne's novel, with his desperate desire to resolve his narrative before interrupted by death, Richardson was revising again with new but unavailing urgency. On the day of his death in 1761, the texts of *Pamela* and *Clarissa* were left in a state that was no more definitive or final than on the day of their first publication—and if Richardson were alive today we can hardly doubt that he would still (and with hypertext) be revising. As *Clarissa* stands in practice, the closing word may well be the edition of 1792 (still largely unexplored), the title page of which claimed on unknown authority to incorporate "the last corrections by the author."

In the everyday business of reading and teaching, as much as in the theory of copy-text, we have traditionally given priority to "original" or "final" versions—or, to recall a now outmoded theory of copy-text (one of stupendous inapplicability here) to "original" accidentals and "final" substantives. Yet, as the textual histories sketched out above make clear, there is nothing very "original" about the earliest published version of a Richardson novel, which could be separated by years of revision from the first full text. And there is nothing at all "final" about the last lifetime version—which, as Richardson's practice of rolling, open-book revision indicates, marks nothing more significant than the point at which the process stood when arbitrarily curtailed by death. In this situation, the revision of a Richardson novel could only (as Johnson memorably writes of his *Dictionary*) "be ended, though not completed" ("Preface" 317). Nor can we ever be sure exactly where to locate this messy end point, given the likelihood that as well as reflecting authorial alterations the posthumous editions that claimed to do so were also doctored, or even occasionally bowdlerized, by other hands. Smoking-gun evidence survives in letters from the 1780s between Richardson's daughters, who privately discuss the need to "make some further corrections" and "alter some particular phrases, &c." in the authorial copy of *Pamela* then in their hands, thereby leaving Richardson's last revision "re-revised" (see Keymer, Introduction xxxiv).

The consequence is that just as there can be no truly "original" or "final" version, so no criteria can establish that any Richardson novel survives in its definitive or perfect state. We must think of the literary work we call *Pamela* as residing in, or constituted by, the ten different surviving versions of it in which Richardson had a hand, and not in any particular edition, whether the first, the fourteenth, or an intermediary such as the octavo sixth. Once this caveat has been made, however, it is clear that when comparing the earliest and latest versions to have survived of Richardson's novels we do indeed encounter a picture interpretable in terms of the familiar "original"-"final" polarity. To generalize here is to simplify, and in the massive task of rewriting these massive texts (and that is what in extreme cases like the 1751 *Clarissa* and the 1801 *Pamela* it amounts to: rewriting), it can hardly be said that every one of many thousands of changes points systematically in the same direction. Competing trajectories are sometimes in play, and in the swarm of so many detailed adjustments, individual local decisions sometimes pull away from the overall drift. In comparison with later revised versions, however, the basic characteristics of a Richardson novel in its "original" version are clear enough. In matters of linguistic, moral, and social decorum it is typically more provocative and transgressive; and in matters of meaning and interpretation, it is typically more indeterminate and open.

Another way of putting this, of course, would be to say that the "original" versions are riddled with solecisms and incoherent in the messages they convey; and these were very much the objections that assailed Richardson on first publication of each work. Among the qualities for which we now read and teach the novels are their openness to plural construction and the subtle ambiguities with which they represent complexities of motive and conduct. But these same qualities—gleefully exploited in Henry Fielding's alternative account of Pamela as a sham and more sympathetically noted in his *Jacobite's Journal* comment on *Clarissa*'s vexed reception ("*Clarissa* is undutiful; she is too dutiful. She is too cold; she is too fond" [120])—severely threatened the respectability that Richardson craved as a rigorous didact. They had to be brought under control. Later editions of *Pamela* progressively pare away the complicating elements that anti-Pamelists had exploited, while the paratextual apparatus of annotations and abstracts clamped on to *Clarissa* in later editions subjects readers to a machinery of interpretative supervision that settles, once and for all, ambiguities about duty and love.

This is not the fine, leisurely, mature reseeing celebrated by Jack Stillinger in his account of Coleridge's revisions, or by Philip Horne in his study of Henry James's New York edition, but something more pragmatic and reductive. The diffidence with which Richardson typically revised is traceable in surviving correspondence, as Peter Sabor argues in his essay in this volume. When an anonymous writer protested loftily on 15 November 1740 that if Pamela "repeated the Sacred Name much seldomer, it wou'd have so much less the Style of Robinson Crusoe," Richardson's instant response was to alter eighty-five occurrences of "God" (Letter, fol. 34).[3] Having published *Clarissa*, he nervously ran the text past learned acquaintances such as Solomon Lowe, the author of *English Grammar Reformd* (1737) and other such works, asking for corrections to style. Paradoxically, Lowe seems to have had a stronger sense than Richardson at this point of the need not to homogenize the distinctive epistolary idiolects of *Clarissa*'s narrators, and while recommending corrections, he also urged that certain solecisms be left in. Some of the corrections were implemented, and when Lowe also found faults in the heroine's conduct, "objecting to Clarissa's little deceits in ye end of Vol. 2d." (Lowe, fol. 102), Richardson reached again for his red pen, as though to render absolute a moral polarity between Clarissa and her family that originally he had colored with nuance. "What *can* I do?," Clarissa asks herself when threatened with forced marriage, before resolving, in the first edition, "I will begin to be very ill; nor need I feign very much" ([ed. Ross] 341). Even this rather excusable touch of shamming is expunged from later editions, and her desperate question goes unanswered.

When I first studied Richardson as an undergraduate in 1983 with Rita Goldberg, to one of whose memorable asides this essay owes its title, revision was an area of live debate at research level, above all in the deconstructive readings of *Clarissa* then recently published by William B. Warner and Terry Castle. But in classroom practice, we had no more choice over texts of *Pamela* or *Clarissa* than with *Grandison* now, and we worked exclusively with "final" versions. The groundbreaking Penguin *Pamela* had appeared in 1980, edited by Sabor from the 1801 text with an introduction by Margaret A. Doody, setting a new standard in Richardson editing. The Riverside, edited by T. C. Duncan Eaves and Ben Kimpel from the 1740 version, was not distributed in Britain, and in any case its meager apparatus, alongside Sabor's rich annotations and Doody's influential introduction, made it ineligible as a teaching edition. For *Clarissa* it was Everyman or bust—and this edition too was based on a "final" state: the Everyman copy-text is undeclared, but in essence this is the 1751 *Clarissa*, incorporating, though inconsistently, a few further revisions from 1759. Now that good trade editions of both novels in their "original" versions are available (the Penguin *Clarissa*, ed. Ross, and the Oxford World's Classics *Pamela*, ed. Keymer and Wakely), we have real choice. Electronic text also exists, and students with access through their institutions to Chadwyck-Healey's CD-ROM database of *Eighteenth-Century Fiction* or to the Web version of the database available by subscription (http://lion.chadwyck.com), will find hyperlinked texts of *Pamela* and *Clarissa* in early and late versions (the first and octavo sixth editions of *Pamela*; the first and third of *Clarissa*).

My own experience as a teacher, and a decisive factor in determining the copy-text of the Oxford World's Classics *Pamela*, is of a radical mismatch between the tastes of modern students and the tastes of those early readers whom Richardson was most anxious to appease when wielding his revising pen. Students are rarely much engaged by the strain of blunt role-model didacticism that made him swell by twelve pages, in the third edition of 1751, the letter in which Anna lauds her friend's exemplary lifestyle and vows, in hectoring italics, that she will imitate Clarissa's punishing daily regime "as to *morning Risings*" ([3rd ed.] 8: 220). Few are engaged by the retrospective obsession with linguistic propriety that made Richardson edit out so many of the authentically epistolary traits in Clarissa's prose—the lexical freedoms, the grammatical lapses—in favor of a more uniform Augustan correctness. It is a familiar phenomenon in revised versions of *Pamela* that from the outset the heroine begins to sound more like the lady she later becomes than the servant she originally is, but less often observed is that the daughter of the arriviste Harlowes also grows markedly posher: "as a while-away-time" ([ed. Ross] 281) becomes "to give myself employment" in the third edition ([3rd ed.] 2: 148); "fluttered me" ([ed. Ross] 302) becomes "discomposed me" ([3rd ed.] 2: 186); "sooner than it agrees with my stomach" ([ed. Ross] 351) becomes "sooner than I should otherwise chuse" (2: 280). Other kinds of decorum imposed by Richardson on the revised text of 1751 are equally uninviting now, and few readers will prefer the version in which Richardson deletes Lovelace's fantasy of Clarissa "pressing with her fine fingers the generous flood into the purple mouths of each eager hunter by turns" ([ed. Ross] 706)—a moment of baroque eroticism that pornographers like John Cleland could get nowhere near—to make room for an improving footnote "on the important subject of mothers being nurses to their own children" (4: 334n).

Conversely, readers discouraged by the showy didactic armature of *Pamela* (here it can help, incidentally, to point to the "tail-piece of morality" in John Cleland's *Memoirs of a Woman of Pleasure* [187] as evidence that didactic professions need not tell the whole story) often respond more positively to the original than to later versions. The cries of outrage generated by the first edition because of its valorization of low status and style, its covertly pornographic elements, and a strain of methodistic defiance that still gave out a whiff of revolutionary puritanism drew Richardson into a marathon of defensive revision. By 1801, innumerable violations of linguistic, moral, and social decorum had been expunged. Bunyanesque vulgarisms are colorlessly lifted and standardized ("a Mort of good Things" [(ed. Keymer and Wakely) 18] becomes "many good things" [(ed. Sabor) 50]; "a Power of pretty Things" [(ed. Keymer and Wakely) 498] becomes "many pretty presents" [(ed. Sabor) 516]; sexy innuendoes are studiously removed—though Mr. B.'s "I wish . . . I had thee as quick another Way" ([ed. Keymer and Wakely] 70) survives in every lifetime edition, and it may have been Richardson's daughters who cut it at last; Pamela becomes consistently more deferential to her "betters," and altogether less spirited, willful, and ambitious. The attenuation is never total, of course, but in later editions the feistiness that still makes Richardson's heroine speak across the centuries becomes significantly muted. Defensive revision also pared away those elements of ambiguity that compelled so much early debate, and in this respect a great benefit of using the "original" text is that *Shamela* and other items from the controversy of the 1740s become much more comprehensible when one reads the text that provoked them, as opposed to the text that sought to remove their grounds of objection.

It will be clear by now that I am arguing for the value above all of first-edition texts as a teaching resource. But need we make the choice absolutely? Editors of print editions must clearly jump one way or another, and—though this is no place to detail the rationale in full—the in-progress *Cambridge Edition of the Works and Correspondence of Samuel Richardson* will follow first editions of the novels, just as it will retain the original state of Richardson's manuscript correspondence, much of which he later revised with a view to publication. As teachers we have more freedom, however, and as a way of exploring the pressures of conservative tastes on innovative texts and the determining conditions of literary production in the eighteenth-century marketplace for print, we gain a great deal by making revision itself the object of study. We can hardly ask students to read and compare two *Clarissa*s as we might ask them to read and compare, say, both the *Lyrical Ballads* and *Sibylline Leaves* versions of Coleridge's "Rime." We can ask them, however, to look up alternative versions of the passages they find most intriguing as they read. Or we can point to particular cases. One example I sometimes use from *Pamela* (see Keymer, Introduction xxx–xxxii) is the passage in which Pamela encounters a group of gossiping fine ladies. She is at her most truculent here, and her stylistic register plunges as though in defiant reaction to their elegant chat: "And so, belike, their Clacks run for half an Hour . . . " ([ed. Keymer and Wakely] 53). Later editions anxiously tone down these effects, and the whole "Clacks" sentence disappears (see ed. Sabor 86).

In *Clarissa*, among the most revealing passages are those on which the too dutiful–too undutiful debate was focused. Revision was at its most intensive here, and corrective footnotes were deployed. A different and nicely self-contained example comes with the "Rosebud" episode ([ed. Ross] 284–88), which in the first edition not only lures Clarissa into a good opinion of Lovelace but also, teasingly, invites readers to share her mistake. After pro-Lovelace response got out of hand, Richardson works strenuously in the third edition to neutralize the effect through careful local rewording and the addition of a note rebuking readers for giving Lovelace "a greater merit than was due to him" ([3rd ed.] 2: 158). At the same time, Richardson deletes the evidence of Clarissa's sneaking jealousy when she finds, once the seeming innocence of Lovelace's behavior has emerged, that she "can allow the girl to be prettier than before I could" ([ed. Ross] 288). As well as focusing attention on the distinctive areas of debate that preoccupied Richardson and his readers, exercises like this can also throw up large general questions about interpretation and meaning, and particularly about the ontological identity of a literary work whose text will never keep still.

NOTES

[1]See Van Marter, "Second Edition" and "Third and Fourth Editions."

[2]See also, for corrections to the letter edited by Carroll, Eaves and Kimpel, *Samuel Richardson* 681.

[3]See also Eaves and Kimpel, "Revisions" 66.

Teaching *Pamela* and *Clarissa* through Richardson's Correspondence

Peter Sabor

I began teaching Richardson's novels to Canadian students in the late 1970s: first *Pamela* to undergraduates; then *Clarissa* in the George Sherburn abridgment (more lacunae than text, so a frustrating experience); and, finally, when Angus Ross's one-volume Penguin edition of *Clarissa* appeared in 1985, the whole of Richardson's masterpiece to graduate students. As the editor of Richardson's final revision of *Pamela*, I devoted considerable class time to the question of Richardson's revisions of his first novel, which he repeatedly expanded, contracted, continued, and reworked for the last twenty years of his life. In the case of *Clarissa*, similarly, I drew attention to the mass of new material Richardson added to the third edition of 1751, photocopying key passages for the class. In the late 1970s and 1980s, students were turning from typewriters to personal computers and finding parallels between their own new methods of composition and those of Richardson. Like Richardson, who regarded the texts of his novels as malleable, forever open to revision in the light of changed authorial priorities and audience demand, students found that computer-generated texts were far more fluid than those prepared on typewriters or laboriously written out by hand. And they realized that Richardson, as his own printer, was in a position very different from that of his fellow novelists—either in the eighteenth century or today—because he was able to alter the texts of his novel at will, without facing financial penalty or having to gain the approval of a recalcitrant publisher. The link between computer printouts and Richardson's print shop was clearly apparent.

My classes focused on Richardson's compulsive rewriting and became increasingly concerned with what lay behind his rage for revision: the pressure exerted by his readers, with their often conservative and conventional tastes. In many of his letters, the novelist asks his correspondents to tell him what they found "objectible" in the novels; as long as readers objected to aspects of his work, Richardson was prepared to amend the text and eliminate the objection. Each Richardson novel thus exists in a series of revised editions, none of which is more definitive than its predecessors. Richardson was, of course, aware of the problems that his repeated appeals for criticism and consultation could cause. In a letter to Edward Young of 19 November 1747, he reproaches himself for his own malleability:

> What contentions, what disputes have I involved myself in with my poor Clarissa, through my own diffidence, and for want of a will! I wish I had never consulted any body but Dr. Young, who so kindly vouchsafed me his ear, and sometimes his opinion. (*Selected Letters* 84)

Richardson continued, however, to involve himself in contentions and disputes over *Pamela*, *Clarissa*, and *Sir Charles Grandison* and to regard the texts of his novels in the way that others might consider work in progress.

As we studied the relation between Richardson's vast correspondence (some 1,650 letters survive) and the composition and revision of his novels, my students took a strong interest in the letters he was receiving, as well those he was writing. They noted that he would forward letters from one correspondent to another, attach parts of a letter he had already written or received to a new one that he was sending, or send different versions of a letter to a variety of correspondents. The parallels between Richardson's own epistolary practices and those of his epistolary fiction are striking: the intricate systems of composing and delivering letters in the novels, in which an epistle can be written by more than one author and dispatched to multiple recipients, are mirrored in his private correspondence. In the late 1980s, another subject for discussion entered the classroom: the parallels between Richardson's methods of circulating his correspondence, often with the help of amanuenses, and the newly developing technology of electronic mail. As e-mail became increasingly accessible and students ever more adept at employing it, Richardson the correspondent came to seem a much more familiar figure than he had been to a previous generation. And just as students would habitually exchange electronic correspondence among themselves and, eventually, their professors (the latter generally taking to the new medium more slowly), so they became increasingly eager to explore the correspondence of Richardson and his circle. They faced, however, a serious impediment. John Carroll's edition, the only modern selection of Richardson's letters, contains no letters to Richardson, only letters by him, and students of the electronic age wanted access to letters Richardson received as much as to letters he sent. Anna Barbauld's six-volume selection of Richardson's correspondence, first published in 1804, was reprinted in 1966 and is accessible in most university libraries, but, as I warn my students, it contains only some 440 letters—just over a quarter of the total. Barbauld included some 270 letters by Richardson's correspondents, but about 1,100 are known today; over 800 letters by Richardson's correspondents are still scattered among diverse printed sources or, in many cases, remain unpublished.

In a letter to Lady Bradshaigh of 19 November 1757, Richardson raised the delicate question of whether their correspondence—a series of letters exchanged regularly since 1748 and covering the composition and publication of both *Clarissa* and *Sir Charles Grandison*—might be published. It would, he believed, "make the best Commentary that cd. be written on the History of Clarissa" (*Selected Letters* 336). Richardson, I believe, was right. But his project, after almost 250 years, has yet to come to fruition. Richardson's correspondence, both with Lady Bradshaigh and with many other contemporaries who read him repeatedly and with intense attention, constitutes an extraordinary analysis of his novels—a sustained debate on the art of fiction between a practitioner and his readers—and an invaluable teaching tool. Recognizing its importance, Cambridge University Press has commissioned a complete edition of Richardson's works and correspondence, with Thomas Keymer and me as general editors, which is to be published within a decade. Twelve volumes of letters, organized by correspondent or groups of correspondents, will be followed by an index volume, enabling teachers to locate passages dealing with issues raised during classroom discussion and to make this material available to students. The correspondence between Richardson and Lady Bradshaigh and her sister, Lady Echlin, will alone take up three stout volumes: the "best Commentary" on Richardson's fiction will thus be printed at last.

Until the Cambridge edition of the correspondence of Samuel Richardson appears, teachers can assemble key exchanges between Richardson and his correspondents from a variety of printed sources. I combine copies of Richardson's letters from Carroll's edition with copies from standard modern editions of letters by his correspondents, such as George Cheyne, Johannes Stinstra, Henry Fielding and Sarah Fielding, David Garrick, Edward Moore, Edward Young, and Samuel Johnson. I use Barbauld's unannotated and textually unreliable edition (Richardson, *Correspondence*) only in extremis, when no alternative source exists.

Carroll's selection of letters on *Pamela* is disappointingly thin. It includes an important letter from Richardson to Aaron Hill on the "original ground-work of fact, for the general foundation of Pamela's story" (39) with a remarkably precise account of the composition of the novel, including the information that "by a memorandum on my copy, I began it Nov. 10 1739, and finished it Jan. 10 1739–40" (Richardson, *Selected Letters* 39, 41). But for Hill's extensive and often ludicrously hyperbolic commentary on the novel, teachers must for the present look elsewhere: the introduction to the second edition of *Pamela*, in which six of Hill's letters appear in abridgment, together with interlinking remarks by Richardson (rpt. in *Pamela*, ed. Keymer and Wakeley 505–19); the posthumously published *Works of the Late Aaron Hill* (1753); and Barbauld's selection (Richardson, *Correspondence*).

Richardson's two surviving letters on *Pamela* to his physician, George Cheyne, contain material that should lead to animated classroom discussion: for example, Richardson's declaration that he has endeavored "to write a Story, which shall catch young and airy Minds . . . in order to decry such Novels and Romances, as have a Tendency to inflame and corrupt" and that he has "generally taken Human Nature *as it is*, for it is no purpose to suppose it Angelic, or to endeavour to make it so" (Richardson, *Selected Letters* 46–47, 47). For Cheyne's letters to Richardson, however, students should be directed to Charles Mullett's dated but still functional edition. Of particular interest here is Cheyne's concern with the physical appearance of *Pamela*: "I wonder you make your modern Books in so small a Type and so bad Paper. It must certainly disgust it to many, the tender and old who only read Books, and it gives an ill Impression of a Book before its Character is established" (63). On reading this, students will better understand why Richardson went to such pains to make the four-volume octavo edition of

Pamela (1742), with its twenty-nine illustrations by Hubert François Gravelot and Francis Hayman, such a handsome piece of bookmaking, although the costs of production compelled him to charge twice as much for it as for the duodecimo editions. (See Yount's essay in this volume for a discussion of ways to use the illustrations in the classroom.) Readers were, understandably, deterred by the high price, and copies remained unsold for over thirty years.

Teachers using Carroll's *Selected Letters* will find a much richer selection of letters on *Clarissa* and *Sir Charles Grandison* than on *Pamela*, but reading them is akin to hearing only one side of a two-way conversation. Richardson's famous autobiographical letter to Stinstra, of 2 June 1753, is in Carroll, but in heavily abridged form. The first three pages of the original, including an important paragraph in which Richardson explains why he is recounting his life story, are omitted, as are a paragraph on *Sir Charles Grandison*; excerpts from nine admiring epistles on *Clarissa* included with the letter; and Richardson's commentary on these excerpts, a fine example of Richardson's habit of highlighting key parts of letters received and forwarding them in the manner of today's dedicated e-mailer. Students will be better served by reading the entire letter in *The Richardson-Stinstra Correspondence*, edited by William Slattery, in which they will also find the letters from Stinstra to Richardson that elicited his revealing (and deliberately concealing) account.

Among the letters that Richardson had copied for Stinstra is the extraordinary one written by Henry Fielding on reading the fifth volume of *Clarissa*: one of the most remarkable letters that Richardson ever received and perhaps the most important one that Fielding ever wrote. It is published, with an explanatory commentary, in Martin Battestin and Clive Probyn's exemplary edition, *The Correspondence of Henry and Sarah Fielding*. The letter records Henry Fielding's reactions to the major events of the volume—Clarissa's imprisonment and rape by Lovelace, followed by her adamant refusal of his proposal of marriage—in cardiographic style, tracing his alternately tremulous and exclamatory responses: "Here my Terror ends and my Grief begins which the Cause of all my Tumultuous Passions soon changes into Raptures of Admiration and Astonishment"; these are the words of a contemporary reader fully absorbed in the arduous process of reading a Richardson novel (70–71). The letter also raises fascinating and as yet unresolvable questions about the nature of Richardson's dealings with Fielding in 1748. Why had the author of *Shamela* and *Joseph Andrews* been sent an advance copy of the fifth volume of *Clarissa*, and why does he sign his letter "yrs. most Affectionately," while asking Richardson "to send me immediately the two remaining Vols." (72)? It is possible, as I tell my students, that Fielding and Richardson were on much friendlier terms, for a period in the 1740s, than is generally recognized. The *Correspondence of Henry and Sarah Fielding* also contains the extant correspondence between Richardson and Sarah Fielding, including a letter by Sarah Fielding of 8 January 1749 that clearly reveals her authorship of the anonymously published pamphlet

Remarks on Clarissa. I recommend this pamphlet, as well as Sarah Fielding's letters on *Clarissa*, to my students and discuss the Richardson-Henry Fielding-Sarah Fielding triangle in class, pointing out that *Remarks on* Clarissa and Henry Fielding's letter on the novel were written only a few months apart.

Like both Henry Fielding and Sarah Fielding, Richardson inserted compliments to his friends in his novels. Students who persevere as far as the postscript to *Clarissa* will encounter Richardson's graceful tribute to David Garrick, "who deservedly engages the public favour in all that he undertakes" ([ed. Ross] 1497). I direct them to Garrick's response in a letter to Richardson of 12 December 1748, thanking Richardson for a presentation copy of the final volumes: "The honour you have done Me (& I do most sincerely think it a great one) in yr last Volume, has flatter'd me extreamly" (Garrick 95). This leads, in turn, to a discussion of Edward Moore's abortive project to dramatize *Clarissa*, with Garrick cast as Lovelace, and then to Moore's letters to Richardson on *Clarissa*. Moore wrote two letters to Richardson in late 1748, both of the utmost interest, as are Richardson's replies. Moore's first letter, like Henry Fielding's more celebrated one, was written in response to a reading of the fifth volume of *Clarissa*. His analysis here of the "Mischiefs of a Lovelace" (Amberg 395) provokes Richardson into a startling defense of certain aspects of his hero:

> Is he not generous!. . . Is he not ingenuous? Does he not on all occasions exalt the Lady at his own Expence?—Has he not therefore many Sparks of Goodness in his Heart; tho', with regard to the Sex and to carry a favourite Point against them he sticks at nothing?—And are there not many Lovelace's in this Particular?   (Amberg 396–97)

In his second letter, written after he had read the final volumes of *Clarissa*, Moore objected, inter alia, that Richardson had not been "a little more minute about the Death of Lovelace" (Amberg 397). This generated an exceptionally detailed reply, even by Richardson's standards. I direct students to these letters, as well as to Tom Keymer's incisive analysis of the exchange in his *Richardson's* Clarissa *and the Eighteenth-Century Reader* (69–72). Part of a class is thus devoted to discussing a modern critic discussing Richardson's reply to one of his correspondents discussing a key section of the novel. The layering effect is as Richardson would have wished. As he wrote to Lady Bradshaigh on 25 February 1754, in a celebrated passage on the deliberate lack of closure in his fiction:

> The whole Story abounds with Situations and Circumstances debatable. It is not an unartful Management to interest the Readers so much in the Story, as to make them differ in Opinion as to the Capital Articles, and by Leading one, to espouse one, another, another, Opinion, make them all, if not Authors, Car[v]ers.   (*Selected Letters* 296)

"Carvers" (not "Carpers" as Carroll wrongly transcribes the word) is used here to mean those who choose for themselves—readers who participate fully in the transaction with the author and articulate their personal experience of reading his novels.

Students who explore the ways in which Richardson's contemporaries responded to his fiction are, I believe, more likely to become "carvers" themselves. For this reason I encourage them to read some of the creative responses to *Clarissa* made available in modern editions: Aaron Hill's "Specimen of New Clarissa," a much revised abridgment of the opening letters that provoked Richardson to justify his novel's longueurs; Lady Echlin's alternative ending to the novel, in which Clarissa is no longer raped and Lovelace is converted to pious Christianity, a document that likewise elicited a vigorous letter from Richardson; and Lady Bradshaigh's extensive annotations on *Clarissa*, together with Richardson's sometimes admiring, sometimes indignant replies (see Barchas, *Annotations*).

If room can be made in a course for both *Pamela* and *Clarissa*, it is intriguing to show students Richardson's mounting unease with his first novel, which he came to regard as unworthy of its successor. In January 1747, Hill termed *Clarissa* "the younger sister of a *Pamela*," while warning Richardson that some readers might be disappointed in the new work "from Effect of that inimitable Excellence that lies before them for Comparison" (Letter, fol. 83). In his reply, Richardson writes of *Pamela* that "its strange Success at Publication is still my Surprize" (*Selected Letters* 78), attributing Hill's enthusiasm for the earlier novel to his kindheartedness and fondness for the author. Both Pamela and Clarissa are intended to be exemplary figures, but the new work has a loftier purpose: "in her Preparation for Death, and in her Death, I had proposed to make this a much nobler and more useful Story than that of Pamela; *As all must die*" (*Selected Letters* 83). None of Richardson's other correspondents shared Hill's concern that *Pamela* might eclipse *Clarissa*. More typical was Edward Young, who wrote to Richardson in February 1746, when the novel was still in progress: "my thoughts run all on Pamela's younger sister, Clarissa; and I promise myself no small satisfaction from conversing with her in March" (E. Young 224). After Young had read volumes 3 and 4 of *Clarissa* in April 1748, the comparison became more blunt: "Clarissa has put Pamela's nose out of joint" (E. Young 300). Richardson's own attitude toward *Pamela* became increasingly condescending, even while he attempted to defend the novel in letters to his correspondents, and between 1753 and 1758 he labored on the full-scale revision that he hoped would give it a dignified place in his canon. None of Richardson's correspondents ever saw the final version of *Pamela*, which was at last published at the behest of his daughter Anne, forty years after his death, but it does answer many of their criticisms.

Among the most encouraging letters that Richardson ever received was a memorable one from Samuel Johnson, occasioned by the fourth, octavo edition of *Clarissa*, published in April 1751 and containing much additional material. Johnson, who received an advance presentation copy in March, wrote not only to congratulate Richardson on the handsome appearance of the octavo edition, with its larger paper and more generous type, but also to advise him not to be deterred by critics' complaining of its excessive length:

> Though Clarissa wants no help from external Splendour I was glad to see her improved in her appearance but more glad to find that she was now got above all fears of prolixity, and confident enough of Success, to supply whatever had been hitherto suppressed. I never indeed found a hint of any such defalcation but I fretted, for though the Story is long, every let-ter is short.   (1: 47–48)

Reading this letter aloud to students before they begin their immersion in *Clarissa*, with due emphasis on that quintessentially Johnsonian word "defalcation," should help head off any complaints about the thickness of the book they have before them. *Clarissa*, as Johnson declares, "is not a performance to be read with eagerness and laid aside for ever, but will be occasionally consulted by the busy, the aged and the studious" (1: 48). I hope that after reading *Clarissa* students will take Johnson at his word, and in their later lives make what had once been merely a prescribed text in a university course matter for at least oc-casional consultation.

Samuel Richardson: Printer-Novelist

Keith Maslen

While Richardson's novels have never ceased to attract or provoke, interest in his printing developed only slowly. For a long time it was enough to wonder that a London tradesman could escape the "sordid views" of his class to write with art and passion of the workings of the female heart, setting his realistic narratives in a social domain from which he was by birth and occupation excluded (James Harris to Richardson in Richardson, *Correspondence* 1: 163). Richardson himself tried to keep the two parts of his life separate. In 1753 he insisted to Johannes Stinstra in Holland that he had written only "at such times of Leisure" as did not interfere with his strenuous attention to the printing business he operated from 1720 until his death in 1761 (*Selected Letters* 230).

The study of Richardson as printer and writer combined came about once editors and textual critics began seriously to consider how texts were transformed in the printing house. Richardson offered an extreme example of an author able and willing to control every stage in the printing of his own novels. Two scholarly works were published in 1936 linking printer and novelist: Alan D. McKillop's *Samuel Richardson, Printer and Novelist* and William Merritt Sale, Jr.'s *Samuel Richardson: A Bibliographical Record of His Literary Career with Historical Notes.* Sale's bibliography focused on Richardson's printing of his own writings.

Sale went on to publish *Samuel Richardson: Master Printer* in 1950. His aim was to draw the character of the press and its master, chiefly by compiling a list of the "books" that Richardson printed (2). Richardson had licensed such an approach by excusing himself to a correspondent in 1743: "I seldom read but as a Printer, having so much of that, and a Head so little able to bear it" (qtd. in Eaves and Kimpel, *Samuel Richardson* 570). As master, Richardson would have been familiar with the texts he gave his compositors to set; he would also have done much reading of proofs, especially in earlier years. It was not unreasonable to suppose that something of what Richardson thus read sank into his mind to resurface in his writing.

Sale's work remained for fifty years the authority on Richardson as printer, and close students of the novels gained comfort from his leading ideas. Sale claims, for instance, that "from the outset of his career Richardson began to exercise choice over the books that he printed," and "as he became more and more independent, the exercise of this choice became more clearly a measure of his preferences and his prejudices" (*Master Printer* 3). The argument, if true, seems to justify drawing an intellectual profile of Richardson from the works he printed, and perhaps even from those he did not print, although Richardson is known to have refused work only when desperately busy. He wrote to an aggrieved author, Philip Skelton, in 1754, while busy with the printing of *Grandison*, "But what did I not do to serve you to the utmost of my power? I parted with three pieces of work. . . . I refused Dr. Leland's last piece" (Richardson, *Correspondence* 5: 238). T. C. Duncan Eaves and Ben D. Kimpel in their critical biography pursued this line of reasoning, remarking that "[t]he known products of his press [are] overwhelmingly pious and . . . free from either scepticism or immorality" (*Samuel Richardson* 69). Such arguments are tempting, but their legitimacy depends on the quantity of the evidence on which they are based. One contrary instance throws them in doubt.

It matters therefore that Sale's record of Richardson's printed output was incomplete. Although Sale knew he fell short, he did not know by how far or in what ways, mainly because his means of identifying works from Richardson's press were severely limited. Like other printers of his day, Richardson put his name only to a small percentage of the works he printed, chiefly those that he had some share in publishing. No Richardson printing accounts were available, apart from Treasury accounts for his official House of Commons printing, and Sale made little use of these. Richardson's scattered correspondence is scanty before the late 1730s, and what is known deals little with his printing. Peter Sabor and Tom Keymer's forthcoming *Cambridge Edition of the Correspondence of Samuel Richardson* is certain to offer important new material. Sale's means for recognizing Richardson's workmanship were the decorative handcut printing ornaments then much in fashion, which left unique fingerprints on many of the printed pages. However, Sale hampered his search by relying on a relatively small selection of the ornaments he found. Moreover, although he discussed the three known categories of Richardson's printing—books and pamphlets, newspapers, and official printing for the House of Commons—he formally described only the first.

I first suspected Richardson to be a much more productive printer than had been shown when in 1951 I bought a schoolbook, not listed by Sale, containing a host of ornaments. In it appeared some ornaments that had already been reproduced by Sale interspersed with many others not yet identified as Richardson's but presumably also his. This discovery led in 2001 to the publication of my *Samuel Richardson of London, Printer: A Study of His Printing Based on His Ornament Use and Business Accounts*. This volume offers a books list containing approximately twice as many items as Sale, a much more extensive parliamentary list of Richardson's official and unofficial House of Commons printing—the unofficial printing a line of work now first made available to Richardson scholars—and a newspaper list based on the examination of 7,522 issues of six newspapers. I reconsider all items listed by Sale, adding details of imprint, format, collation, full ornament record, and location in all but a few problematic instances. Of my many sources, some were new, including previously unused Richardson printing accounts and of course *The Eighteenth-Century Short Title Catalogue*. Besides the business accounts, my main means of verification were the printer's ornaments, totaling 526. I traced the ornaments through every Richardson work in which they appeared, recording their details by means of a relational database so that patterns of use could be interpreted. These ornaments are reproduced with tables showing frequencies and dates of use, dimensions, signs of wear and tear, and so on. A lengthy introduction surveys Richardson's forty years as a master printer, discussing the various categories of work and the range of customers. Richardson can now be viewed as one of the great London printers of his time.

The major find is Richardson's unofficial parliamentary printing, which comprises both private (and local) bills and a peripheral group of printed papers, the work of lobbyists. Why did all this work remain unknown for so long? Richardson can take some blame for not being more explicit. For example, when in that rare autobiographical letter to Stinstra he looked back over thirty-three years as a master printer:

> I began for myself, married, & pursued Business with an Assiduity that, perhaps, has few Examples; & with the more Alacrity, as I improved a Branch of it, that interfered not with any other Person; & made me more independent of Booksellers (tho' I did much Business for them) than any other Printer. (*Selected Letters* 230)

Richardson's early years as a printer are obscure. It now appears that he began in the late summer or autumn of 1720, taking over the printing business of John Leake some months after Leake's death in February. He had previously been acting as Leake's overseer and then the firm's manager, but for how long is not clear. The following year he married Martha Wilde, daughter of the John Wilde to whom he had been apprenticed. All through the 1720s he had striven to establish himself; it took him until 1725 to pay Leake's heirs for the business. No wonder that years later he recalled how eagerly he had made the best of his opportunities. He acknowledges the "much Business" he did for the booksellers. Indeed, he would have been foolish to ignore the wholesaling and retailing booksellers of London who dominated the British book trade. Eaves and Kimpel conjecture, not unreasonably, that Richardson's main associates before the publication of *Pamela* were his fellow members of the Company of Stationers of London—although as I suggest below this view needs to be qualified. Well over two hundred town and country booksellers are named in imprints in my books list, linking Richardson with many of the leading firms of his day. The range of authors whose work he printed likewise has been extended.

However, in this short piece I want to focus on important areas of Richardson's work as printer that have been given little or no attention by Richardson scholars. The clue, long visible, is Richardson's reference to that "Branch" of work that he personally had developed, one neither handed to him as a gift of booksellers nor shared with other printers. Sale thought it was a newspaper that enabled Richardson to take his "first step toward . . . emancipation" from the dominance of the booksellers (*Master Printer* 34). And, yes, between 1723 and

1746 Richardson was involved in the printing of all or part of six newspapers. However, except during the mid-1730s, he had only one newspaper at a time in printing, and this cannot have made him rich. Eaves and Kimpel were closer to the mark when they opted instead for Richardson's official printing of public bills, reports, and other papers for the House of Commons (*Samuel Richardson* 56). My objections are that Richardson did not begin this work until 1733 and that its quantity (not counting his printing from 1743 of the retrospective volumes of the *Journals of the House of Commons*) was not that great. A third suggestion, which I am of course convinced is correct, relates to a branch of business that Richardson can be shown to have "improved" from his earliest days as a printer (see Maslen, "Samuel Richardson as Printer" and "Samuel Richardson's Private Acts").

That Richardson had "conducted an extensive business in the printing of private bills" was first noticed by the parliamentary historian Sheila Lambert ("Printing" 35). When, by tracking down and examining copies, I discovered just how much of this work Richardson had printed from first to last, I realized that this was the "Branch" of business Richardson had in mind when writing to Stinstra. There was enough of it to confer a considerable measure of independence from the booksellers. The word "improved" was shrewdly chosen. Richardson did not initiate this trade. Private bills had been required to be printed since 1705, and the few private bills I have seen dating between 1715 and 1719 appear from their ornamental initials to have come from the printing house of Richardson's predecessor, Leake. Richardson saw the potential of this line of work while working for Leake and determined to carry it on. As the traffic in private bills continued to increase during the century, Richardson profited accordingly. His determination not to let any of this trade slip out of his hands may be imagined. Nearly the full extent of Richardson's private-bill work between 1720 and 1761 is revealed in my parliamentary list, where I describe 868 private bills and 178 local bills, also customarily classed as private, making a total of 1,046. By comparison, Richardson's official printing between 1733 and 1761 of House of Commons public bills, accounts, and papers amounts to no more than 276 items. Since the total number of private and local bills enacted between 1720 and 1761, as revealed by the House of Commons journal, was approximately 1,300, it is clear that Richardson enjoyed by far the greatest share of this trade. Richardson did not have a monopoly. Between 1720 and 1761, the Bowyers, father and son, are known to have printed 66 private bills (Maslen and Lancaster). A few other printers were probably involved. It is probable that Richardson printed more than I have found, especially local bills, copies of which have proved notoriously elusive. It must also be noted that behind each act finally approved and printed by the King's Printer there were commonly two or three printed drafts often varying considerably in text and hence requiring much resetting. The printer charged for all this work, hence most private bills were worth more to Richardson than might appear from their size as shown by surviving copies of a particular draft. This is not all: whereas Richardson charged his bookseller customers a markup of fifty percent on top of wages, for all parliamentary work the markup was double. This work demanded exceptional accuracy and dispatch, but the rewards were commensurate.

It is tempting to speculate how Richardson may have reacted to the contents of these private bills. Concerned in the main with what can be broadly described as family matters, their purpose was to allow individuals and groups who were rich or influential enough to alter the course of their lives through the passing of legislation. Many occasions called for the remedy of a private bill. There were estate bills to enable an individual or trustees or guardians to dispose of property; enclose common fields; alter wills; dissolve marriages; restrain lunatics from marrying, aliening, or incumbering their estates. Marriage settlements might require changes in the law. "John Earl of Grandison in the kingdom of Ireland" petitioned in 1729 to settle family estates consequent on the marriage of his son, Lord Villiers, and his wife, Jane (Maslen, *Samuel Richardson* 173–74). Some fourteen years later, in 1753 and in another country, Richardson could safely borrow so choice a name for the hero of his last novel! The family affairs of the rich and noble were often intimately exposed, as in the "Act to dissolve the marriage of Godfrey Wentworth, Esquire, with Dorothea Pilkington, his now wife," which cites the wife's "criminal intercourse, and an adulterous conversation" (Maslen, *Samuel Richardson* 235). Richardson's familiarity with such legal documents might license the speculation that he had become fascinated or horrified by the doings and misdoings of members of the upper classes long before he came to write about Mr. B. and Lovelace. Clarissa's tragic history, after all, began with her grandfather's will (said to be open to dispute), by which she inherited a too desirable estate.

Private bills brought independence from the booksellers because they were printed for a set of private clients, lawyers who knew how to feed such things into the parliamentary system. (For public bills and other papers, Richardson's client was the House of Commons, which gave the order for such things to be printed.) The names of nineteen such persons for whom the Bowyers printed their 66 private bills are known, though only a few have been adequately identified. These persons belong to a new class of parliamentary agent, whose undoubted leader was Robert Harper of Lincoln's Inn. Harper's career, spanning an astonishing fifty years and neatly encompassing Richardson's, was exposed to view in 1971 by Lambert in *Bills and Acts*. Between 1720 and 1761 Harper drew about 600 bills of which Richardson printed almost 500. He was therefore Harper's major printer, though not his only one.

A second lawyer for whom Richardson printed a good deal of this sort of work has recently been identified (Maslen, "Samuel Richardson's Private Acts" 7). This was the attorney James Blew, for whom, between December 1720 and May 1730, Richardson printed 112 works. Many of these had to be reprinted, resulting in a total of 204 distinct pieces. Not one is listed by Sale. The document containing this interesting new information came into being following Blew's early death in late May or early June 1730, when a family dispute brought Court of Chancery proceedings and Richardson was required to submit details of his business dealings with Blew. Richardson copied out Blew's account into a notebook for submission as a Chancery master's exhibit. The court proceedings, although not as protracted as Jarndyce and Jarndyce in Dickens's *Bleak House*, dragged on until 1769 (see Blew). The Blew account is not one of Richardson's own printing-house ledgers, such as those that exist for several of his contemporaries, but is the most substantial of his extant printing accounts, apart from the treasury record of his official parliamentary work.

Thirty of the 112 are private and local bills dealing with the usual wide range of topics: enclosures, marriage settlements, road improvements, bridge building, and river navigation. However, most aim to influence the vote on or character of proposed legislation. Their titles confirm their purpose: "The Case of the Levant Company, in relation to the bill now depending before this Honourable House [of Commons], for Performing Quarentine"; "Letter to a Member on the New Privileges of the East India Company"; "Reasons humbly offered for regulating the importation of tobacco into this kingdom" (Maslen, *Samuel Richardson* 66, 103, 120). Lambert explains that those who felt themselves affected by legislation before parliament, themselves probably the promoters of bills, "often published statements of their positions, usually in the form of broadsheets which could be handily distributed to members in the lobbies and no doubt had a wider circulation" (*House of Commons* 1: 28). The Blew notebook shows that the numbers printed of such pieces usually did not much exceed the combined membership of both houses. Lambert further explains that many such papers are listed in L. W. Hanson, *Contemporary Printed Sources for British and Irish Economic History, 1701–1750*, which Lambert recommends because it provides "a very valuable adjunct to the formal records of the House" (*House of Commons* 1: 89). Although many of the items printed for Blew are in Hanson, many remain unidentified, even though the legislation to which they refer is readily recognizable.

Blew was a good customer for just over ten years. Richardson had presumably inherited him when he took over Leake's printing house in 1720, since Blew had been in business at least since 1714. For work done for Blew during 1721 Richardson received about £100, of which one-third or more would have been gross profit. Here is yet another substantial body of material with which Richardson was closely concerned and which needs to be weighed for its bearing on our assessment of Richardson. Did others continue Blew's activities, and did Richardson print for them?[1]

There is often something maddeningly slow about the printing of books. Authors know this well enough, and yet they too with one eye on posterity delay even further the printing of their magnum opus. Richardson, it can now be seen, spent much of his time on other kinds of work where speed was of the essence. Throughout his entire career he was caught up in what may be described as "printing to the moment," analogous to the "writing to the moment" of Richardson's characters.[2] The deadlines for newspapers and for parliamentary bills are measured in days if not hours. The Blew notebook records that in early 1726 Richardson printed and reprinted the Kensington Road bill on no fewer than five occasions: 30 March and 1, 23, 28, and 30 April. At one time the workmen were paid extra "for Expedition being all Night" (Maslen, *Samuel Richardson* 254–55). A corresponding urgency attended the printing of the para-parliamentary cases, reasons, and the like that feature so plentifully in Blew's account. On 20 July 1721 there is an entry for printing 600 copies of a "sheet relating to prevention of Infection, by Running of Goods," followed by 300 "of ye same, [with] Alterations & additions," and 200 more "with Great Additions" (Maslen, *Samuel Richardson* 118). From our historical perspective, it is hard to sense the impact of such works on Richardson's contemporary readers, just as we struggle to recall how last month we lived through the successive stages of a breaking news story, now almost forgotten. I would not go so far as to claim that Richardson learned from these special pleaders how to write to the moment, but he certainly knew from experience that printing was not necessarily more permanent than speech.

Perhaps our old knowledge of Richardson's life as printer, which showed in black and white a poetic writer and a prosaic tradesman, was more comfortable. However, I think a new critical agreement has been reached that Richardson can only be properly understood in the light of everything that he achieved. Above all there is a growing appreciation that he was an intensely political being. The new material enlarges the possibilities for exploration of the printer-novelist whose works, in Terry Eagleton's words "intertwine with commerce, religion, theatre, ethical debate, the visual arts, public entertainment" and reach "into the most inconspicuous crevices of middle-class culture [and] the most august of state ideological apparatuses" (6, 8).

During my lengthy investigation of Richardson as printer I was encouraged by the hope that others would use my work to make connections guessed and unguessed between the printer and his novels. The most challenging body of new material is undoubtedly Richardson's printing of private parliamentary bills. There are parallels to be drawn between the dramatis personae of two sets of narratives, the factual and the fictive. Consider for instance the surnames Richardson chose for his array of fictional characters, suiting their rank and class, found rather than invented, and contributing to his realism. Did he borrow names other than Grandison from the bills he printed, and if so what might such borrowing tell about the workings of his creative imagination? And did he perhaps derive his grasp of legal terminology from these same sources?

My books list is another field for harvesting. What works did Richardson print that Sale does not catalog? Is it still true that Richardson would not print works that he disapproved of? He wrote scathingly of Eliza Haywood's scandal fiction, as Tom Keymer noted in his introduction to *Pamela* (Keymer, Introduction xi–xii). Yet I show that in 1732 he printed two of the four volumes of the third edition of her *Secret Histories* (*Samuel Richardson* 90). Perhaps this shared printing job provided the ground for Richardson's opinion. Will my lists justify further speculation as to the evolution of Richardson's political ideas? Sale, who identifies as Richardson's earliest customer (from 1719) Archibald Hutcheson, the Tory member of Parliament and persistent opponent of the proposals by the South Sea Company to redeem the National Debt that led to the bursting of the South Sea Bubble, argues that "Richardson's political position in the early 1720s accords closely with that of Hutcheson" (*Master Printer* 37). While I would not go so far as to doubt Sale's conclusion, I must question his assumption that like was somehow attracted to like, for Hutcheson had first been Leake's customer and Richardson merely acquired him by purchase. There is a deeper issue here. I cannot do better than quote the words of that great bibliographer W. W. Greg: "Every item of historical evidence performs a two-fold function: positively it enlarges the basis we have to build on, and enables us to extend the structure of valid inference; negatively it is often of even greater service in limiting the field of admissible conjecture" (x).

A final question or two for those with an interest in the visual arts. Why did Richardson use so many printer's ornaments: headpieces at the head of chapters and other textual divisions, tailpieces to fill blank spaces at the end of such divisions, initials and factotums (in which any letter could be inserted) to pick out the first letter of text? In the mid-sized schoolbook I mention above, thirty-five Richardson ornaments are used one hundred and ten times. Perhaps in this instance Richardson's compositors were simply following the current fashion. But since Richardson bought most of this material, it may be guessed that sometimes he chose the designs. One ornament that portrays Europa being carried off by Jupiter in the form of a bull was first used in volume 5 of the third edition of *Clarissa*. The ornament was used not merely in the customary manner as decoration but to underline for the alert reader the significance of Clarissa's rape. Here author and printer were working together as one. Again, in the mid-1740s Richardson begins to use a new class of pictorial ornament, and it would be interesting to know why. These questions and others, I would hope, can be answered by consulting the corpus of Richardson ornaments collected by Maslen (which surely does not include all that Richardson ever used). This corpus may also help researchers identify yet more works from Richardson's press (see *Samuel Richardson*).

NOTES

[1]Richardson's considerable dealing with a third attorney and parliamentary agent has recently been revealed by Keymer ("Parliamentary Printing"). It appears that between 1725 and 1729, Richardson printed cases and other legal work for William Martin,

brother of the well-known banker Thomas Martin, in the amount of £179.4s.6d, half as much again as for Blew over the same period. The too trusting Richardson was swindled out of his due payment. One of the jobs in question can be identified as *State of Mr. Bagenal's Title to, and the Conveyances and Securities from Him of the Irish Estates to Mr. Martin and Trustees, 1725* (Maslen, *Samuel Richardson* 142).

[2]Compare "written, as hoped, to Nature & the Moment" (Richardson to Lady Echlin [Richardson, *Selected Letters* 316]).

Vegetable Loves:
A Defense, in Part, of Mrs. Jewkes

Patricia Brückmann

What needs to be emphasized most to new students of Richardson, and even to advanced ones, is Richardson's use of detail to point his fictions. How old, for example, is the heroine of *Pamela* when she arrives at B-hall? When she is abducted to Lincolnshire? How far away and in what kind of circumstances do her parents live? What was a guinea worth in 1740? What was her father's occupation? What is his job now, and how much does it pay? How long has her mistress been dead when the novel opens? Does this period have any significance in ordinary ritual? When does Pamela change the clothes handed down to her from Mr. B.'s mother? Where does she get her new ones, and what do they cost? What are the meanings of "linen"? What are clocked stockings and Spanish leather? Where is Mr. B.'s southern house and why does Richardson locate the gloomy old mansion that dominates most of the novel in Lincolnshire? Finally, why do the answers to these questions matter? I offer some illustrations.

I knew I had found a good reader when, at the beginning of my lectures on *Pamela*, a young woman who had already reached the Lincolnshire garden and the sunflower correspondence appeared at my door with a question about a passage: "Does this mean what I *think* it means?" Because we began the course with the *Pilgrim's Progress* and *A Journal of the Plague Year*, the group already knew about the way that gardens, garden history, and pastoral oases figure in the eighteenth-century novel. They also knew that Mr. B.'s establishment in Bedfordshire was a pleasant property, whose garden, in a detail supplied later in the novel, has a fashionable "pretty canal" and other water features, all artful imitations of nature and all very expensive (470). His house in Lincolnshire, the oldest of his extensive holdings (he also owns a London flat and a small farm in Kent), is by contrast no *locus amoenus*. Accordingly, the presiding figure, Mrs. Jewkes, is no mother substitute. This more northerly garden contains only a sunflower and a rosebush, vital to Pamela as devices for her clandestine correspondence with Parson Williams. The class and I would later spend some time on both these, especially the sunflower, a flower appropriate for a plain country garden yet with a tradition of its own.[1]

But my student, interested neither in sunflowers nor in rosebushes, focused on Pamela's discussing the growth of beans "planted" the day before. "Do you think," Pamela says to Mrs. Jewkes, "that any of my Beans can have struck since Yesterday?. . . Here, said I, having a Bean in my Hand, is one of them; but it was not stirr'd. No, to be sure, said she: and turn'd upon me a most wicked Jest, unbecoming the Mouth of a Woman, about Planting, &c." (134). We were then using the T. C. Duncan Eaves and Ben D. Kimpel edition of the novel. In the newer, Thomas Keymer and Alice Wakely edition, the note on this passage suggests that it is

> perhaps best glossed by "Roger Phfuquewell's" account . . . of the ceremonies of planting observed by the men of Merryland, which involved "prostrating themselves on their Faces, and muttering many Ejaculations in praise of the Spot they have chosen . . . then he sticks his Plough in it, and falls to labouring the Soil with all his Might."   (528 n134)[2]

Keymer and Wakely also note Fielding's use of "&c." for female sexual organs in *Shamela*. Although this gloss helps with the possible obscenity of the passage, it says nothing about "stirr'd," although that is the word that starts Mrs. Jewkes on her jest and that, together with the shape of the horsebean, struck my student. As Pamela holds the motionless bean in her hand, she fully understands the jest, however "unbecoming the Mouth of a Woman." Later in the novel, Sir Simon, who is given to sexual insinuation, responds to Lady Jones's wish that he say nothing to make ladies blush, saying, "They blush, because they understand" (298), which is taken from Jonathan Swift's *Cadenus and Vanessa*, a poem that, as Keymer and Wakely remind us, Richardson admired (566).

We need not reach quite so far afield for a gloss as Thomas Stretzer's *Merryland*, because a long literary tradition of planting and sexual activity already existed. Gordon Williams cites "the *Young-Mans Answer*," by Samuel Pepys, where a young man asks a "pritty Lass" to "let me your Garden view, And what fine flowrs you do want, ile plant them o'er anew" (Williams 2: 1052).[3] Nathaniel Bailey similarly "records the Lat. 'HORTUS in some *Writers* the Privy Parts of a Woman'" (Williams 2: 581).

Encouraged by my visitor, I began our class meeting that day with the beans, then went on to talk of the very different garden with which the novel begins. This, as I have noted, is in Bedfordshire, the home county where Mr. B. has built his newest house, with its Georgian windows, summerhouse, library, and pleasant gardens in the style, we can conjecture, of the mid-century.[4] The order and openness of the house are reflected by the servants remaining from the reign of the former Mrs. B., especially by Mrs. Jervis, whose past status seems to have been rather more elevated. But while not all my students were as sharp as my earlier visitor, many were quick to perceive Pamela's attraction to Mr. B. because of her perpetual delay in leaving even after his designs are clear. (Others in the household, including the heroine herself, do not see the attraction.) They also saw how useless the apparently motherly chief of the B-hall servants really is, for it takes Mrs. Jervis a long time to see her master's plots and not just because he has so far run an "orderly and well-governed household" (128). Conversely, and probably because they are country people as well as anxious parents, Mr. and Mrs. Andrews realize what is going on. When one student spluttered that *her* parents would have jumped into the car and come to fetch her, another pointed out that, after Mr. Andrews's descent from schoolmaster to a shilling-a-week fence-post-hole digger, they are, after all, poor as well as twenty-three miles away.

But Pamela is in no real danger in Bedfordshire. If the staff are ineffectual, they are also numerous and for the most part well intentioned. The abduction, which occurs only a quarter of the way through the novel, is essential—not only to effect Mr. B.'s ultimate design but also to bring Pamela from an upper-class pastoral world to the central problem of the book. By "problem" I mean the maintenance of a family "as ancient as the best in the Kingdom" (257). Mr. B.'s family is now down to its last male, not just through marriage but, as the text makes clear again and again, through the sexual encounters that will continue the line. Pamela does not need admirers of what is essentially a fugitive and cloistered virtue; she needs an antagonist who will bring her to clarity about her future. In other words, she needs Mrs. Jewkes and her landscape.

Robert A. Erickson's *Mother Midnight*, a study, as his subtitle announces, of "birth, sex, and fate in eighteenth-century fiction (Defoe, Richardson, and Sterne)," provides useful contexts for the Lincolnshire housekeeper from the world of midwifery and brothel keeping in literature and art. Reading Erickson provides students with an important detail from eighteenth-century social history. Mrs. Jewkes's origins, as Pamela rather sniffily observes, lie in the world of innkeepers, and Mrs. Jewkes has a sister nearly as doubtful in reputation as she. Pamela implies Mrs. Jewkes is not the right sort of person for a teenager (Pamela arrived at twelve and is now fifteen) who has been surrogate daughter for three years to Mrs. B., an upper-class a woman whose clothes and shoe size she shares. But although Mrs. Jewkes is later seen tipsy (at least in Pamela's account) and no one would call her beautiful, my class was quick to note that we cannot entirely trust Pamela's caricature of Mrs. Jewkes's goggling eyes, skin "pickled a Month in Salt-petre," and arm as thick as her own waist (114). More than one student was moved to think of Juliet's bawdy nurse, and once in search of what might lie beneath the caricature, students were struck by other dimensions in Mrs. Jewkes. As Pamela knows from comparisons made early in Bedfordshire, her keeper may be bad at keeping accounts.[5] But as later passages will show, she is practical with bandages for maids caught in collapsing walls and useful as doctor to the master to whom she is devoted. Unlike the Bedfordshire crew, she is also capable not only of realistic assessments about the consequences of actions but also of indirect determinations about where platonic love must end if life and estates are to continue.

The students and I looked at the historical context of the Lincolnshire garden scene where Mrs. Jewkes is fishing. Pamela remarks that she is planting life, whereas her antagonist is destroying it. Although untrue, her remark sets up the jest that establishes Pamela as the potentially fruitful terrain. Was there any historical or literary significance, asked one student, to the fishing? There was. Eighteenth-century readers would certainly recognize a richly obscene allusive tradition in the scene of fishing and fishponds, even if they were no longer enthusiastic readers of John Donne. Fishing, as Williams notes, is "a perennial image" (see *fishpond*, 1: 494–97).[6] The sunflower appears from Ovid onward. Pamela is not planting life but advancing her plot for rescue; she is also not simply planting a vegetable with a suggestive shape but planting horsebeans, which were used for fodder, not for human food. Mrs. Jewkes's amusement (and she likes to see Pamela amuse herself) may suggest that she is aware of her charge's ineptitude as gardener. I told students that if they read *Clarissa* they would find another witch-midwife in the character of grotesque brothel keeper, who has none of the features that take the edges off Mrs. Jewkes. Were there also gardens in *Clarissa*, asked one? I told them about the garden in Mrs. Sinclair's establishment, "crammed . . . with vases, flowerpots and figures without number," its profusion and confusion an image of the house itself (470).

But while this earlier garden, as neglected as its walls and the household chapel turned junk room, may not teem, the wicked jest in *Pamela* signals another production—the main matter of both the abduction and the novel as a whole,[7] that is, the union of Pamela and Mr. B. That much the students implicitly agreed on, for nobody ever liked Parson Williams. While not actually preferring energetic, aspiring rapists to clerical wimps and though sympathetic to Parson Williams's endangered position as Mr. B.'s dependent, students noted with approval that Pamela does "not love a Parson" and wished for more aggressive action from Mr. B. (143). This was despite my warning them about Richardson's problems with Lovelace and his insertion of footnotes into *Clarissa* meant to discourage those too much taken (like the heroine herself) by Lovelace's considerable charms.

No year passed in which a student did not inquire after the cucumber, a vegetable that turns up in the text just before the joke about the beans. Pamela is trying to "come at [her] Sun-flower" (128) when, as a device to get rid of the maid, she says, "Pray, step to the Gardener, and ask him to gather a Sallad for me to Dinner . . . and pray tell him I should like a Cucumber too, if he has one" (128). Searches in databases and dictionaries for how the word *cucumber* was used in the eighteenth century produced initially only documentation of the common phrase "cool as a cucumber"; commentaries on the fragility of cucumber frames; and the use of *cucumber* as a synonym for tailors, who did not expect to do well in that off-season called "cucumber time."[8] The students, who had already reflected on the cucumber and its shape, were by now quite taken with the notion that they might find common sense echoed by the history of images and ideas.

The best source came through the serendipity of college chat. After a class, I told a colleague about our Richardson discussion. A few days later, back came a note advising me to try Ralf Norrman and Jon Haarberg, *Nature and Language: A Semiotic Study of Cucurbits in Literature*. In the first part of the book, entitled "Pregnant Gourds and Delirious Pumpkins," the authors map out what we might call the cucurbitic terrain. Such vegetables are ubiquitous in literature and in art, they suggest, because of their "anatomy" and "the cucurbitic tradition" (14). They grow with exceptional speed, the cucumber most rapidly of all according to Athenaeus's *Deipnosophistae*, the oldest Western cookbook. Cucumbers, says Athenaeus, "grow in gardens when the moon is full, and their growth is as visible as that of sea-urchins" (1: 321). Their "associations," Norrman and Haarberg suggest, are "with summer, sunshine, well being, vitality, fertility, rejuvenation, luxury and abundance" (14). For instance, Cinderella's fairy godmother's transformation of a pumpkin to advance her heroine's cause would seem to have vegetarian folklore behind it.[9] Most readers of *Pamela* sense the presence of this fairy tale in the background. Norrman and Haarberg cite Pliny on cucumbers and fertility in a passage from another encyclopedic work, the *Natural History* (22). The Loeb translation, from which I give a longer quotation, reads, "It is thought that conception is aided by cucumber seed if a woman keeps it fastened to her body without its having touched the ground; while labour is easier if, without her knowledge, the seed, wrapped in ram's wool, be tied to her loins" (7). Williams notes that cucumbers are proverbially associated with coldness, but adds, "However, the vegetable's roughly phallic shape has given it a contrasting significance in [this] proverb . . . 'He is pleased with gourds and his wife with cucumbers,' glossed as 'A Proverb by which is expressed that both the man and his wife are vitious much alike.'" Thomas Middleton hints as much in *A Chaste Maid in Cheapside* when Allwit declares, "My wife's as great as she can wallow . . . and longs For nothing but pickled cucumbers and [her lover's] coming" (qtd. in Williams 1: 348).

My class and I agreed it would be ridiculous to assume that Pamela, in calling for a salad, singles out the cucumber because she knows the history I have just sketched out. And while she understands Mrs. Jewkes's gloss on the beans, without, we assume, herself glossing the "&c.," it takes the crone's joke to alert her to the obscenity. The cucumber simply adds to the vegetable landscape that is building up in the garden. It is not quite Alexander Pope's bravura turn in *The*

Rape of the Lock about maids, bottles, and corks (54), but the sexual implication seems plain, given the scenery and the cast of characters. I guess that I admire Richardson for keeping Mrs. Jewkes quiet and thus leaving the implications to the reader.

Would my class have done all this research if Richardson had bought specified the vegetable as a bean? Perhaps. But that Pamela herself specifies the meaning of them increases the sexually suggestive quality of the scene, as well as providing a proper (or improper) backdrop for Mrs. Jewkes, a character who looks like everyone's nightmare of a "wicked Procuress" (109). This wide-of-the-mark phrase belongs to Pamela, who finds it increasingly convenient to project wickedness onto Mr. B.'s arithmetically challenged agent, a lightning rod to deflect judgment from the hero.

On the most obvious level, Mrs. Jewkes and the landscape in which she functions isolate the heroine and give her a force against which to react. The result is that Pamela becomes necessarily more inventive, livelier, stronger—and much more attractive. Mr. B. will say in the end (whether we believe him or not) that he has fallen in love with her physical person but marries her because of her mind and character. But we concluded that another important effect of removing her from the artificial proprieties of the south to a natural country world is that her attention and ours is increasingly drawn to production and reproduction. That is, to borrow from Erickson, we are drawn not to the world of the witch but to the world of the midwife. Although we will find Pamela reading John Locke's treatise on education in the second part of her story, her chief function is not to reproduce knowledge but to continue Mr. B.'s line.

While Mr. B. annoyed my students with his comments about clockwork (369) and his flowering into a pastoral poet (495), he deliberately enlarges the implications of the kitchen garden and the preoccupations of his northern housekeeper when he says that he likes Pamela's small waist but wants it to swell. This sounds like the double entendres of the neighbors, as aware of squirearchical imperatives as Pamela is of wicked jests.[10]

When we went on to *Shamela*, I suggested Eric Rothstein's splendid annotative essay "The Framework of *Shamela*." As we know, Henry Fielding did not like *Pamela*, but, as Rothstein points out, *Shamela* is an "exploitation rather than an exposé of its older soberer sister" (399). The essay both gave students pleasure in scholarly detective work and demonstrated in a practical way how eighteenth-century texts respond to one another. But when students read Fielding's arch comment in *Shamela* about Pamela's wedding night—"this was the Letter which is lost" (H. Fielding, *Apology* [ed. Baker] 64)—they asked whether anyone, outside what they were prepared to believe was an exceptionally colorful libertine tradition of writing in the period, would write an account of a wedding night, however suggestive the surrounding text? Overt sexual reference is, quite simply, not Richardson's style. And yet Richardson provides sensual details that make this scene (and other parts of the novel) highly suggestive.[11] The Lincolnshire estate is in sharp contrast to Bedfordshire; there is no Georgian symmetry in the novel. Because that other wicked jester, Mrs. Jewkes, is the central figure of these spaces, she is in her own way the agent if not the architect of the union between hero and heroine. George Saintsbury remarked long ago, "I am much mistaken if there are not in Richardson more than a few scenes and situations the 'impropriety' of which positively exceeds anything in Fielding"(103).[12] The vegetable loves of Lincolnshire are among these scenes. In 1801, the cucumber and the wicked jest about the beans disappear, a negative confirmation of their allusive quality.[13] This later deletion (not unlike other transformations in the evolution of the text) confers a gentility foreign, I think, to what Richardson wanted to represent in a novel that my students were prepared to rank as lively and humane.

NOTES

[1]For recent studies, see Mancoff 40–60; Druick and Zegers 75–77, 376. Works of this kind put students in touch with the ways in which fine-art traditions inform fictions. The sunflower is vigorous and, in the seventeenth century, illustrates "many forms of devotion and constancy . . . of a subject to a patron, a wife to a husband, a child to a parent, or a lover to his or her beloved," as Mancoff observes (49). The emblem tradition extends this devotion to sacred love as well. It would have been hard not to have been aware of this tradition. As Harris has told us, Louis XV took the sunflower as his emblem (*Samuel Richardson* 32–33).

[2]*A New Description of Merryland* was written by Thomas Stretzer. The obscene implication of the invented author's surname will be clear enough; his first name is obscene too.

[3]See also Partridge 638.

[4]One of my former students, Katherine Spencer-Ross, a double major in English and art history, wrote a senior essay on the houses and gardens of some novels before 1832. Since she was, at the same time, working on the English landscape garden, she drafted a persuasive sketch of the Bedfordshire house based on details in the novel. A student in the following year sketched a plausible plan of the Lincolnshire estate. See my "Prisons and Palaces: The Settings of *Pamela*."

[5]On eighteenth-century women and accounts, see Hunt (58–59) and Connor.

[6]Most students, even the advanced ones, need to be told about the existence of dictionaries like Williams's, as well as Chambers's *Cyclopedia*, dictionaries of canting words, Grose, and Partridge on slang and unconventional English. None of these details appear in the abridgments of 1769 or 1790.

[7]Some students went on to read *Pamela II*, where Pamela rapidly becomes the mother of seven, five boys and two girls, just right for a landowner who wanted both to continue his line and to extend his property. They found Janet Aikins's essay on the second part especially useful (see "Re-presenting the Body").

[8]Searches like this provided an opportunity to remind the class about the usefulness of the Chadwyck-Healey database.

[9]For a later text, Norrman and Haarberg cite a passage in *Nicholas Nickleby* where the throwing of the cucumbers over the wall is "a gesture of courtship" (134–35).

[10]For a lively corrective to readings of Richardson that seem to leave out his sense of the body, see Juliet McMaster; see also Harris, *Samuel Richardson* 28, 160–61.

[11]See also "the great Nasty Worm" (128) and the "supposed Bulls" who turn out to be "only two poor Cows" (134).

[12]I owe this quotation to Brian Corman.

[13] My thanks to Sara Salih for pointing this out.

Teaching *Pamela* and the History of Sexuality

Jeremy W. Webster

Students are often shocked to discover the eighteenth century's frankness about sex—they generally come into a course on literature and the history of sexuality in the period convinced that no one wrote about sex until the 1970s. After a sampling of John Wilmot, the Earl of Rochester's poetry has disabused them of that idea, students are ready for a more sophisticated discussion of eighteenth-century sexual mores that includes such issues as the way that people thought of gender and sexual roles, how one's sex usually dictated one's sexual activities, and the differing consequences of sex for men and women. Samuel Richardson's *Pamela* is a particularly useful text for teaching these issues because it illustrates transitions between the premodern and modern systems of constructing gender and sexuality. As Michael McKeon argues, during the Restoration and eighteenth century "personal worth was relocated in the common woman, the repository of a normative honor that had been alienated from an undeserving male aristocracy and that would be apotheosized in the domestic virtues of the modern heterosexual family" ("Historicizing Patriarchy" 310). *Pamela* exemplifies this relocation of personal worth and the contemporaneous valorization of domestic heterosexuality in its depictions of the family, patriarchy, femininity, rape, and the sexuality of women. A comparison of closely read passages from the novel with other works from the Restoration and eighteenth century helps the students in my course on historicizing sexuality in eighteenth-century literature better understand these transformations in English sexuality.

The issue of what constitutes a family is a major theme throughout Richardson's novel. Lawrence Stone argues that

> the four key features of the modern family—intensified affective bonding of the nuclear core at the expense of neighbours and kin; a strong sense of individual autonomy and the right to personal freedom in the pursuit of happiness; a weakening of the association of sexual pleasure with sin and guilt; and a growing desire for physical privacy—were all well established by 1750. (8)

Pamela demonstrates the rise of such a modern, nuclear family as the fundamental social unit, but the word *family* means at least two different things in the eighteenth century. On the one hand, it means roughly what it does today, that is, parents and their children, as when Mr. B. tells Mr. Peters that "he would send his Coach for [Mr. Peters] and his Family" (364). On the other hand, *family* can also mean the entire household, including servants, as when Mr. B. asks Mrs. Jervis whether Pamela is "of any Use in the Family" (28). Being useful to this larger group is one of Pamela's goals. As she writes just after her marriage to Mr. B., "When all these tumultuous Visitings are over, I shall have my Mind, I hope, subside in to a Family Calm, that I may make myself a little useful to the Household of my dear Master, or else I shall be an unprofitable Servant indeed!" (497).

The issue of Pamela's usefulness in the family raises several questions worth pursuing with students. What skills were expected of Pamela as servant and wife? We learn in the first paragraph of the novel that Pamela's former mistress taught her "to write and cast Accompts, and made me a little expert at my Needle, and other Qualifications above my Degree" (11). How do these skills affect Pamela's "use in the family" and shape the direction of her relationship with Mr. B.? How does Mr. B. define use? Are his judgments based on her use value or do his criteria for evaluating her change over the course of the novel? How does the novel ultimately define family? Does it choose one definition over the other? What does it mean that Pamela still thinks of her husband as her master and herself as his servant? The answers to these questions can be tracked throughout the novel. One possible reading activity would be to have students mark each use of the word *family* and then compare the number of times and contexts in which it is used to mean a nuclear family or an entire household.

Stone points out that the eighteenth century's move toward "companionate marriage" and its tendency "to put the prospects of emotional satisfaction before the ambition for increased income or status" led to greater equality between husband and wife (325). *Pamela* portrays the development of this larger autonomy for married women. To begin with, Mr. B. repeatedly asserts his right as head of the household to use Pamela as he sees fit, an assertion in keeping with traditional patriarchy as articulated by Robert Filmer in *Patriarcha*. But the first of John Locke's *Two Treatises of Government* had demolished Filmer's argument that the head of a family, like the king, had almost absolute power over his dependents. *Pamela* not only dramatizes the debate between these two ideologies but also works toward a synthesis of them. Throughout the novel, Pamela argues for her right to self-determination: as Jocelyn Harris points out, "Each time that Mr. B abuses his authority as a domestic king, Pamela responds with Locke's 'Fundamental, Sacred and unalterable Law of Self-Preservation'" (*Samuel Richardson* 18). Mr. B., who slowly comes to accept the argument that Pamela alone has a right to determine her affective and sexual relationships, eventually proclaims that "a voluntier [sic] Love" is the most important characteristic in a wife and that "true Love" is his only motivation for asking her to marry him (270).

Richardson's attitudes toward women's autonomy are most clearly visible when Mr. B. offers Pamela a written contract guaranteeing her compensation for her sexual services. When we are about halfway through the novel, I introduce Nancy Armstrong's thesis that *Pamela* rewrites the assumed sexual contract between men and women by "empower[ing] the female to give herself in exchange with the male" (112). I help students see this point by walking them through Armstrong's comparison of this contract with an early-seventeenth-century Puritan marriage pamphlet. Armstrong presents a chart that clearly delineates gender roles:

HUSBAND	WIFE	
Get goods	Gather them together and save them	
Travel, seek a living	Keep the house	
Get money and provisions	Do not vainly spend it	
Deal with many men	Talk with few	
Be "entertaining"	Be solitary and withdrawn	
Be skillful in talk	Boast of silence	
Be a giver	Be a saver	
Apparel yourself as you may	Apparel yourself as it becomes you	
Dispatch all things outdoors	Oversee and give order within	(110)

I then ask students to compare this chart with the sexual contract offered by Mr. B. (188–92), just as Armstrong does, and to think about several questions: How do Pamela's responses to her master's contract challenge the division of labor inherent in the Puritan marriage tract? What does it mean that Mr. B. even offers her a contract—does this signal that he has already lost the battle of the sexes? What does the contract assume about relations between men and women? What do Pamela's responses suggest that she values? To what extent does Pamela follow these Puritan tenets? Does she "talk with few" men? How many and what kinds of men does she talk to over the course of the novel? What are the consequences of these conversations? Is she "solitary and withdrawn" or is she "entertaining"? How does she behave in social settings with Mr. B.'s relatives and friends? Is she "silent"? To whom does she speak? How does she speak to them? What are the consequences of her speaking? Does she apparel herself "as it becomes" her? When does she change clothes? Why? What is the effect of her clothes on Mr. B., especially when she returns to her rustic garb early in the novel? All these questions prompt students to consider the novel's representation of women's autonomy in marriage.

Family duty clashes with women's autonomy in the novel's resolution, because the same rhetoric of individual autonomy that Pamela espouses throughout her trials is incompatible with the duties of a wife. As Ann Louise Kibbie points out:

> In the transformation of Pamela's character by marriage, the heroic rhetoric of personal freedom, with which Pamela has resisted becoming another's property and asserted her right to self-possession, must be replaced by a new rhetoric of subjection. (566)

Now that Mr. B.'s character has been refashioned into a loving husband, Pamela's must be refashioned into a dutiful wife. Not only does Pamela continue to refer to Mr. B. as her "master" and herself as his servant (497), she explicitly gives up her claim to self-possession. As she promises her fiancé, "I will resolve, with these sweet Encouragements, to be, in every thing, what you would have me be! And I hope I shall, more and more, shew you that I have no Will but yours" (351). I ask students to consider Pamela's transformation in the latter portion of the novel. Why is self-possession not an acceptable trait for a wife in this period? What instructions does Mr. B. give her for her future conduct as his wife? How do these compare with those traits listed in the Puritan pamphlet?

As Mr. B.'s transition from sexual predator to loving husband shows, *Pamela* also participates in its culture's argument that marriage is the appropriate set-ting for sexual pleasure. In a novel that repeatedly refers to Mr. B. as a libertine, *Pamela* is in many respects the story of his domestication. As Vincent Quinn reminds us, "Libertines were particularly associated with sexual misconduct—they were represented as rakes who corrupted married women and ruined vir-gins" (540). Mr. B. admits he has "acted too much the Part of a Libertine" in his behavior toward Pamela (341). Indeed, his attempts to rape her, first in Mrs. Jervis's chamber (63–64) in letter XXV and later at the Lincolnshire estate just after he has offered his contract in return for her services (202–203), confirm him as a libertine. In the middle of his second attempt, however, Mr. B. inexpli-cably pauses and demands to speak with Pamela:

> I must say one Word to you, Pamela; it is this: You see, now you are in my Power!—You cannot get from me, nor help yourself: Yet have I not offer'd any thing amiss to you. But if you resolve not to comply with my Proposals, I will not lose this Opportunity: If you do, I will yet leave you.   (203)

This passage raises several questions that I ask my students to think and write about. Why does Mr. B. pause? His response to Pamela's fear and subsequent fainting place him in marked contrast to other libertines in Restoration and eighteenth-century literature, for instance Aphra Behn's Willmore in *The Rover*, who also attempts to rape women—twice. But Willmore, like Mrs. Jewkes, interprets women's struggles against rape as little more than foreplay. I ask students to identify other ways in which Mr. B.'s libertinism differs from Willmore's. How has libertinism changed as a cultural signifier from the 1670s to the 1740s? What libertine acts does Mr. B. actually perform in the novel? Are the most obvious features of libertinism—seducing wives and ruining vir-gins—still in place or have they changed?

The most tangible signs of Mr. B.'s libertinism are his attempts to seduce and ultimately rape his maidservant, an issue in the novel that must be discussed with extreme care. When Mr. B. rejects the opportunity to rape the uncon-scious Pamela, his reluctance to use violence contrasts markedly with previous aristocratic discourse about rape. Another text for comparison here is Alexan-der Smith's (probably apocryphal) story "Madam Clark, Mistress to the Earl of

Rochester." Having read selections of Rochester's poetry earlier in the term, my students often see Rochester in particular and libertinism in general as liberating male and female sexuality despite the inherent misogyny of some of his work. These students are therefore usually surprised to read Smith's account of the earl's rape of a young countrywoman he meets after she has been thrown from her horse. Having fallen in love with her, Rochester pursues Madam Clark's love, but when she refuses to satisfy his desire, "he began to use Violence" (20). When Madam Clark's grandmother hears her scream, she runs upstairs to her granddaughter's bedroom,

> where finding a Tryal of Skill betwixt the Earl and the young Gentle-woman, and being one that lov'd to see Generation Work go forward, she piously gave an helping Hand, by holding her Legs 'til his Lordship had robb'd her of that Jewel which never could be retriev'd again.   (20–21)

Madam Clark becomes Rochester's mistress until his untimely death. Destitute and ruined, she is forced into prostitution and soon dies at the hands of a greedy pimp. Thus *Pamela* opens up a difference between Mr. B.'s libertinism and Rochester's, at least as libertinism is constructed by one early-eighteenth-century writer, for whereas Madam Clark is ruined with the help of her grandmother, Pamela retains her virtue despite Mrs. Jewkes and even marries her would-be rapist. The trial of H–J– for rape, in 1722 (see "H–J–"), anthologized in Robert DeMaria's *British Literature, 1640–1789*, offers an analogous plotline for students to compare. Here, a man is acquitted of "assaulting, ravishing, and, against her Will, carnally knowing Mary Hicks, Spinster," despite the testimony of Hicks and two witnesses confirming her story, because the accused was able to call a witness who claimed that Hicks said she would rather marry her attacker "than hang him" (617, 618). These texts raise several questions for students to process. What attitudes toward both rape and virtue does each of these texts convey? How do these attitudes reflect cultural visions of libertinism? How does Pamela avoid Mr. B.'s attempted rape? Why does he not rape her after she faints? What relation between rape and marriage do these texts suggest?

Finally, *Pamela* also illustrates changes in the construction of women's sexuality during the period. On the one hand, as I state above, Pamela exemplifies McKeon's argument that "personal worth was relocated in the common woman"; that is, she represents a modern discourse of virginity that equates a woman's worth with her virtue. Pamela's parents advise her to "resolve to lose your Life sooner than your Virtue," since "It is Virtue and Goodness only, that make the true Beauty" (20). After Pamela takes this advice to heart, her virtue is rewarded, as the novel's subtitle tells us, when she marries Mr. B., assuming status and position in return for her virtue. Her fate stands in marked contrast to that of Sally Godfrey, with whom Mr. B. has had a child out of wedlock. Godfrey's story is typical of earlier eighteenth-century amatory heroines, including

Fantomina, Eliza Haywood's protagonist in a story of the same name. While Pamela is rewarded for preserving her chastity, Fantomina and Godfrey are punished for losing theirs. Having fallen in love with Beauplaisir, a handsome young libertine, Fantomina yields to his advances. When he proves inconstant, she disguises herself in a series of costumes to seduce him repeatedly. Her game succeeds until her mother returns from abroad and finds her unmarried daughter pregnant. After giving birth to her child, Fantomina is consigned to a convent to atone for her waywardness. Godfrey similarly succumbs to Mr. B.'s advances and after bearing his child moves to Jamaica to avoid the "Shame" of her "former Fault" (482). Thus *Pamela* essentially rewrites the romantic narrative of earlier amatory fiction by offering its heroine as a positive example of sexual virtue.

If Pamela exemplifies the modern system of thought about what is appropriate behavior for women, Mrs. Jewkes represents an older system of thought that espouses greater sexual fluidity, including lesbianism and premarital sex. As Terry Castle points out, "Mrs. Jewkes is perceived by the heroine in their first encounters as a powerful, yet oddly hermaphroditic figure, a 'man-woman'" ("P/B" 480). Pamela suspects that Mrs. Jewkes is sexually interested in her, and indeed when Pamela first arrives at the Lincolnshire estate, Mrs. Jewkes offers to kiss her. Pamela rejects the advance, saying, "I don't like this Sort of Carriage, Mrs. Jewkes; it is not like two Persons of one Sex" (108). By contrast, when Mrs. Jewkes argues for Pamela's capitulation to their master's overtures, she strongly resembles Madam Clark's grandmother. As she reasons, "Are not the two Sexes made for one another? And is it not natural for a Gentleman to love a pretty Woman? And suppose he can obtain his Desires, is that so bad as cutting her Throat?" (110). Again, when his attempt to rape Pamela fails, Mrs. Jewkes urges her master on, insisting that he make the most of Pamela's fainting spell.

John Cleland's *Fanny Hill; or, Memoirs of a Woman of Pleasure* provides a striking comparison, for, unlike Pamela, Fanny typically accepts sex outside marriage as good fun. Cleland also indulges in male fantasies concerning lesbianism, specifically in the scene in which Phoebe initiates Fanny into sex with men (48–49) and thus plays a role that Castle calls "enwomaning" (480) and that Mrs. Jewkes hopes to play for Pamela. Mrs. Jewkes's failure is partly due to her manliness—Pamela describes her as "a broad, squat, pursy, fat Thing" who "has a huge Hand, and an Arm as thick as my Waist" (114). These differing representations of anxiety about lesbian sexuality can be productively compared. What characteristics does Pamela associate with lesbians? In what other ways does Mrs. Jewkes transgress acceptable sexual boundaries for women? And since Pamela finds Mrs. Jewkes threatening, how does the threat she poses influence the direction of Pamela's relationship with Mr. B.?

My students respond enthusiastically to the issues raised by *Pamela*. Richardson's other works would, I believe, be equally fruitful in any course on the history of sexuality, because Clarissa's attraction to, rape by, and rejection of Lovelace and Sir Charles Grandison's difficulty over his divided but pure heart raise many of the same issues as Richardson's first novel. Whichever work one chooses, Richardson's voice is indispensable, because his fictions vividly represent significant shifts in sexuality at a time when English culture was revising its notions of the family, patriarchy, and the sexual behaviors of men and women.

Naughty Pamela's "Sweet Confusion"

Felicity A. Nussbaum

In teaching Richardson's *Pamela; or, Virtue Rewarded*, I place the novel in the context of eighteenth-century conduct books and sermons that address women's moral dilemmas and prescribe appropriate behavior in compromising situations.[1] The immediate result is that the novel's dual goal of instructing and pleasing looks controversial, compared with its ostensible didactic agenda of advising "the modest Virgin, the chaste Bride, and the obliging Wife" (3). Thus I make the focus of our class discussions fiction's precarious balance between edification and entertainment, which extends to the lascivious for some readers. To display these contradictions, I offer substantial samplings from the anti-Pamela controversy to emphasize how the reader is enticed into imagining and elaborating on Pamela's erotic desire while being denied its explicit fruition. To show how other eighteenth-century fictions accentuate the gendered complexities of employing text to titillate, I assign passages from Laurence Sterne's *Tristram Shandy*, a novel in which Madam Reader is teased into acknowledging her secret understanding of the narrator's ribald jokes, and John Cleland's *Memoirs of a Woman of Pleasure*, popularly known as *Fanny Hill*, an erotic tale that overtly arouses sexual desire. Some have even taken Cleland's novel to be another parody of *Pamela*. For further contrast, I provide selections from the deadly dull but highly instructive *Pamela II*, Richardson's own sequel to the 1740 novel, in which the heroine becomes a proper domestic subject. By bearing seven children, Pamela seeks to regain the power exchanged for the use of her body, which marriage to the philandering and often abusive Mr. B. has legitimated. The students generally cannot accept, however, that a reformed rake makes the best husband. Their view is confirmed by reading selections from *Pamela II*, in which the heroine seems to succumb entirely to Mr. B.'s will and his double standard. By marrying Mr. B., Pamela also compromises the apparent authority she had gained in refusing his former advances. The sexual tension so crucial to the original *Pamela* dissolves into the heroine's tedious moral tutoring of her apparently incorrigible husband, who teasingly entertains thoughts of adultery with a countess whose visits Pamela is forced to endure. In short, comparison of these various texts arms students with material to specify the ways in which, as one conduct book cautions, an eighteenth-century woman's thrill in reading and experiencing romance requires "suppression of all irregular desires, voluntary pollutions, sinful concupiscence, and of an immoderate use of all sensual, or carnal pleasures" (Wilkes 30). Romance does, however, incite exactly those passions.

I then encourage my students to determine whether they fall into the anti-Pamela camp and consequently mock, like Henry Fielding's *Shamela* (published in April 1741), the heroine's wish to make a great fortune by her "Vartue" through marriage (Fielding, *Apology* [ed. Keymer and Sabor] 97). We also consider the way in which the popular movie *Pretty Woman*, the story of a beautiful whore with a heart of gold who falls in love with her wealthy client, repeats yet revises Pamela's story of a poor girl's finding her unlikely prince. I encourage them to note that like the contemporary film, *Pamela* borders on pornography, because the virtuous Pamela is encouraged to succumb to a similarly compromising relationship with Mr. B., to become his "harlot" (41) and thus his property (126). Just as in *Pamela*, the success of *Pretty Woman* requires the heroine's failed self-recognition of her desire to achieve a higher class, together with her naïveté—or at least ambivalence—about her secret affection for the prince until he offers marriage. Drawing parallels between the novel and familiar cultural fables enables students to recognize both the historical imperative to moral behavior in the eighteenth century and the heedless fascination that romance continues to inspire in the modern moment.

Richardson's claim in writing *Pamela* was that he hoped to dissuade youth from romantic fantasy by introducing "a new species of writing that might possibly turn young people into a course of reading different from the pomp and parade of romance-writing, and dismissing the improbable and marvellous, with which novels generally abound, might tend to promote the cause of religion and virtue" (Richardson to Aaron Hill, in Richardson, *Selected Letters* 41). Readers enthralled by Pamela's predicament often found instead that her story excited the impossible dream of exceeding one's class while maintaining one's innocence. (As Jocelyn Harris points out, however, readers may well have divided along gender lines in their response to the novel.)[2] Richardson's wish to turn away from "romance-writing," an ambiguous genre assumed to be especially alluring to frivolous and idle women readers whose habits he wished to reform, is especially remarkable since a chambermaid's marrying her master rather than being merely the object of his sexual assault appears to be particularly "improbable and marvellous." Similar romance formulas continue to attract a willing audience today, as is obvious from television shows such as HBO's *Sex and the City* and a recent ABC program in which two- dozen women competed for a handsome wealthy bachelor. Students are quick to recognize, however, both the appeal of a romance tale that leads to wedding the prince and its ripeness for parody.

These romance conventions, classically defined by Ann Snitow in a still valuable essay, "Mass Market Romance: Pornography for Women Is Different," lend themselves to lively discussions of the genre's contamination then and now. Snitow believes that contemporary romance is especially directed at women to encourage their willing submission to bourgeois family life and its inequities. She observes that romance plots, replete with edgy expectations, emphasize sexual difference and mystify the opposite sex. Most frequently, the romance heroine is increasingly isolated from sympathetic friends and family in an artificially bounded space and time. In addition, the heroine's adventures are largely confined to the pursuit of marriage, and her feelings remain a mystery to her. In *Pamela*, as with most romances, the hero's apparently cold, heartless, swelling masculinity eventually gives way to a marriage proposal once the heroine recognizes her own passion, which could not be revealed until his declaration of love. Masculine tyranny is simultaneously repellent and indescribably seductive, but, in a typical romantic resolution, Mr. B.'s obduracy softens into intimacy, into a willingness to negotiate a position that seems to encompass the woman's prerogatives more fully. In Pamela's case, social status is traded for obedience. But her writing to the moment in an eternal present makes the novel resemble romance, in that women's preoccupation with daily trivial pursuits heightens sexual feeling and makes it relevant to every encounter.

Several of the sequels, extensions, and parodies of *Pamela* warmed to the novel's subtext and treated it as furtively erotic. Curiously, Aaron Hill reports a rumor that Richardson and his partners may have published one of those parodies, *Pamela Censured,* as a marketing strategy for the original novel.[3] In addition to Fielding's *Shamela,* sequels to *Pamela* include Eliza Haywood's *Anti-Pamela; or, Feigned Innocence Detected* (June 1741) and Charles Povey's lesser-known *The Virgin in Eden* (Nov. 1741). Povey's treatise claims to unfold its moral by reinterpreting potentially inflammatory passages and reveals "PAMELA's Letters [that] proved to be immodest Romances painted in Images of Virtue" (81). Among other anti-Pamelists is J– W–, author of *Pamela; or, The Fair Imposter.* This satire, reminiscent of Alexander Pope's *Rape of the Lock,* mocks Pamela's alleged virtue and misogynistically generalizes her duplicity as characteristic of all women:

> But such the Falshood of a Womans Heart,
> So dark their Cunning, and so deep their Art;
> So certain to deceive, where Honour binds,
> Such Frailty taints their undetermin'd Minds,
> Who's most oblig'd, is soonest insincere,
> And she's most faithless, who is held most dear:
> Nor would the best, could she her Fame secure,
> One Hour deliberate, to play the Whore.
> (lines 156–63)

Once married, the poem alleges, the greedy strumpet Pamela first turns cold and haughty and then engages in an affair with Mr. Williams, Mr. B.'s Lincolnshire chaplain. In both of these texts, the poem claims, Pamela's protestations of innocence turn into flirtatious greed.

In Eliza Haywood's *Anti-Pamela*, Syrena, the energetic and crafty heroine, displays none of Pamela's moral ambiguity. Like many other readers of Richardson, Haywood, who claims on the title page that her narrative is founded in "Truth and Nature," accuses Pamela of a knowing duplicity. Yet Richardson would have

us believe that Pamela's gift to Mr. B. is "an experienced truth, a well-tried virtue, and . . . [an unequaled] natural meekness and sweetness of disposition"
(337), which serve as an appropriate exchange for his riches. Pamela protests
that she would embrace "Rags and Poverty" (15) rather than forfeit her virginity, a temptation that her father believes would "set [her] so above [her] self"
(13). Indeed, before her wedding day, Pamela expresses sexual anxiety about
actually marrying "the lord of her wishes." But here the erotic undercurrent
rises to the surface when Pamela's internal debate, produced and reflected by
cultural ideologies and resolved in the text through marriage, becomes manifest
in Lady Davers's rude question, "Have you not been a-bed with my brother?"
(396). Pamela again affects innocence by interpreting the question as a simple
inquiry into whether she is married. Such antagonism between women over
men and money has been previously limited to the servants Mrs. Jewkes and
Mrs. Jervis. But near the end of the novel it is elevated to a higher class status
in Lady Davers's antagonism to a future sister-in-law who stands to inherit the
family's wealth.

In a related vein, several influential critics have associated the emergence of
mercantile capital in the mid-eighteenth century with the growing popularity
of representations of sexual feeling in romance (Lovell), because women's pleasure is simultaneously stimulated through the purchase of commodities—the
pleasures of shopping—and regulated through impossible moral injunctions
(Guest; McKendrick, Brewer, Plumb). Snitow also connects romance novels to
women's "shopping" for men, as well as to capitalism's reliance on women's willing submission to the "sexual contract," Carole Pateman's term for the power relations of heterosexual difference inherent in the social contract. Female desire
is channeled into pleasures that advance the goals of capitalism, argues Snitow:

> When women try to picture excitement, the society offers them one vi-
> sion, romance. When women try to imagine companionship, the society
> offers them one vision, male, sexual companionship. When women try to
> fantasize about success, mastery, the society offers them one vision, the
> power to attract a man.   (149)

Similarly, Pamela, like other romance heroines, reaps psychological satisfaction
from remaining true to cultural expectations of femininity even as she struggles
against its injustice. (Class difference evaporates, however, once desire is routed
into a wedding.) That is, for characters in romance, contact is highly sexualized
but does not taint the reader's moral distance. That dichotomy may help to explain *Pamela*'s complicated and contradictory reception.

The comparison of romance to pornography, although not always apt, bears
further elaboration because both genres can arouse a perverse thrill through the
depiction of violence against women. Examples from *Fanny Hill* and *Pamela*
encourage students to note unwitting arousals of sexual feeling in the heroines'

suitors through self-display and attention to dress. Pamela's fraught anticipation of Mr. B.'s attentions might even be said to initiate what Snitow calls "the foreplay of romance" (149).[4] Pamela takes great pleasure in having captivated her "wicked, wicked master" (202), whom she once likened to Lucifer. Indeed, she even acknowledges that Mr. B. had originally intended to rape her. In an evocative passage mocked in nearly every sequel, Pamela adorns herself in her straw hat, "home-spun gown and petticoat, and plain leather shoes" and regards herself with pleasure and apparent pride in the mirror before preparing her three parcels (55). This scene invites the parody hinted in the later novel *Fanny Hill*, when the young country lass, "tricking [herself] out for the market" (14), succumbs to the temptation of using her body to compensate for her poverty. Fanny, after lingering over a description of her universally desirable figure and face, belatedly enjoins herself to affect modesty:

> This is I own, too much, too strong of self-praise; but should I not be ungrateful to nature, and to a form to which I owe such singular blessings of pleasure and fortune, were I to suppress, through an affectation of modesty, the mention of such valuable gifts? (15)

Pamela similarly justifies her self-admiration in her humble garb as perfectly appropriate: "To say truth, I never liked myself so well in my life" (55).

In another passage that also signals the erotically charged, even pornographic, elements in *Pamela*, Mrs. Jewkes is complicit in allowing Mr. B. access to his servant's bedside. Pamela's heaving breast, together with her panting, swooning, and fainting, fires the imagination and acts (as one author satirically suggests) as ironic "Excitements to *Virtue*" (Keymer and Sabor 2: 56), though the threat to virtue intermingles with the dream world to become fantasy. Mrs. Jewkes dismisses Pamela's terror, assuring her that her "master's more hideous actions" are "but a *Dream,* as well as that: and when it was *over,* and [Pamela] was well awake, [she] should laugh at it as such!" (167). At that moment, Pamela simultaneously experiences and denies sexual desire, confirming Mr. B.'s assumptions about her veiled longings. Likewise, when Fanny Hill is initiated into prostitution, the violence of a "fine gentleman" brought forward as a prospective husband aims to incite sexual feeling in the reader, even though Fanny claims to be disgusted:

> Snorting and foaming with lust and rage, he renews his attack, seizes me, and again attempts to extend and fix me on the settee; in which he succeeded so far as to lay me along; and even to toss my petticoats over my head, and lay my thighs bare, which I obstinately kept close, nor could he, though he attempted with his knee to force them open, effect it so as to stand fair for being master of the main avenue. (19)

While Fanny's elderly client prematurely ejaculates, Pamela successfully resists the attempted rape that serves as a turning point in her power relation with Mr. B., thus deflecting a more lascivious reading of the scene.

Pamela's virtue, intelligence, and apparent honesty, all of which are revealed to Mr. B. when he scrutinizes her journal, are the principal softening agents in domesticating him. Pamela's ability to express an independent subjectivity distinguishes her from women who are willing to be the objects of men's desires. It helps her negotiate the differences between incompatible kinds of empowerment and turns the violence directed against her into sociable sentiment. Her writing, like her moral stature, effectively humanizes her man so that she can claim him as an object of romance, while her preoccupation with an eternal present directs potential sexual feeling into acceptable channels. Pamela persuades her aristocratic lover to thrill to the honest, naked subjectivity of her journal instead of her bare body. As she says, "For now he will see all my private thoughts of him, and all my Secrets, as I may say" (226). And yet, she has used subtle and strategic deception when she deposited her letters without his knowledge. Having snagged Mr. B. and persuaded him to acknowledge and affirm her principles, she exemplifies women's insistence that love is a precondition for sexual intimacy. Ultimately, because Mr. B.'s change of heart keeps Pamela's eros sufficiently aroused, she happily accepts the less salubrious aspects of marriage and motherhood in exchange for a higher social class. In short, Richardson turns the pornographic threat of romance, manifest in the sequels and *Fanny Hill*, into novelistic domesticity. Pamela is not the passive or willing agent typical of much pornography, even though her trading of virtue for fortune persistently threatens to resemble it. Most readers who remain unconvinced by her reasons for remaining in the household nevertheless admire her saucy resistance to Mr. B.'s expectations. In the end, as the dicta of conduct books are fulfilled, all the characters in the novel, unlike those in pornography, acknowledge her value and worth: "She, who forfeits her chastity, withers by degrees into scorn and contrition; but she, who lives up to its rules, ever flourishes, like a rose in *June*, with all her virgin graces about her" (Wilkes 29).

Thus, interpreting *Pamela* as a popular romance novel in a context of pornography offers the chance to debate the significance of historicism and to distinguish an eighteenth-century heroine from a twenty-first-century one. Students are intrigued by the possibility that Richardson based *Pamela* on an actual love affair between Hannah Sturges, a coachman's sixteen-year-old daughter, who in 1725 married Sir Arthur Hesilrige, seventh Baronet of Northampton. But they usually protest that such an incident would not carry the same cultural resonance today, at least in most European countries and North America.[5] The excruciating injustice of the double standard that forced Pamela to forgive Mr. B.'s affair with Pamela's less canny precursor, Sally Godfrey, also distinguishes this novel from those of the current moment. Despite her servant class, the character Pamela Andrews understood only too well that the distinction between a good girl and a bad girl in 1740, the year Richardson's novel was published, rested merely on a thin hymeneal membrane. William Dodd's sermons to "penitent prostitutes" brings this point home:

> For, though, the great author of our being hath, for wise and good ends, implanted the same passions in either sex, and therefore transgression is as possible, and of consequence as excusable on the weaker side, as it is on the stronger; yet fact abundantly demonstrates to us, that men, for the most part, are the seducers. . . . And it is well known how much harder that case, in this particular, is with the female sex, than with our own. One false step for ever ruins their fair fame; blasts the fragrance of virgin innocence, and consigns them to contempt and disgrace!   ("Fourth Sermon" 89)

These richly varied fictional and nonfictional writings, published in the mid–eighteenth century and close to *Pamela*'s time, spark impassioned discussion among students about the reader's complicity in anticipating Pamela's sexual responses, about the heroine's motivations, and about the similarities between romance and pornography. Set alongside *Pamela*, these texts illuminate exactly what is at stake in maintaining heterosexual difference and its alignment with patriarchal authority in the past and in the present.

NOTES

[1] Armstrong, who argues that the novel is a seduction tale framed within a conduct book, demonstrates that the sexual contract is political, as Pateman first articulated.

[2] Harris helpfully demonstrates that in *Clarissa* especially, Richardson purposefully referred to contemporary erotica to erase and recast its erotic content for women readers (Introduction lxxii–lxxvi).

[3] Keymer and Sabor convincingly float this theory in the introduction to *The* Pamela *Controversy* (2: xv).

[4] Snitow evocatively employs this term in relation to Harlequin romances.

[5] The parallel is drawn in *Memoirs of the Life of Lady H.*

Reading the Domestic Servant-Woman in *Pamela*

Kristina Straub

This essay on teaching Richardson's *Pamela* is in one sense an exercise in point-ing out the obvious: that the titular character is a domestic servant-woman. Un-packing the implications of this fact is a helpful way of introducing students to some of the historical conditions that often distance them from this novel, puzzling and frustrating them. Why doesn't she just leave? is my students' com-mon response to Pamela's claustrophobically contained verbosity. It is telling that they are especially amused by Henry Fielding's parody *Shamela,* whose heroine takes "writing to the moment" to the point of scribbling during one of Booby's abortive rape attempts. A girl who writes at times when, in students' opinions, she ought to be exerting some form of agency, such as packing her bags, hailing the next stagecoach, or reporting an attempted rape to the local authorities, makes *Pamela* a text that seems implausible, unrealistic, and often just plain boring to many students. Why does she write so much? And nothing really happens! they say.

The most frequent problem that I encounter teaching this novel is how to steer students toward understanding the historically specific cultural condi-tions that grant Pamela's agency its particular, textual form: her letters.[1] The approach to teaching *Pamela* that I outline here contextualizes the heroine's epistolary agency through eighteenth-century debates about domestic servant-women's economic opportunities and material conditions. My goal is not so much to teach students what a servant-woman's working life was really like as to offer them textual evidence of pervasive cultural disputes over her economic agency. I use short, fairly easily available texts culled from a large collection of pertinent texts from the late seventeenth into the nineteenth century concern-ing what Bridget Hill and many others have called the servant problem.[2] Here that debate can be seen crystallizing around Richardson's wildly popular and viciously attacked novel of 1740.

Eighteenth-century writers tend to agree that they were living through a time of crisis about domestic servants. To Daniel Defoe, for example, London is the center of corruption for servants:

> London, like the Ocean, that receives the muddy and dirty Brooks, as well as the clear and rapid Rivers, swallows up all the scum and filth of the Country, and here they need not fear of getting Places; what Servants are likely to come out of such Nurseries is not hard to suggest, nor is it any breach of Charity, to suppose that this helps to fill the Town with a generation of Whores and Thieves. (*Great Law* 86)

Defoe's language reveals a harried, conservative response to the extensive eco-nomic and demographic changes affecting domestic service in England during the early eighteenth century. "The Town" afforded many displaced workers a market which to sell skills and labor for a higher standard of living than that of a changing English village economy, or so they must have hoped. This urban "Ocean" of available labor is tainted not only by the "scum and filth of the Country" but by its conditions of economic opportunity ("they need not fear of getting Places"). London offered servants an economic agency that, in the opinion of writers like Defoe, all too easily slid into criminality ("Whores and Thieves"). For Defoe, London had become a "paradise for Servants" in which "order is inverted, Subordination ceases, and the World seems to stand with the Bottom upward" (*Great Law* 17). Whatever the actual material conditions of domestic service throughout England, the literature on London servants reveals what employers most feared in their servants: a new and threatening economic independence.

The domestic servant-woman occupies a particularly interesting position in the servant problem because her new, dangerous economic agency so readily meshed with the illicit sexuality already associated with her. The conduct literature shows a consensus that the servant-woman is a walking sexual target. As the seventeenth-century adviser Hannah Woolley warns the prospective female cook, "beware of the solicitations of the flesh, for they will undo you; and though you may have mean thoughts of your self, and think none will meddle with such as you; it is a mistake, *Hungry Dogs will eat dirty Puddings*" (217). For many writers, however, the sexual magnetism of the servant-woman is understood not only as a social and moral problem, a view rooted in misogynist framings of laboring women's sexuality, but also as a byproduct of such women's (sexually saturated) social volition, yet another twist in the problems allegedly created by servants' economic agency and social mobility. The maid's sexual attractiveness gives her a certain range of dangerous choices. In his *Directions to Servants*, Jonathan Swift satirically debates which lovers a chambermaid should take: "Your usual Lover, as I take it, is the Coachman; but, if you are under Twenty, and tolerably handsome, perhaps a Footman may cast his Eyes on you" (75). More pointedly, Swift's maid uses her sexuality to gain social mobility, for she may aspire to rise up the family hierarchy:

> If you are handsome, you will have the Choice of three Lovers; the Chaplain, the Steward, and my Lord's Gentleman. I would first advise you to chuse the Steward; but if you happen to be young with Child by my Lord, you must take up with the Chaplain.   (82)

Thus the London maid's sexuality is knitted rhetorically into the problem of her alleged social mobility and economic agency. The maid's ability to attract desire across class lines made her a disturbingly mobile figure in literature on service.

Defoe's *Augusta Triumphans; or, The Way to Make London the Most Flourishing City in the Universe* is a rhetorically overheated polemic against the immorality of London servants in which he particularly targets women domestics. Defoe expresses his dismay at the growing practice among London servants of giving warning: if a servant was displeased with his or her master or mistress, the servant could, Defoe huffs, simply find another position. This mobility was made possible by an urban labor market in which servants did not find themselves bound by traditional loyalties to their employer families but could sell their labor to the highest bidder in conditions of relative anonymity. Significantly, Defoe reads servant-women's economic agency, the simple ability to leave an unsatisfactory job for a potentially better one, as a threat to both the moral fiber of the family and the social fabric as a whole. Even more significantly for our understanding of *Pamela*, this economic mobility cashes out, willy-nilly, as the worst form of illicit sexual opportunism. Economic agency makes Defoe's maid a whore, "slippery in the tail," and able to rove

> from bawdyhouse to service, and from service to bawdyhouse again, ever unsettled and never easy, nothing being more common than to find these creatures one week in a good family and the next in a brothel. This amphibious life makes them fit for neither, for if the bawd uses them ill, away they trip to service, and if their mistress gives them a wry word, whip they are at a bawdyhouse again, so that in effect they neither make good whores nor good servants.   (*Augusta Triumphans* 8)

Needless to say, Defoe's florid prose makes for some lively discussion among my students. What does he mean by a "good whore"? they ask. It also makes clear that the morally uncompromising right of a domestic servant-woman to sell her labor to her own best advantage is not a universal or ahistorical assumption. That belief may be culturally available to twenty-first-century readers, but not to Defoe.

To us, Pamela's situation looks like a good job gone bad, an experience any student who has bagged groceries for summer money recognizes, or rather misrecognizes, as a matter for individual action. She should simply find another job, they say. Defoe's quickness in conflating this acceptable form of individual agency with an unacceptable form of women's sexual agency—prostitution—suggests that a reading that does not account for historical differences in the perception of labor distorts Pamela's options. Pamela's concern about how to return to her parents, once Mr. B.'s nefarious intentions are clear, looks less like pointless dithering and more like a reasonable response to current assumptions, such as Defoe's, about what it means for a young woman to leave her place:

> Sometimes I thought to leave them [her belongings] behind me, and only go with the Cloaths on my Back; but then I had two Miles and a half, and a By-way, to go to the Town; and being pretty well dress'd, I might come to some harm, almost as bad as what I would run away from; and then

may-be, thought I, it will be reported, I have stolen something, and so was forc'd to run away; and to carry a bad Name back with me to my dear poor Parents, would be a sad thing indeed!   (*Pamela* 24–25)

Leaving her job means exerting an economic agency that exposes her to victimization or criminal charges: she is either perceived as a thief, constructed as a whore because of her situation as an unprotected woman, or is sexually vulnerable to rape ("some harm, almost as bad as what I would run away from").[3]

Richardson's novel can thus be read as constrained by cultural assumptions about the kinds of agency available to women servants, but it is also possible to read it as an important intervention in public-sphere discussions over that agency. Richardson is asking his readers to put themselves in the shoes of a young woman who is not, by nature, "slippery in the tail," not a sexual outlaw or object, but rather someone who wishes to exert moral agency despite her economic and material constraints. For Pamela to find herself another job would fly in the face of these constraints and effectively give her the appearance of guilt. Hence, writing is one of Richardson's few available options for endowing Pamela with moral agency. Pamela's letters, then, are not mere by-products or reflections of her moral consciousness; given Defoe's concerns about the domestic servant-woman's economic agency as socially and sexually transgressive, they are the only form that her moral agency can take. In other words, writing is a way of exerting moral agency without also claiming the economic agency that would land her in the guilty position of Defoe's "amphibious" maid. Pamela's letters are simultaneously revolutionary and conservative in that they grant the capacity for moral consciousness and agency even as they work within cultural assumptions about the servant-woman's limited rights to sell her own labor on an open market.

The instructor can alert students to the possible effects of Richardson's intervention in public discussions of the domestic servant-woman's moral, sexual, and economic agency by having them read excerpts from Eliza Haywood's *Present for a Servant Maid*, published in 1743, three years after *Pamela*'s debut. Unlike Defoe and like Richardson, Haywood makes rhetorical space for the servant-woman's moral consciousness, while still acknowledging the constraints on her economic agency. Haywood agrees with Richardson (and many others) about the sexual vulnerability of the servant-woman, no matter how circumspect she might be: "Being so much under his [the master's] Command, and obliged to attend him at any Hours, and at any Place he is pleased to call you, will lay you under Difficulties to avoid his Importunities, which it must be confessed are not easy to surmount" (Haywood 45). Her catalog of the men from whom the maid must defend herself includes the master, the master's son, the gentleman lodger, apprentices, and male servants—in short, all the male members of the family (Haywood 45–50). In this text, Haywood follows Richardson's innovative installation of moral agency in the domestic servant-woman while still frowning on any servant's attempt to exert economic control over the sale of her labor. Leaving one's place is a last-ditch, perilous course of action that would expose the servant to even greater moral danger than her master's seductions. Of course, she must somehow avoid the sexual predations of the men in her family, but Haywood is hard put to imagine what the maid might actually do if pressed. She writes only, "A steady Resolution will enable you; and as a vigorous Resistance is less to be expected in your Station, your perservering may, perhaps, in Time, oblige Him to desist and acknowledge you have more Reason than himself" (Haywood 45).

Haywood's phrase "perhaps, in Time" would hardly have been reassuring to any women servants who wished to follow her advice. It also makes evident to students the lack of real, material power accompanying a servant-woman's newly installed moral agency, so that they can place Pamela's responses to Mr. B.'s rape attempts in the novel within contemporary discourses on service. Haywood is no clearer than Richardson about exactly what material power the servant-woman might deploy, given that she must avoid exerting an economic agency that would bring her, as Pamela says, to sexual "harm, almost as bad as what [she] would run away from." In the novel, Pamela's moral agency prevails over Mr. B. only when she hands control to a higher power. This solution tends to obfuscate the contradiction revealed by Haywood's more practically minded advice, which counsels that the maid is responsible for exerting moral agency but loses the rectitude on which this agency is grounded the minute she resorts to economic and physical mobility. Pamela's fainting and loss of consciousness during those moments when she most needs physical control over her own body, as well as her almost superhuman ability to spring from Mr. B.'s grasp at other critical points in the novel, can be read as Richardson's Christian, spiritual detours around an ideological contradiction that cannot be resolved in material terms. Writing is an earthly strategy complementary to this spiritually granted strength because it does not require Pamela to exert economic control over her labor and body, a control that automatically compromises her morality. The letters Pamela writes for her mother and father are the most material form that her moral agency can take. Although Richardson, as an author and printer, dealt in texts as economic commodities, Pamela's writing assumes moral authority because of its detachment from economic motives and thus from sexual motives.

By contrast, Shamela firmly reattaches the servant-woman's writing to economics when she writes to her mother, a bawd who advises her daughter on the best way to Booby's fortune. Shamela's economic mobility is a form of sexual agency—an even more dangerous, because plausibly concealed, version of Defoe's slippery prostitute of a maid. But Shamela does not simply repeat Defoe's stereotype of servant-women, because, as with Pamela, her capacity for sexual desire, as opposed to desirability, fails to mesh seamlessly with her economic motives. Whereas Defoe's servant-woman prostitutes herself for reasons that seem entirely economic, Shamela likes sex for its own sake, at least with her dear

Parson Williams. The issue of women's sexual desire coarsely echoes Pamela's muted and delicately expressed responses to Mr. B.'s attractiveness and is shown to be a force independent from economic motives. Indeed, it is Shamela's sexual desire, coupled with the evidence of her letters, that finally derails her economic agenda. (Haywood repeats this narrative in her *Anti-Pamela* when the heroine Syrena Tricksey becomes overly interested in sex for her own physical gratification—she manages to screw, quite literally, her chances at gaining a fortune, or even a livelihood. Her letters to her mother, like Shamela's, are the means to her exposure.)[4] The servant-woman's sexual desire, a very different matter from her desirability, opens a rhetorical space in the literature on service that is pointedly free from economic motives. In *Pamela*, this desire points the way to the limited, domestic-sphere agency that Nancy Armstrong attaches to the middle-class domestic manager. To read Pamela as a domestic servant as well as the model domestic manager she later becomes in the sequel is to illuminate the separation of economics and sexuality on which this agency depends.[5] Pamela's modestly expressed desire for Mr. B., if indeed it is innocent of economic motives, can be read as a recommendation rather than a liability. Similarly, her letters are the means to wielding a moral authority over Mr. B. and his family. Since Shamela's desire and writing are linked to her aspirations to gain economic power, they work against her: they spell out the message that the woman servant can have no culturally legitimate control over her labor that is compatible with the moral authority of womanly virtue invested in her by Richardson. What emerges from this juxtaposition of texts, less surprising to instructors than to students, is the overwhelming early modern bias against the notion that servant-women own their labor in the sense that Marx would suggest a hundred years later. This realization makes an important difference in the way that students read Pamela and her apparently obsessive letter writing. Furthermore, the literature on the servant problem also reveals the important role played by sexuality in cultural narratives that rhetorically shape the domestic servant-woman's economic and moral roles. The illicit sexuality of the maid marks her economic agency as off-limits because literacy becomes a means to detecting criminality. Conversely, desire and literacy reward the servant who eschews forbidden economic motives while simultaneously embracing the moral imperative of virtue. Ignoring Pamela's status as a servant gives an ahistorical credibility to the epistemological separation of labor and sexuality, economics and desire, a separation that Richardson was radical in beginning to legitimate.

NOTES

[1]Thomas Keymer and Peter Sabor's *The* Pamela *Controversy: Criticisms and Adaptations of Samuel Richardson's* Pamela, *1740–1750* is an invaluable aid in helping advanced undergraduate and graduate students historicize Richardson's novel. While this

collection of materials does not focus on the issue of servitude, it gives students a strong sense of the novel in its immediate discursive context.

[2]Texts that provide helpful historical background on domestic service and the history of various crises in servant-master relations over the course of the eighteenth century are J. Jean Hecht's *The Domestic Servant Class in Eighteenth-Century England* and Bridget Hill's *Servants: English Domestics in the Eighteenth Century.*

[3]See Harris (*Samuel Richardson* 14–20) for an illuminating discussion of Mr. B.'s power to manipulate Pamela's identity into that of criminal, either whore or thief.

[4]This text is available as volume 3 of Keymer and Sabor, *The* Pamela *Controversy.*

[5]See two sequels to Richardson's novel, John Kelly's *Pamela's Conduct in High Life* and Richardson's own sequel, *Pamela; or, Virtue Rewarded, in a Series of Familiar Letters from a Beautiful Young Damsel to her Parents: Afterwards, in her Exalted Condition, between her, and Persons of figure and Quality, upon the Most Important and Entertaining Subjects, in Genteel Life.*

Making *Pamela* Real for Undergraduates: Sexual Harassment and the Epistolary Form

Nicky Didicher

When Samuel Richardson made his famous attempt at a "new species of writing, that might possibly turn young people into a course of reading different from the pomp and parade of romance-writing" (*Selected Letters* 41), he deliberately chose a setting and a style recognizable to his readers, regardless of their class or gender. But for today's undergraduates, especially those outside Britain, the setting and the style are neither realistic nor familiar. Most of these first-time readers of *Pamela* find the heroine's language extremely formal and old-fashioned instead of homely and colloquial, and her situation as a servant in a grand house makes her story seem as strange and exotic as any of the romances Richardson famously deplored. Although T. C. Duncan Eaves and Ben Kimpel argue that Richardson's characterization is masterful because "the Pamela he caused to speak and write is a real woman" (*Samuel Richardson* 104), I suggest a series of in-class and out-of-class activities that help make Pamela's style and situation seem more real, more accessible, and more sympathetic to the average North American undergraduate student.

Since the time of the Pamelist and anti-Pamelist factions, readers have tended to divide themselves into camps—so do my classes (unlike Florian Stuber's fashion design students; see "Teaching *Pamela*"). Some students begin by feeling sympathetic toward Pamela because she experiences sexual harassment in the workplace, but generally become less sympathetic because of the book's length and lack of incident in the second half and because Pamela marries her harasser. Other students are irritated with Pamela from the start, suspecting her credibility because of her self-praise and becoming increasingly enraged each time she faints or flings herself at her master's feet.[1] I therefore approach "making *Pamela* real" for the students through two main issues: sexual harassment and the novel's epistolary form. To engage students, I suggest in-class activities and ways to incorporate what students learn about these issues into work outside the classroom. My pedagogical goals are, first, to reengage those readers who lose interest and sympathy because of what they perceive as the novel's length or the plot's repetitive, slow-moving pace; second, to engage those readers of *Pamela* who immediately dislike Richardson's style or Pamela's personality; and, third, to use the currency of sexual harassment to stimulate student thinking about Richardson's novel, while remaining sensitive to students for whom this is a very personal or emotionally stressful subject.

I begin my in-class discussion of eighteenth-century letter writing by showing replicas of Pamela's equipment—liquid ink, quill, penknife, and sand jar. Then we review her lists of materials (see *Pamela* 50, 100, 112); examine Joseph

Highmore's first illustration for *Pamela,* "Mr. B. finds Pamela Writing" (see www
.tate.org.uk/servlet/ViewWork?workid=62138&tabview=image); and discuss the
plausibility or implausibility of Pamela's being able to produce a text from such
limited supplies. Using the passage about Pamela's writing under cover to her
parents (279), I demonstrate how to fold a letter into a cover and seal it with
a wafer, and I show the difference between wafers and sealing wax. When a
smaller class size permits, I have the class members divide into groups and
compose a letter to another group, which they write in imitation of eighteenth-
century prose style and with nib pens, then sand, fold, seal, and deliver. I also
acquaint students with some other aspects of eighteenth-century letter-writing,
such as the fact that it was common to make copies of letters, as Pamela does.
We discuss letters as communication and the advantages and disadvantages of
using letters to make up a novel.

A comparison of the conditions of Pamela's writing with those of contemporary office workers, who use e-mail that an employer can secretly monitor, leads
to a discussion of personal letters and privacy. How do we feel about someone's
reading our mail without our knowledge? Do we see it as a wrongful act, an
invasion of our privacy? Do we react differently to the reading of letters written by one fictional character to another? Pamela claims that "what one writes
to one's Father and Mother is not for every body" (228–29), and her parents
say that "there are in these Papers twenty Things nobody should see but ourselves" (278). Is Richardson then encouraging us into voyeurism? Will any epistolary novel generate a voyeuristic tendency in the reader? At this point I bring
in Tassie Gwilliam, who in *Samuel Richardson's Fictions of Gender* remarks
that *Pamela* is "perhaps the fantasy of a man imagining himself a woman being
watched by a man" (41). Here we can also discuss the different effects that
Richardson's epistolary strategy may have on readers of different genders and
sexual orientations and connect those effects to the issue of privacy.

I include two kinds of out-of-class activity related to epistolary form: reading journals and specific creative projects. Reading journals take on a new significance as we study *Pamela.* Students have been making honest, informal,
to-the-moment reports of their responses to course texts at semiregular inter-
vals and analyzing their reactions to the novel. They trust to the privacy of that
communication on the understanding that I will not share their journal entries
with other members of the faculty or class, unlike Mr. B., who passes around
Pamela's journal among his friends (I refrain from giving any quotations here
from student journals for just this reason). A few students realize that their
endeavor resembles Pamela's, and I usually point this out to the others in my
marginal responses.

Creative projects include having students conceive of an epistolary virtue-
in-distress novel, set on their own campus and in their own time. I ask for an
outline of plot and characters, an annotated list of the correspondents, a break-
down of their novel's structure, and a few pages of manuscript, as well as an

explanatory essay that covers intended audience, students' adaptations of plot conventions, the problems students encountered, and their solutions for them. Another project focuses on *Pamela* and asks students to choose a key scene or group of scenes and imagine they are Mr. B., writing letters to a friend in London. Students base their letters on Pamela's version of the incident, including her report of Mr. B.'s style of speech. One woman student, who remarked that trying to see the summer-house scene from Mr. B.'s point of view was at first difficult, found that as she continued to work on her letters she became more understanding of and sympathetic to his position, even though she had determined beforehand to portray him as an outright villain. Considering changes in their own thinking thus helps students understand Mr. B.'s comparable conversion.

Seeing the villain-hero's point of view is also central to my first in-class activity on sexual harassment. Here I show a Pepe Le Pew cartoon entitled *Heaven Scent*, in which Pepe mistakes a cat with a stripe of paint for a female skunk, pursues her relentlessly, and tries to make love to her (other Pepe Le Pew cartoons will work, but I find that this one combines the characteristics in which I am most interested). Students then note similarities and differences between *Pamela* and the cartoon. Beyond the obvious similarity of a male character in sexual pursuit of an unwilling female, students often remark that although the Warner Brothers characters are two different species, the skunk is misled by the cat's appearance to treat her as another skunk. They compare this to Pamela's appearance, which is refined and elegant even though she is from a lower class. Also, the cat goes through alternating periods of limp passivity and frenzied scratching to get away, in much the way that Pamela sometimes faints and sometimes talks back or runs away. Finally, because the cat never has a voice or even a name, we sympathize not with her but with Pepe; in contrast, Richardson uses Pamela's voice to make us incline toward her point of view. We discuss what effect the different narrative strategies have on readers, who are forced to see the stories from the point of view of the harasser (Pepe) in one instance or the harassed (Pamela) in the other.

As a second in-class activity on this topic, I work with the class to create an outline on the board of what constitutes sexual harassment in Western society today. Many students have studied this topic in other classes or have been made aware of it in workplaces and can collaboratively put together a good working definition. They may not know the difference between treating harassment as a civil and a criminal offense. However, students' definitions usually specify that the offensive behavior must be both unwanted and repeated and that it can include physical contact; verbal comments and suggestions; and offensive visual material, such as pornographic calendars or posters. Students know that an employer who threatens to fire an employee for refusing to consent to a sexual act or who offers a raise or promotion conditional on such consent commits harassment. Mr. B. engages in many of these behaviors. I make clear that the term *sexual harassment* and its current legal boundaries are a product of our culture, not Richardson's, but that the behavior described by the term is universal. Today we may be quick to allege harassment, yet even so, some employees are unwilling to take steps to prosecute. I also point out that most people in our society would recognize Mr. B.'s behavior as immoral and unjustifiable, whereas eighteenth-century readers would have been more varied in their responses, largely because Pamela's social position as a servant makes Mr. B.'s actions less objectionable than they would have been toward a woman of his own class. If students are also reading *Joseph Andrews*, I point out that in our society it is rarer and more difficult for a male employee to take action against a female employer for harassment; often, people will not believe him. Similarly, eighteenth-century readers would have found Lady Booby's harassment difficult to believe. Students will likely find the gender reversal central to Henry Fielding's comic objective, reversing Richardson's objective of sympathetic tears for Pamela's plight.

Richardson has Pamela specifically comment on how common it is for an upper-class man to seduce a servant girl (70). I give students a generalized outline of Pamela's legal situation at a time before women were persons under the law: she would need support from a respectable man such as Mr. Williams or Sir Simon Darnford for any legal action regarding a breach of the peace or a rape, and Mr. B. might still socially (though no longer legally) have a right to use her sexually through his authority as head of the household. Also, I explain that Mr. B.'s position as justice of the peace puts him in charge of the local legal system. Pamela herself feels that she has grounds for a complaint but knows she cannot take action: "Is there no Constable, no Headborough, tho', to take me out of his House? for I am sure I can safely swear the Peace against him: But, alas! he is greater than any Constable, and is a Justice himself" (60). Students generally find it easy to sympathize with a young woman who finds herself subjected to sexual harassment in the workplace and who has nobody to tell. They also find the portrayal of Mrs. Jewkes as both an assistant to Mr. B. and as a same-sex sexual harasser disturbing, both because of the negative portrayal of a masculinized woman and because this means that Pamela no longer has support, even from other female servants. If the group's dynamic is such that students feel comfortable discussing examples of comparable situations in their own lives, I try to ensure that the class treats the subject with respect and sympathy. By considering their own visceral reactions to Pamela's suffering, students develop questions about the way that Richardson manipulates our reading of the text, about whether the text makes us feel imprisoned or harassed, regardless of our personal experience with harassment. As Albert J. Rivero points out, our "reading is shaped by . . . other readings—Mr. B.'s, Pamela's, Richardson's—embedded in the text, readings we can accept or resist" ("Place" 32). Students will find it helpful not only to perceive ways that their reading of *Pamela* is affected by other readings embedded in Richardson's text but also to realize that their resistance to that text is appropriate. That is, it is helpful for them to see their resentment and anger toward Mr. B. for his behavior, toward Pamela for her acceptance of him, and toward Richardson for writing the book in the way he did as evidence that *Pamela*, instead of aestheticizing rape, may be purposely engendering moral outrage.

My out-of-class activities on harassment are based mainly on research. For example, students can inquire into the current legal definition of sexual harassment and then use *Pamela* as a test case, exploring the exact points early in the text at which Mr. B. commits acts that could be tried in a civil or criminal court today. (We assume that Pamela's account is accurate.) Or they can conduct research into Stockholm syndrome, in which kidnap victims find themselves supporting the cause of their kidnappers and sometimes feeling love for them. Fully aware that *Stockholm syndrome*, like *sexual harassment*, is a new term to categorize a preexisting behavior, they then analyze Pamela's Lincolnshire experience in the light of that modern diagnosis.

Epistolary method and sexual harassment link together through issues of voyeurism and sexual manipulation to provide stimulating, sometimes intense, class discussions. Once students can imagine Pamela as a real girl behaving realistically, they become more sympathetic, more willing to continue reading her story. As Michael McKeon points out in *The Origins of the English Novel*, the realistic elements of *Pamela* stand in a complex dialectic relation with its romantic or less realistic elements (358–64). The class activities I have suggested are not meant to push the balance toward the domestic and the realistic. Rather, they offer students who find the novel romantic and therefore unbelievable a complementary way of experiencing *Pamela*.

NOTE

[1] I generalize here, drawing on class discussions and entries in reading journals, in both of which I encourage students to speak honestly and openly, provided they feel comfortable doing so.

Resisting Richardson: Student Skepticism and Teaching Strategies for *Pamela*

Robert Markley

Samuel Richardson is a crucial figure in most courses in the eighteenth-century novel, but his works can provoke skeptical, even cynical responses from students who resist his depiction of virtue in distress as the foundation of women's identity. In my classes, I try to use this skepticism to have students explore their sense that his novels often fail in their self-professed didactic aims. Drawing on essays about *Pamela* from an undergraduate course in the eighteenth-century novel (at the University of Virginia in 2000) as well as two articles on Richardson by graduate students that had their beginnings in seminars I taught at the University of Washington (in 1987 and 1990), I want to suggest that the perceived failure of Richardson's didactic program can become a powerful heuristic tool for teaching his novels—precisely because such student responses cut against the grain of much of the criticism published on his novels during the last fifty years. Although as teachers of eighteenth-century literature, we may be committed—institutionally as well as individually—to demonstrating the aesthetic quality and historical significance of Richardson's works, we can use class time profitably to examine the values and assumptions that underlie his novels. In this respect, students' resistance to Richardson offers a means to rethink how we teach and write about eighteenth-century literature and how we approach competing historicist reconstructions of his novels.

My strategies for teaching Richardson's novels have changed over the years, partly in response to student skepticism about his heroines. Instead of trying to persuade students that they are "wrong" or that they should learn to appreciate his novels, I ask them to articulate the aesthetic and ideological grounds for their resistance to the view—one defended by some feminist critics—that Pamela and Clarissa are exemplars of virtue and are convincing psychological creations. This process is a complex one because the aesthetic value of *Pamela* often is not self-evident to undergraduates. Richardson's didacticism, or, as many students experience it, heavy-handed coercion, cuts closer to the bone for twenty-something readers than for many of their middle-aged teachers. Pamela is too much a creature of her parents' desires to convince most students that she has a mind of her own. Consequently, teaching strategies that treat her as a convincing and sympathetic character—whether noble heroine or relatively passive victim—can be counterproductive. While teaching *Shamela* after *Pamela* provides students with a historical context for assessing the rivalry between Henry Fielding and Richardson, it does not, in my experience, alter the basic dynamics of their resistance to Richardsonian ideology. The most productive encounters with Richardson's novels, I have found, depend on students learning to recognize the ways in which the novels construct rather than reflect a modern psychological subject, as Nancy Armstrong has argued in the case of *Pamela*. Such a recognition can emerge dialogically in the classroom if student skepticism is an integral part of discussions and writing assignments.

I teach either *Pamela* or *Clarissa* in graduate courses, and my students' responses in these classes have shaped both my understanding of undergraduates' skepticism and the strategies I have developed to use it productively. The unabridged *Clarissa* occupies three to four weeks in the middle of a seminar usually entitled Sexuality and the Novel, 1660–1820. Although the syllabus varies from year to year, we read Richardson after novels by Aphra Behn, Daniel Defoe, and Eliza Haywood and before Frances Burney's *Cecilia* and a Jane Austen novel.[1] Students consequently have a solid grounding in the history of the novel before they encounter Richardson, and they have done extensive reading in the social and economic history of the period. Two articles published by former students, Martha Koehler and Daryl Ogden, began as seminar papers in different iterations of this class, their readings of Richardson, in some measure, stand for fifteen years of conversation and often intense discussion about his novels. I now use excerpts from their articles to begin discussions about readerly resistance to *Pamela* in my undergraduate courses. Undergraduate and graduate students characteristically employ different rhetorics to describe their experiences as readers: undergraduates respond cynically to Richardson's ideological values and assumptions because they find them socially and psychologically unconvincing; graduate students want to explore critically the workings of Richardson's aesthetic and sociopolitical commitments. Where undergraduates often see the gap between Richardson's stated intentions and his characters' actions as an artistic failure to craft a realistic novel, graduate students (like recent critics such as Cope, Hinton, and Gordon) see such fissures as characteristic of a coercive, masculinist ideology, one in which Richardson is complicit. As one comment on an anonymous course evaluation put it, "Clarissa is an archaeology of how a 'good girl' learns to repress herself." Although many apologists for Richardson may blanch at such comments, this view is one that I have heard repeatedly over the last fifteen years from students who reject the possibility that he was critiquing this same ideology.

Not one of my graduate students has bought into a Richardsonian ideology that identifies female psychological interiority—a woman's "integrity"—with masculinist notions of chastity, virtue, and daughterly obedience. The critical essays that I typically assign for the seminar have varied since the 1980s; over the years, however, the ones that work most effectively are those that challenge views of Richardson as a sympathetic protofeminist, offer feminist critiques of the novels, or explore the sociohistorical contexts in which he wrote. In different ways, Koehler's and Ogden's articles respond to this tradition of cultural studies criticism and then explore the tensions in the novel between didacticism and narrative art. Drawing on recent narrative theory, Koehler argues that Clarissa's seemingly fundamental oppositions between virtue and sin, good and evil, generosity and self-interest, and passivity and aggression are always in the process of breaking down into parasitic, triangular exchanges. To maintain his heroine's "moral perfection," then, Richardson paradoxically must isolate "Clarissa from the gender she is supposed to exemplify" (165). Clarissa can be a model of female virtue only because she exhibits none of the feminine weaknesses that contemporary moralists deplore. In effect, Koehler offers an intriguing strategy for beginning to understand why many students are put off by Richardson's heroines: if the novelist were successful in his didactic aims, his novels would be of little interest—merely cynical efforts to excite and then repress the ghosts of female desire. It is only in his failures that a space of aesthetic interest and political intervention can be created.

In a similar vein, Ogden suggests that "Richardson's Clarissa actually writes against Richardson himself" (50); in his view, the paternal fantasy of the daughter who must defend her virtue even to martyrdom is disrupted by a visual semiotics—Clarissa's desire to be gazed on only by Anna Howe—that is crucial to the expression of (repressed) desire. The heroine's will, he argues, discloses a rupture in a heteronormative narrative of marriages sealed and chastity vindicated: "if Clarissa's tiny locket [containing her image] symbolically seals Hickman's and Anna's eventual marriage, Clarissa's lifesize portrait [bequeathed to Anna] dwarfs it, thus sealing a far more overwhelming affirmation of her desire for Anna" (50). The repressed lesbian desire that Ogden sees as crucial to the dynamics of the novel suggests strategies that allow students to think through the implications of Richardson's heroines as both confined in and yet never contained by the paternal fantasy of daughterly virtue—of the daughter who resists all temptation and sexual aggression precisely to conform to the absolute desire of the father. My point in using these excerpts in the classroom is not to insist that students accept Koehler's or Ogden's arguments or to suggest that their feminist-Lacanian approach should take precedence over discussions of aesthetic value. Instead I emphasize that their readings both encourage and extend a dialogical classroom experience that provokes rather than forestalls discussion. Richardson paradoxically becomes most compelling when his didacticism provokes skepticism, cynicism, and resistance.[2]

Koehler's and Ogden's articles also offer a cautionary strategy for those writing or reading essays in this volume, *Approaches to Teaching the Novels of Samuel Richardson*. Student responses always evade, exceed, or invert teacherly intentions. In discussing the interplay between my classroom approach and undergraduates' reactions to *Pamela*, then, I want to concentrate on written responses as a means to provide something of an empirical basis for my argument. Because I was a visiting professor at the University of Virginia, none of the students—three-quarters of them English majors and all of them juniors or seniors—had taken a course with me before; only a handful had taken other courses in the eighteenth century. Consequently, there were few expectations about what approaches I might take or what I might "want" on papers and exams. My course on the eighteenth-century novel was as close to a laboratory experiment on teaching Richardson as one could imagine.

Having used a number of handouts early in the semester to introduce students to eighteenth-century debates about property law, the role of women in society, and social and class divisions, I began our discussion of *Pamela* by asking students to characterize the heroine's relationship to her parents in their first few letters. I then asked them to select subsequent scenes that either led them to modify or reinforced their characterizations and to analyze them in short, in-class freewriting exercises. The most popular scenes should be familiar to teachers and critics of the novel: Pamela in front of the mirror, Mr. B. in drag, and Pamela and Mr. B. trading insults. The short paragraphs then became the basis for subsequent discussions. Finally, I introduced excerpts from Koehler's and Ogden's essays (quoted in part above), and we talked about how these critical perspectives might affect students' responses to Pamela. As the students' choices may indicate, the tenor of class discussion favored the view that the novel was a "paternal fantasy" (F13)[3] that substituted parental authority—typically described as rigid and absolute—for a believable portrait of feminine desire. I used a similar strategy to begin discussions of other novels, notably Burney's *Evelina*. Students compared the opening letters between Villiers and the heroine with those between Mr. Andrews and Pamela and then were asked to discuss how their reading of *Pamela* reinforced or challenged this comparative approach.

Rather than offer after-the-fact reconstructions of these responses, I want to focus on essays written for an in-class midterm exam. Students could choose one of four questions to answer and had options to write on other novels. Seventeen of twenty-five students (thirteen women and four men) chose to answer the following question (and agreed to be quoted in this essay):

> Compare Pamela and Evelina as eighteenth-century "teenagers." Which one is a more believable—or successful—character? Why? Be sure to define what you mean by "believable" or "successful." Keep in mind that "teenager" is a historically and culturally specific term that became current only in the twentieth century.[4]

Their willingness to tackle the problem of *Pamela*'s didacticism suggests that students felt reasonably confident that they could explain differences between the narrative strategies of the two novelists. The students' writing to the moment excuses some of the stylistic haste evident in their responses, and it indicates as well their willingness to engage both aesthetic and ideological questions. Although their responses varied, none of the students thought Pamela was either a more "believable" or "successful" character than Evelina. The essays, in this respect, reflected the tenor of class discussions.

Not one student interpreted Pamela's actions in the way that Richardson insists his readers should. One woman suggested that, given "the sexual tensions pervading Pamela's pleas for her continued virtue, Richardson provides the reader with more scenes of entertainment than true instruction—[yet] he fails to connect with his reader" because his heroine does not behave "as a real teenage girl" (F3). "Real" in this description, I think, does not necessarily imply an ahistorical judgment about the novel but indicates that this reader remains unconvinced by Richardson's ventriloquizing of an idealized daughter's protestations. After reading Behn and Haywood, students are wary of accepting Richardson's views as indicative of sociocultural reality in the eighteenth century; Richardson describes "the way things, like daughters, should be, rather than how historians think they were" (F2). Unlike Evelina, who "questions authority like a real teenager," Pamela acts "on blind faith, never questioning the desires of her parents" (F2). This obedience makes Pamela's character "contrived, annoying, or unrealistic" and leads to this devastating assessment: instead of being moved to sympathy and admiration, this student became "bored with Pamela's theatrics and her inflated self-esteem" (F10). Significantly, such "cynicism" produced by Pamela's "unrealistic nature" (F3) suggests criticisms different from those that inform Fielding's *Shamela*. Instead of seeing Richardson as a hypocrite or a naive apologist for a gold-digging heroine, many students argued that he "failed to make [Pamela] real [because] her exaggerated and unstable emotions" (F7) do not jibe with either their experience or their perception of the social world described by Behn, Haywood, and Burney. Even at "her most pathetic, Pamela is never anything [more] than the personification of virtue" (F5); therefore, she often seems "false [because] no daughter is without fault, blemish, or impure thought, except in a father's mind" (F11). These comments register insights akin to those voiced by some recent critics: as an "abstract embodiment of virtue" (Lee 39), Pamela gives fictional shape to the sadomasochistic construction of feminine identity in a patrilineal society (Hinton). Instead of returning to the arguments advanced forty years ago by Morris Golden, this criticism calls our attention to Richardson's ideological investment in displaying his heroine's disinterested virtue by compelling his readers to weep disinterestedly for her fate (Gordon 179–93). The spectacle of Clarissa's suffering produces such skepticism in part because Richardson makes admonitions and precepts the basis of his moral psychology (Cope). In part, then, the skepticism of many female students stems from the fact that they have heard similar rhetoric before, if not from their parents then from latter-day promoters of abstinence. As one wrote, "there's no 'Pamela,' a flesh-and-blood person actually suffering, there's only an imagined character put through trials by the author" (F8).

Such responses to Pamela could be attributed to students' ignorance of the cultural and historical contexts of the eighteenth-century novel. Yet the exams indicate that these students had a good enough grasp of socioeconomic conditions, legal strictures, and gender politics to argue intelligently that "property law usually took precedence over moral law" (M4) and that "love was dependent on all sorts of social-financial demands" (F13). Because students were asked to compare Evelina and Pamela, they had the opportunity to define a sociocultural as well as psychological basis for assessing the two characters' behavior. For most students, Pamela's inaction spoke louder than her words. While *Pamela* depicts women as "passive, weak individuals . . . incapable of making their own decisions," *Evelina* "subverts these anti-feminist assumptions." Consequently, Burney's "is a more realistic work, especially for modern readers, because her female characters are more assertive and independent" (F13). It is significant that students frequently used arguments about "realism"—obviously a loaded term and one that I always ask students to define—to historicize Burney's female characters but not Richardson's. Mrs. Selwyn looms large in such responses, yet Evelina herself is described as more "believable and more fun" (F5) than Pamela. Despite the social conservatism that many students noted in Burney's novel, all agreed that it was a more effective didactic text than *Pamela* because it seemed less coercive psychologically and morally: "Burney allows the reader to undergo the same introspection as does Evelina, without being told what should and shouldn't be done" (M3). The widespread emphasis on "realism" as a standard by which to judge the two novels suggests that Evelina's "natural virtue" is more instructive than Pamela's "learned virtue" (M2) because "the reader can never live up to Pamela's 'standards,' but she can imagine herself being forgiven in *Evelina*" (F12). Because Pamela "is too extreme to be convincing," (F6) Richardson's didacticism seems shrill and dogmatic, ultimately reproducing the anxieties that the novel is intended to assuage.

In contrast, Burney's heroine is "a much more convincing [model] for readers to imitate" than Pamela (F12), because she is "more honest" (F1). Burney's didactic aims, accordingly, seem "far broader" (M1) and encompass social and interpersonal relationships as well as "abstract virtue" (F4). In short, for these students, "Evelina is a "well-developed character" (F9), one who "give[s] readers what they cannot get from Pamela: realism" (F8). Ultimately, the students' tendency to translate the question's phrasing—"believable" or "successful"— into "realism" suggests that their aesthetic judgments are deeply implicated in their perceptions of social behavior and psychological experience with which they can empathize. Pamela fails, in their minds, on both accounts.

There is, of course, a pied-piper argument to be made about my students' responses to Richardson: "Markley made his biases clear, and the students simply gave him what he wanted to hear." Fair enough. But a counterargument needs to be considered as well: traditional Richardsonians also make their biases clear, leave little room for resistance, and consequently are handed back what they want to hear. In short, student responses to *Pamela* and *Clarissa* suggest a range of strategies for self-critical examination about how we teach Richardson and the eighteenth-century novel more generally. Most readers of this essay have experienced the frustration of comparatively low enrollments in courses in the

eighteenth century and have had to deal with student expectations that all novels should adhere to "mall-rat realism" (F10). But it would be shortsighted and
ultimately self-defeating for readers of this essay to dismiss these students' criticisms of Richardson as the product of ignorance, substandard education, or a
naive fascination with women writers at the expense of a novelist who, for years,
was credited as a spokesman for his heroine's dignity and moral authority. If
student skepticism can be turned to advantage in the classroom and student
resistance harnessed to rethink the teaching of Richardson's novels, we can
begin to give students a sense of belonging to a community of readers—from
Richardson's contemporaries such as Fielding and Haywood to current critics such as Ogden, Koehler, and Gordon. This movement from cynicism to a
historically and theoretically informed skepticism ultimately may lead to reas-
sessing the significance of such resistance to eighteenth-century literature. One
of the comments on the teaching evaluations I received put Richardson in his
literary-historical context as follows: "I thought this course was going to be su-
per-boring, but much of it was really very interesting. Except Pamela. . . . She
should have been more like Fantomina."

NOTES

[1] In addition to the graduate surveys I have taught at my home institutions, I have
also done versions of this course as a visiting professor at the University of Oregon
(1990), Tulane (1991), and the University of Virginia (2000). My thanks to all these
students for their invaluable feedback over the years. In a sense, this essay is as much
theirs as mine.

[2] These include essays by Stephanson; Straub; Nussbaum; and Cope and sections from
Armstrong; McKeon's *Origins*; Cook; and Thompson.

[3] Responses are noted by gender (F for female, M for male) and numbers to indicate
which students are commenting.

[4] The term *teenager* had been discussed in class in response to arguments advanced
during a graduate colloquium that some of the undergraduate English majors had
attended.

Pamela Illustrations in the Classroom

Janet Aikins Yount

Terry Eagleton has explained the mid-eighteenth-century *Pamela* vogue in the terms of modern cultural studies: "Like Superman, *Pamela* is the name for a diverse set of social practices, an emblem encountered at every turn, a domestic talking-point and public declaration of faith." Like the popular comic strip, *Pamela* "is not merely to be read: it is to be dramatized, displayed, wielded as a cultural totem, ransacked for moral propaganda or swooned over as love story, preached from the pulpit and quoted in the salons" (5). In fact, the sixth, corrected edition (1742)[1] of Richardson's novel contained twenty-nine illustrations that display the superheroine, frame by frame, in her valiant attempt to fight evil with unparalleled virtue, as if anticipating the superhero comic-strip genre.

Scholars believe that Richardson selected both the novel's illustrators and the scenes to be depicted.[2] The artists who designed and engraved these illustrations were the virtuoso French illustrator Hubert François Gravelot and his younger associate Francis Hayman, who accomplished their work during the very time when Richardson was writing and revising volumes 3 and 4 of his text.[3] Remarkably few readers have seen these pictures, which have never been republished in later editions. Fortunately, all twenty-nine engraved illustrations, and the pages they face, are online at www.unh.edu/english/faculty/yount/pamela_illustrations/pamela_illustrations.html.

At the top of each image, the engraver identifies the placement of each illustration by volume and page number, thereby suggesting that each picture manifests a direct correspondence to the page of printed text it faces. As explained on the Web site, the last illustration is unique. It is the only one that corresponds to two numbered pages of text (Richardson [6th ed.] 4: 474–75), and in different copies of volume 4, the final illustration appears to have been variously bound to face either page 474 or page 475. For example, the illustration faces page 474 in the copy of the text at the William Ready Division of Archives and Research Collections, at McMaster University; however, in the copy at the Cambridge University Library, the illustration faces page 475. Moreover, this image not only corresponds to two pages of the text but also evokes two separate moments in the narrative by referring the reader to page 417 in the same volume. The Web site provides the printed text of page 417, thereby enabling students to speculate on the significance of and dynamic created by such dual visual representation in a sequential narrative. The Web site also provides the printed text of volume 3, page 2, with which the illustration designed for volume 3, page 11 was "usually bound" (Sale, *Bibliographical Record* 31) so that students can discuss the interpretive implications of this mistake in binding.

At the bottom of each image, the engraver identifies the artist responsible for its design, and I find that students welcome the challenge of identifying differences between the twelve illustrations by Hayman and the seventeen by Gravelot. Moreover, classroom study of the interplay between word and image prompted by the pictures gives students access to what Marcia Allentuck calls the "associatively and emotively pictorial" nature of Richardson's narrative (875; see also Brown). The guiding questions for such study are, first, in what ways do the illustrations constitute a substantive part of Richardson's text, and, second, what do they actually depict both individually and collectively?

From an editorial standpoint, the shock value of *Pamela* resides not in the titillating encounters between the reluctant heroine and the overbearing Mr. B. but in the student's amazed discovery that there are several different *Pamela*s, each one contending for authority. Is the "real" *Pamela* the unillustrated two-volume first edition that Richardson began writing on 10 November 1739, when his wife was pregnant with their last child, and that he published (made public through sale by booksellers) on 6 November 1740? That novel ends after Pamela's marriage to Mr. B., when the heroine wins acceptance into the B. family; but the conclusion may be deemed unsatisfying if we attend, as most critics have not,[4] to the sudden revelation that Mr. B. has an illegitimate daughter, Miss Goodwin, whom he staunchly refuses to take into his family. At the other extreme, students will ask whether they should regard the illustrated four-volume edition of 1742 as the genuine *Pamela*, because its two additional volumes resolve Miss Goodwin's fate and depict Pamela's life as a wife and repeatedly pregnant mother. The illustrations provide engaging vehicles through which to address such questions and to debate the relative merits of these two very different versions of a single novel.

As students embark on this discussion, they soon discover that the pictures by Hayman and Gravelot evoke events in the story that Richardson chose to exclude from the represented action. For example, the last illustration in volume 2 (fig. 1) places the history of Sally Godfrey, Miss Goodwin's mother, squarely before our eyes, even though the woman herself does not appear either in Gravelot's illustration or in Richardson's text. In the text facing the illustration, after Pamela asks Mr. B. if Miss Goodwin "stand[s] in nearer Relation to you than a Niece," the following exchange ensues between Mr. B. and his new wife:

> 'Tis even so, my Dear, reply'd he; and you remember my Sister's good-natur'd Hint of Miss *Sally Godfrey*. I do, well, Sir, answer'd I: But this is Miss *Goodwin*. Her Mother chose that for her, said he, because she would not be called by her own.   (*Pamela* [6th ed.] 2: 404)

Miss Goodwin's false name and identity, to which Mr. B. here refers, evoke his former transgression with Sally Godfrey and the "Particulars of the Affair," which Mr. B. then proceeds to explain. After hearing his "moving Tale" Pamela

Figure 1. Illustration designed by Gravelot and text from the 6th ed. of *Pamela*, 1742, 2: 404.

remarks, "The Words, [']Mother *is* of no mean Family,['] gave me not to doubt the poor Lady was living" (Richardson [ed. Keymer and Wakely] 480–82). Suddenly, here, Sally Godfrey comes into existence as a live being. Moreover, by displaying the scene in which Pamela meets Miss Godfrey's illegitimate daughter for the first time, the illustration forces the sight of Miss Goodwin on the reader. The illustration thus prompts students to discuss Richardson's reasons for ending his narrative in the first edition with Miss Goodwin's fate still unresolved.

This episode connects thematically with the incident that initiates the entire plot: the death of Mr. B.'s mother, which is announced in the opening sentences of the novel, although, again, the event is not represented in the action. In her first letter to her parents, Pamela announces that her mistress has died; however, she adds a telling consolation for her parents: "God . . . put it into my good Lady's Heart, on her Death-bed, just an Hour before she expir'd, to recommend to my young Master all her Servants." Most important, the expiring Mrs. B. recommended that Pamela, who "was sobbing and crying at her Pillow," be singled out for special notice. In this letter Pamela gives us our only access to the voice of Mr. B.'s mother, recalling her words as follows: "Remember my poor *Pamela!*—And these were some of her last Words! O how my Eyes run!—Don't wonder to see the Paper so blotted!" (*Pamela* [ed. Keymer and Wakely] 11). In

Richardson's text, both the former Mrs. B. and Sally Godfrey are absent mothers whose voices are not heard and whose lives remain unnarrated; Pamela's first letter to her parents and the illustration featuring Miss Goodwin make the existence of these absent mothers palpable and introduce alternative female points of view into an epistolary fiction otherwise dominated by Pamela's voice.

Students should also seek to differentiate the visual details invented by the artists from those that correspond to actual descriptions in Richardson's text. For example, the penultimate illustration in volume 2, facing page 305, features Pamela kneeling beside an elaborate bed, begging Mr. B.'s sister for acceptance. On a wall in the background hangs a portrait of a woman (fig. 2). In the pages immediately following the illustrated scene, an outraged Lady Davers says to her servant:

> *Beck* seest thou that Bed? That was the bed that I was born in; and yet that was the Bed, thou sawest as well as I, the wicked *Pamela* in this Morning, and this brother of mine just risen from her!

Lady Davers here demands that we all view the bed Mr. B. calls his "Bridal-bed" (Richardson [ed. Keymer and Wakely] 421). Mrs. B. gave birth to her children, Mr. B. and Lady Davers, in this bed. In the illustration, the bed is, essentially, the

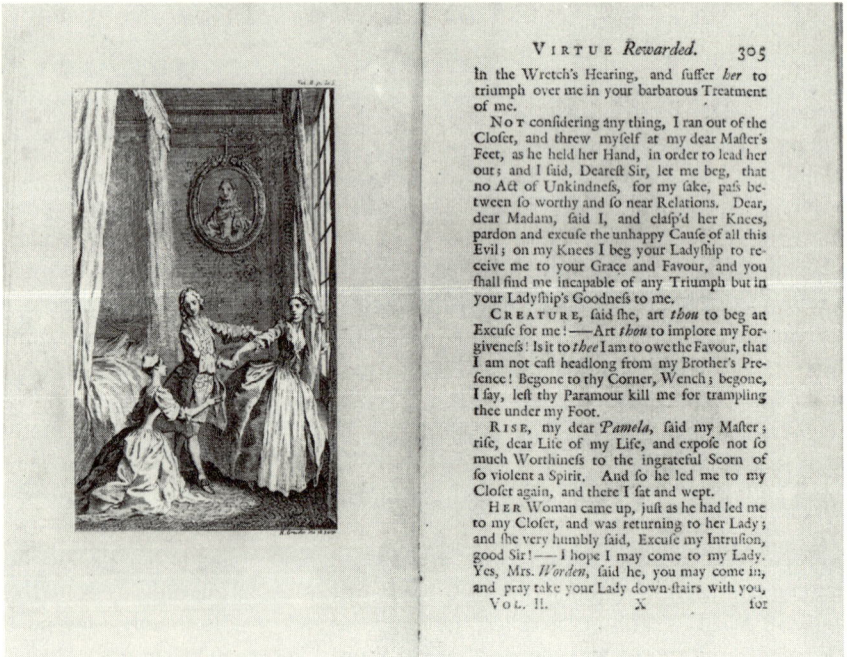

Figure 2. Illustration designed by Gravelot and text from the 6th ed. of *Pamela*, 1742, 2: 305.

protagonist. Unlike the bed, which the text actually mentions, the framed portrait of a woman was Gravelot's invention. We can assume the image depicts the former Mrs. B., whose painted representation witnesses the altercation between her son and daughter as well as the consummation of her son's marriage to Pamela. By including the portrait in his illustration, Gravelot reminds us that *Pamela* offers a verbal portrait of a newly emergent Mrs. B., a former servant who has supplanted her predecessor, Mr. B.'s mother, whose only direct appearance in the text occurs in Pamela's retrospective account of her deathbed directives.

Working with the illustrations also encourages students to notice the classroom edition they are using. The Norton edition, first published in 1958, was based on the first two of four volumes of the "eighth" duodecimo edition of 1761 (Sabor, "Cooke-Everyman Edition" 361), the last to have been printed during Richardson's lifetime. Other modern editions, by T. C. Duncan Eaves and Ben Kimpel, and Tom Keymer and Alice Wakely, reproduce instead what Richardson initially viewed as his complete text, the two-volume first edition of 1740. The Penguin edition follows still another editorial line of thought, offering something close to Richardson's final revisions of the text by printing a modernized version of the first two of the four volumes of the 1801 London edition. As Peter Sabor explains, that edition was printed from a copy, now lost, of the 1742 illustrated octavo edition of *Pamela* interleaved by Richardson with loose pages containing revisions and additions written during the 1750s. After his death in 1761, this copy was preserved by his daughters, who brought about its publication in 1801 (Sabor, "Note"). Unfortunately, the Penguin edition omits volumes 3 and 4, despite their publication in 1801 as part of a four-volume whole.[5] The question students may ask is why any of this matters. The text of *Pamela* provides the answer.

As a highly successful printer, Richardson understood the power of the printed word, as does Mr. B. In the first pages of the novel, Mr. B. comments on one of the heroine's letters, "I see my good Mother's Care in your Learning has not been thrown away upon you. She used to say, you lov'd Reading; you may look into any of her Books to improve yourself, so take care of them" (Richardson [6th ed.] 1: 4). His remark is anything but simple praise of Pamela's education, for he has gained access to this letter by suddenly entering what Pamela calls "my late Lady's Dressing-room," where she had been writing. By choosing the "Lady's Dressing-room" as the site for this encounter, Richardson surely wants us to recall Jonathan Swift's scandalous poem of male voyeurism ("The Lady's Dressing Room" 1730). Pamela tells her parents that when her "young Master" burst in, she went to "hide the Letter in my Bosom," of all places. Her startled reaction has provoked the intruder to pluck the letter from its intimate hiding place and read her penned words, which were not intended for his eyes. Students who thoughtfully examine the accompanying illustration soon realize that Hayman designed it not only as a picture of the two characters but also as the figuration of the postscript of her letter to her parents, in which Pamela registers her dismay at her master's intrusion and his assault on her body and her letter. In her commentary on the picture, Allentuck describes Pamela as "demure," her eyes cast down on her quill pen, and Mr. B. as "impassive," his eyes focused on Pamela's letter (883); however, the true subject of the illustration is textuality. That is, Hayman's composition provides a literalized image of the postscript, a penned afterthought whose very subject is the technology of writing and the importance of reading.[6]

Richardson would have us realize that the turn of a phrase can wield enormous power, as the variant texts of *Pamela* readily demonstrate. Students who compare the page of text facing Hayman's illustration with that of the first edition will discover a significant revision. In the first edition Pamela writes, "O how I was sham'd" by Mr. B.'s behavior, but in the sixth edition her remark is, "O how asham'd I was!" The revised wording conveys a subtle sense of guilt, not mere shame or embarrassment. By locating changes of this kind, students can explore the ways in which Richardson's revisions effected substantive changes in character and action.

Strictly speaking, the Hayman and Gravelot illustrations do not constitute a causally sequential narrative, and students can refine their understanding of narrative probability by attempting to define their alternative coherence. After students have read the novel but before they have viewed any of the illustrations, I ask them to imagine which scene Richardson and his illustrators were most likely to have chosen as the first picture. Typically, students think first of what Eaves calls the "somewhat sensational if not perfervid scenes" in the novel, such as Mr. B.'s attack on Pamela in the summer house (354). When confronted with the actual first illustration, the one in which Mr. B. reads from Pamela's letter, students sometimes react with surprise and then produce instructive responses when asked to provide a rationale for their choice of a second illustrated scene. During this exercise, a class of mine correctly concluded that the second image would feature Pamela confiding in a woman, most probably Mrs. Jervis, because our opening view of the heroine depicts Mr. B.'s rude intrusion on her privacy. One student even proposed that Mr. B. would appear in some way as a spy in the image. These remarkably accurate speculations arose from our prior analysis of the narrative logic guiding the first illustration and its accompanying text.

Even for those who do not press on to volumes 3 and 4 of *Pamela*, the later illustrations offer valuable material for study. For example, on page 94, the text facing the second illustration in volume 3, we read Pamela's transcript of a letter from her friend, Polly Darnford (fig. 3). In the original typography, Richardson flagged each line of the transcription with double quotation marks, a reminder that we are reading Pamela's copied version of her friend's written words:

> The Truth is, my Papa has been much disordered with a kind of rambling Rheumatism, to which the Physicians, learnedly speaking, give the Name of *Arthritica vaga*, or the Flying Gout; and when he ails ever so little, (it

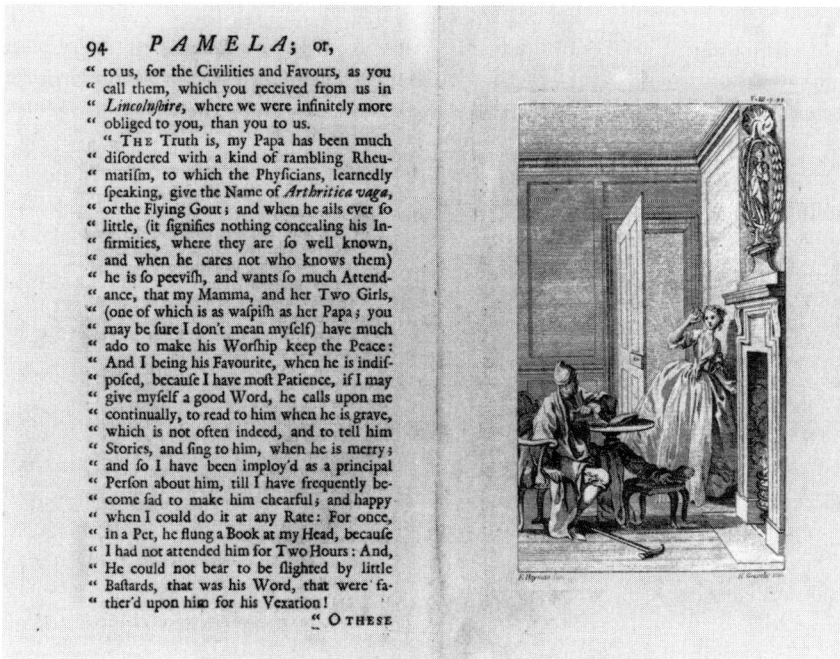

Figure 3. Illustration designed by Hayman and text from the 6th ed. of *Pamela*, 1742, 3: 94.

signifies nothing concealing his Infirmities, where they are so well known, and when he cares not who knows them) he is so peevish, and wants so much Attendance, that my Mamma, and her Two Girls, (one of which is as waspish as her Papa; you may be sure I don't mean myself) have much ado to make his Worship keep the Peace: And I being his Favourite, when he is indisposed, because I have most Patience, if I may give myself a good Word, he calls upon me continually, to read to him when he is grave, which is not often indeed, and to tell him Stories, and sing to him, when he is merry; and so I have been imploy'd as a principal Person about him, till I have frequently become sad to make him chearful; and happy when I could do it at any Rate: For once, in a Pet, he flung a Book at my Head, because I had not attended him for Two Hours: And, He could not bear to be slighted by little Bastards, that was his Word, that were father'd upon him for his Vexation! (Richardson [6th ed.] 3: 94)

That one long sentence reveals the selfish and overbearing character of Polly's "Papa," whose gesture of throwing a book at his daughter's head constitutes a graphic pun on the use and abuse of literature. Students should analyze what the length and style of the sentence reveal about teenage Polly's character and state of mind. They should also consider the signification of the double quotation marks beside each line of transcribed text (see fig. 3), for these markers invite us to think about what Pamela herself must have been thinking as she copied each word of this shocking epistle. By implication, the quotation marks prompt us to imagine Pamela at her writing desk, whereas the words she copies describe the scene between Polly and her father that is displayed by the illustration opposite. The portrayal of Polly, in both word and picture, seems a comic anticipation of the tragic paternal abuse suffered by Clarissa Harlowe. In *Pamela*, the portrayal of Polly amplifies the debate about fatherly duties to daughters that Richardson introduces in the Miss Goodwin subplot. As this exercise suggests, students can use the later illustrations to test their speculations about which aspects of volumes 1 and 2 possessed the greatest potential for development both in the later volumes of *Pamela* and in Richardson's other fiction.

Stephen A. Raynie has proposed that many of the illustrations function as anti-Pamela texts slyly embedded in the novel. Picking up on this hint, students working with the pictures in small groups enjoy searching for compositional elements that complicate Richardson's text. For example, those with access to the engravings of William Hogarth may notice in the illustration of Pamela's reunion with her father (vol. 2, facing p. 89) an ironic visual allusion to plate 2 of Hogarth's "The Harlot's Progress," in which a young prostitute overturns a tea table to prevent a lover from noticing the presence of his rival (Shesgreen, print 19). Indeed, suggestive allusions to Hogarth occur more than once in Hayman's and Gravelot's illustrations.

In addition to the works of Hogarth, the illustrated edition of Aesop's fables, which Richardson edited and published in 1739, served both the artists and Richardson as a shadow text for *Pamela*.[7] As Sale points out, advertisements identified this edition of Aesop as the one quoted in the novel (3–4). If Pamela draws direct connections between her circumstances and various fables, the artists at times reinforce such parallelism in their compositions. For example, in the text facing the illustrated fishing scene, the heroine says to Mrs. Jewkes:

> I was thinking this poor Carp was the unhappy *Pamela*. I was likening you and myself to my naughty Master. As *we* hooked and deceived the poor Carp, so was I betrayed by false Baits; and when you said, Play it, Play it, it went to my Heart to think I should sport with the Destruction of the poor Fish I had betray'd; and I could not but fling it in again.
> (Richardson [6th ed.] 1: 214)

Here Pamela has lured Mrs. Jewkes to the fishing hole on false pretenses, her real motive being the retrieval of hidden letters in the garden. Hayman's illustration coyly places Mrs. Jewkes at the end of Pamela's line so that she appears "hooked" on both the fishing line and the "line" of Pamela's disingenuous argument. The presentation of this episode in the narrative also parallels the layout of printed fable books. That is, Richardson first provides a picture (both the illustration and the description of the scene in Pamela's words), then a mini-narrative (the story of the carp's capture and near destruction), and finally an explicitly stated moral drawn from the combined picture and text. Students will locate other illustrations that, when combined with the text, follow a similar pattern.

In answer to the guiding questions posed at the start of this essay, the illustrations for the 1742 edition of *Pamela* formed an integral part of the text as its author knew it. The revisions of the 1750s, interleaved by Richardson into a copy of the 1742 text but not published until long after his death, contain extended passages of description perhaps written so that some future edition could simulate in words the effects rendered visually in 1742 by Hayman and Gravelot. Indeed, their illustrations trigger participatory reading, instead of merely depicting subject matter.

Thus the illustrations to *Pamela* enable students to perform a multifaceted exploration of John Locke's claims for the educative and pleasurable force of illustrated books (*Some Thoughts* 212).[8] As if to expose this controlling theme throughout the series of pictures, the very last illustration (fig. 4), which shows Pamela telling stories to her children and her servants, depicts in an interactive

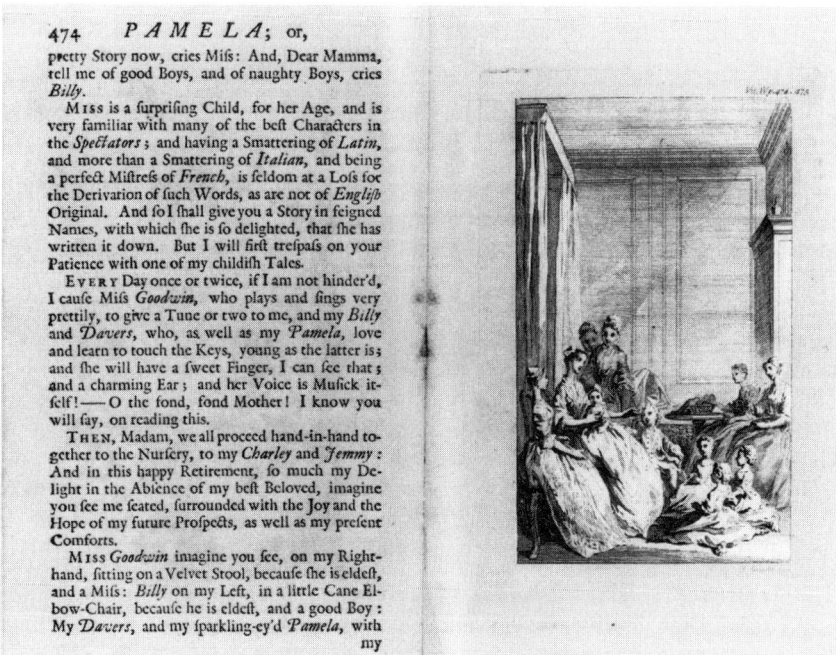

Figure 4. Illustration designed by Gravelot and text from the 6th ed. of *Pamela*, 1742, 4: 474–75.

manner the powers of narrative. In the two-page text accompanying the illustration, Richardson reinforced the importance of a reader's or listener's active engagement by inserting a footnote referring us to *"this Vol.* p. 417" for an explanation of the "Rule of Two Ears * to One Tongue" (Richardson, 6th ed., 4: 475). As Pamela says, "Knowledge is obtained by *Hearing*, and not by *Speaking*, . . . So you must be sure to mind, that you *hear* twice as much as you *speak*" (417). In the 1742 edition, Hayman's and Gravelot's illustrations enable readers to *"hear* twice as much" as Richardson speaks. Today's students may read the novel's verbal text, but only through classroom engagement with the pictures will they fully realize the interactive and intermedial narrative that is set into motion by the heroine's words.[9]

NOTES

Permission for the use of the illustrations from the 1742 edition of Pamela granted by the William Ready Division of Archives and Research Collections, McMaster University Library, Hamilton, Ontario, Canada. The funding for the reproduction of the illustrations on the Web site was provided by the College of Liberal Arts, University of New Hampshire.

[1]On the composition, printing, and publication of *Pamela* in its various editions, see Sale; Sabor, "Richardson's Continuation."

[2]Eaves fully documents Richardson's initial attempt to employ William Hogarth in the creation of two frontispieces for the second edition of *Pamela* and his subsequent choice of Gravelot and Hayman for the twenty-nine illustrations. Eaves also provides a list of the plates for which Hayman, as opposed to Gravelot, provided the original design (Eaves 351–54).

[3]Richardson wrote volumes 3 and 4 of his novel after becoming outraged at the appearance of spurious sequels to volumes 1 and 2. He began the manuscript of volumes 3 and 4 in April 1741, completed it by 8 October (Sale 28), and published a first edition of the later volumes in duodecimo on 7 December 1741. He then made extensive revisions in what would become "the third edition" of volumes 3 and 4, described on its title page as "Embellish'd with Copper Plates, Design'd and Engrav'd by Mr. Hayman and Mr. Gravelot," which he printed between December 1741 and May 1742. On 10 May he published these two volumes together with the sixth, corrected edition of volumes 1 and 2. Clearly, he regarded these four illustrated octavo volumes as a single work.

[4]Recently this unsettling element in the story has received more attention. See Harris, *Samuel Richardson* 13–14; Sussman; Schellenberg; and Rivero ("The Place").

[5]The Penguin omission reflects the general critical opinion that because Richardson wrote these two volumes in response to spurious sequels to his own volumes 1 and 2, the later volumes are more properly regarded as a sequel. Hayman's and Gravelot's illustrations, however, invite us to question the assumption that the second half of *Pamela*, sometimes called *"Pamela II,"* should be viewed as a separate work. The history of *Pamela* editions may explain why most modern critics have judged Richardson's extension of his novel to be inferior in quality to his original text, for throughout most of the twentieth century, the only readily available edition of volumes 3 and 4 was the Every-

man (1914), which reproduced the bowdlerized and at times incoherent Cooke edition of 1811. Fortunately, *Literature Online* now has made the full text of the sixth corrected edition (1742) readily available at lion.chadwyck.com, along with that of the first edition of *Pamela* (1740).

[6]For fuller analyses of illustrations discussed here, see Aikins, "Richardson's 'Speaking Pictures,'" "Re-presenting" and "Picturing"; Brown.

[7]For a discussion of this aspect of *Pamela*, see Keymer, "*Pamela*'s Fables."

[8]Richardson may well have drawn his rationale for illustrating *Pamela* and other books he printed from Locke's *Thoughts concerning Education*, which Pamela herself consults on the subject of child rearing throughout volume 4. Locke wrote as follows: "If [a child's] *Aesop* has Pictures in it, it will entertain him much the better, and encourage him to read, when it carries the increase of Knowledge with it" (212; see also Aikins, "Pamela's Use").

[9]Wagner has proposed "intermediality" as a term to describe "those fascinating works that combine visual art and prose fiction . . . , urging the reader not to give preference to one medium but to consider both" (18).

Richardson's *Pamela* and Political Allegory

Michael McKeon

We often think of Richardson's *Pamela* as the first domestic novel in English. My aim in teaching it in the way I describe here is to give students a sense of what this priority means not only on the level of content but also in formal terms. To this end, *Pamela* needs to be read in a course that also reads a political roman à clef of the preceding period, ideally Aphra Behn's *Love-Letters between a Nobleman and His Sister* (1684, 1685, 1687). If necessary, *Love-Letters* can be excerpted to make it more accessible to the average undergraduate. It is also helpful to include John Bunyan's *The Pilgrim's Progress*, part 1 (1678) and Defoe's *Robinson Crusoe* (1719) in the sequence of texts.[1]

Whether this is a course on narrative, the novel, or on Restoration and early-eighteenth-century literature, we read the texts chronologically. This means that we come to *Pamela* after *Love-Letters* and can read it in the context of Behn's work. I urge students to attend closely to prefatory material in all these texts, because it is crucial to the author's efforts to prepare the reader for the reading experience that will follow. Contemporary readers, I point out, will not have the generic expectation of a novel, although with hindsight we can look back to see how these disparate sorts of narrative contribute to the establishment of that genre in the middle of the eighteenth century. A fruitful exercise can have students juxtapose two or more of the prefaces, by Behn, Richardson, Bunyan, and Defoe, to appreciate how widely they differ in the expectations they seek to create. At the same time, this exercise helps students see the different prefaces as instances of the same basic sort of writing, whose purpose is to establish a framework of expectations. This can help prepare them for thinking about the more complex purpose of the novel genre.

Love-Letters is preceded by a dedicatory epistle and by a summary of the "argument" of part 1. The most important aim of these two prefatory sections is their claim that the following narrative is a translation from the French of a collection of letters about contemporary politics and warfare in high places, written by the actual aristocrats involved. To disguise the scandalously public nature of this subject, the narrative pretends throughout to be speaking about private, even intimate, love affairs, and the characters are given fictitious names taken from old romances. The letters are said to have been discovered in the private cabinets of the principal correspondents. However, hints in the dedicatory epistle, not to mention the annotations of modern editors, quickly make it clear that this claim is a fiction. Behn in fact writes about contemporary English politics and aristocrats, using these elaborate devices to distance her writing from its real topic, which is too dangerous to address directly (the events of the exclusion crisis were unfolding even as she wrote). But the pretense that she is speaking only about private matters—love, sexual desire, romance fictions—

rather than about matters of great public moment is justified by more than the wish to avoid legal prosecution. Behn also writes in a tradition based on the belief that common readers will best grasp the complexities of great affairs of state if these affairs are cast in ordinary terms. She thus constructs an allegorical plot whose everyday events and concerns stand for and signify the elevated affairs of the great.

In teaching *Love-Letters* along with *Pamela*, I emphasize this belief because it gets to the heart of what makes the first narrative relatively hard to follow and the second easier. I do not simply mean that it is harder to make sense of allegory than of literal narrative. It is also difficult for us to credit Behn's attitude that public affairs involving heroes, royalty, and events of world-historical importance are more significant than private ones, which are best used as a means of reaching the higher end of understanding great affairs. *Love-Letters* gives plenty of opportunities to experience this allegorical imbalance between the private and the public. A central theme is the conflict between the passionate desires of young lovers (Silvia, Philander, Octavio, Calista) to possess each other and their elders' resolve to arrange their marriages for the financial and political interests of the family. The conflict between the two sides is carried out in the close and overheated confines of domestic interiors, where the passionate desires of the principal characters create an atmosphere of claustrophobic and clandestine excitement. But the allegorical structure of Behn's narrative obliges us to keep in mind that its private events stand for the contemporary public conflict between the will of the people and the authority of the king, which was being fought out in the open, in the public spaces of parliament, court, and the battlefield. So, as in all allegories, we read on two levels. In Behn the private conflict between forced marriages of alliance and marriage for love resembles, and tacitly figures forth, the public conflict between absolute authority and the liberty of the subject (or, between the benign paternalism of the king and the unruly license of the people). The experience of reading *Love-Letters* is so compelling on its own private terms that Behn often tempts us to linger, as it were, on the level of the signifier. The more we do this, however, the more we are inclined to take the private story of love as self-sufficient—interesting and important enough to justify our staying there for a while.

Broadly speaking, the first two parts of the work focus on narrating private affairs of love, relying on scattered allusions to remind us of the political and military activities to which they refer, whereas the third part narrates more of these public "French" engagements directly. But the difference between the private and the public plots is not so easy to distinguish as this might suggest. Although Behn's basic allegorical structure is clear, there is no one-to-one correspondence between signifier and signified. Much of our sense of the way the private stands for the public comes through metaphor, not allegory. Drawing on the public plot of the exclusion crisis, the characters compare themselves and each other to tyrants, traitors, judges, criminals, and the like. Silvia fears that "household spies" (90) may betray her love affair with Philander, and the artificial laws of the patriarchal family impinge on the natural freedoms of the lovers. In other words, the translation from the private to the public realm is often achieved within the level of the private itself. And when we concentrate on public events in part 3, we find that the great are as consumed by amatory desire as their underlings are—and, like them, use political metaphors to describe their feelings.

This preoccupation with the private-public correspondence even at the microlevel of metaphor, although it might seem to reinforce the basic signifying relationship, also has the cumulative effect of challenging our ability to tell the relative significance of, and even the difference between, the two realms. I encourage students to experience this as an intentional challenge on Behn's part. Some episodes in which this confusion is strikingly and amusingly acted out are Silvia and Philander's efforts to conceal their affair (51–62), Octavio's arrest for treason and its aftermath (262–70, 280–90), and Cesario's love for Hermione and his success in obtaining the king's pardon (319–36). Although Behn's conventional commitment in *Love-Letters* is to political allegory and its valorization of both the public and the historically factual, she is also interested in testing the boundaries between the public and the private, the factual and the fictional. Read against *Pamela*, this interest bespeaks a growing temptation of Behn's culture to value both the private lives of ordinary people and the narration of things that have no real existence. When we are most caught up in Behn's private intrigues, we are also most inclined to disregard what had seemed at first a crucial justification for our attending to *Love-Letters*: its concern with the factual truth about elevated persons. Having lured us into reading the private plot as a mere romance only to insinuate its actual status as a stand-in for public affairs of great importance, Behn tempts us to find our greatest satisfaction in what might as well be fiction after all.

Read against Behn's *Love-Letters*, *Pamela* seems its mirror image. The material that prefaces the first edition, including Richardson's long title page, announces that *Pamela* is an authentic collection of letters written by real people, not found in a cabinet but communicated to the "editor" for publication (3).[2] The novel was so popular that three months after the first edition, a second edition was published in which there appeared an additional set of prefaces that are less careful to maintain the initial claim to factual authenticity. In this way, Richardson, like Behn, moderates the claim to factuality once it has been thoroughly made. (In his next novel, *Clarissa*, the claim disappears entirely.) Moreover, Richardson's story is also one of private and amatory passions, entirely confined to the hothouse interiors of two country homes: the drawing rooms and bedrooms in which Pamela resists the passionate approaches of Mr. B. and the antechambers and closets in which she documents the minute details of her private emotions. Indeed, the private framework of this story, much like Behn's, is the conflict between internal love and external authority, the latter now embodied not in the parental generation but in the figure of the libertine seducer. And Pamela's metaphoric language, which dominates the novel, repeatedly translates this theme of private conflict into the emotive register of the public and the political: she is a "rebel" (66), a "criminal" (203), a "slave" (126), and a "traitor" (199); Mr. B. inflicts his "lawless Tyranny" over "Pamela through his, "Imprisonment" of her in the Bedfordshire house (147, 208). What is missing in *Pamela*, of course, are not only the open public spaces but also the political allegory and the public level of action itself.

Not that *Pamela* lacks the sort of overarching pedagogic purpose that informs all allegory. Richardson's title page makes clear his ambition to use the story of Pamela "to cultivate the principles of virtue and religion," and the introduction to the second edition applauds him for secreting, "under the modest Disguise of a *Novel*, all the *Soul* of Religion" (9). Moreover, although Behn never published a key to her roman à clef, the moral "applications" with which *Pamela* concludes (409–12) function as a key: they open up or make explicit the identity and meaning of the characters. (Students will be interested to see examples of keys compiled for other contemporary romans à clef, like those of Delarivier Manley. Keys can be reproduced from the following editions of Manley's works: *The New Atalantis* [1710, 1716], *The Memoirs of Europe* [1710], and *The Adventures of Rivella* [1715, 1717]). The difference is that in political allegory like Behn's, opening up identity amounts to assigning the characters an actual (public) identity, whereas in *Pamela* it involves assigning them an ethical (private) personality. "Political character" does not cease to be important in *Pamela*, as the force and persistence of Richardson's political metaphors make clear. But the absence of an allegorical framework of signification means that, for Richardson, significant characterization need not be sought in public exemplars because greatness of character can plausibly be found in the private actions and passions of common people. The public world remains for him an important ethical register, but it is not the crucial framework for identifying human value. Of course, political allegory is only a rigorously structural means of providing a public framework of this sort; the public norm is more broadly evident in the way classic literature tends to confine its most serious attention to the great. A good nonallegorical example of this norm is the Shakespearean double-plotted drama, in which the low plot reflects a debased and comic version of the high plot.

Students need to understand that *Pamela* is not a rewriting of a roman à clef like *Love-Letters*. Rather, I suggest that they see it more broadly as an internalization of the social ethics that obtained for those of elevated social and political status in the premodern world. The normative value that had characterized the public elites of traditional cultures has become a capacity also of the Pamelas of the world. This revaluation is already a feature of *Love-Letters*, reflected in the porosity of the public-private boundary that a stricter allegory would have kept watertight. But the contrast between these two narratives of potential upward mobility is instructive. The exclusion crisis (and therefore also *Love-Letters*) played out the profound problem of status inconsistency on the most public level of royal inheritance: Monmouth-Cesario does not accede to the throne of England because his (private) "true nobility" is not sufficient to overcome the fact of his (public) illegitimacy. The difference in *Pamela* is double. First, the problem of status inconsistency is persuasively enacted at the private level of the serving girl; and second, Pamela's marriage to Mr. B. demonstrates that the (private) virtue of the commoner is able to overcome the (public) disadvantage of low birth. These two differences concern plot content. I connect these differences with the contrast between allegorical and literal narration to give students a palpable sense of how form and content are interactive and correlative elements in literary works.

Students tend to be sensitive to Richardson's pedagogic claims in *Pamela* and to be broadly skeptical (like Mr. B. and Fielding) about the didactic "key" everywhere embedded in *Pamela*. Thus they are suspicious about the sincerity of Richardson's ethical purpose. I welcome a healthy skepticism, but caution against their becoming too easily cynical and thereby missing the complexity and seriousness of the socioethical revision in which Richardson is engaged. But I also suggest another sense in which Richardson's procedure in *Pamela* has the aura of allegorical signification. The passage in which Mr. B. experiences a conversion to Pamela's virtue through reading her "journal" (94; 197–209) permits us to see Richardson's interest in a species of privacy and interiority that is related to, but goes beyond, the realm of virtue and religion. In this passage, Mr. B. becomes, in effect, the ideal reader of Pamela's writings, because he learns to value and take pleasure in the narrative of her defended virtue in a way that avoids the necessity of a strictly literal belief in her version of things. It is not her (public) accuracy regarding actuality that counts but her (private) credibility regarding the affective truth of their relationship. In other words, Mr. B.'s method of reading Pamela serves as an allegory of an emergent mode of aesthetic response, a mode that Richardson would have us emulate in reading *Pamela* and one that foregrounds not just Pamela's rhetorical powers but also her ability to draw him, and us, into the private space of her interior emotions. For this to happen does not require that the vestigial public language of political characterization should disappear; it requires that such language assume an allusively metaphoric force whereby the public is tacitly understood to modify and suffuse the private rather than the private signifying and giving way to the public. With encouragement, students will have recognized that Behn's narrative technique modulates from an epistolary first-person to an increasingly distinct third-person voice over the course of *Love-Letters*. It is worth helping them see how this experimentation lays the ground for Richardson's allegorization of the aesthetic reading process. As the distance between Silvia and her narrator increases, Behn learns how to evoke the inner motives of her protagonist in a way that reveals both Silvia's ethical shortcomings and the affective complexity of her state of mind. Increasingly, we hear the narrator's didactic reflections on Silvia's duplicity as a stirring acknowledgment of her doubleness, her interiority. Richardson's passage from the public to the private register is one from the political to the ethical, but also to the aesthetic.

The argument for including *Pilgrim's Progress* and *Robinson Crusoe* in this sequence is probably obvious enough. The relation between these two texts is a fruitful analogue to that between *Love-Letters* and *Pamela*, an analogue that lays out, in the classic and (even to undergraduates) comparatively familiar terms of religious allegory, the less immediately accessible notion of both political allegory and its privatization. Again, the point is not to claim that Defoe's novel is a literal rewriting of Bunyan's allegory. Rather, it is to conceive the religious appeal from the letter to the spirit—from a literal signifier about the lives of common people to an allegorical signified of eternal life in heaven—as analogous to Behn's secular appeal from the private to the public. Like Behn, Bunyan fashions a familiar signifier so compelling in its circumstantial and emotional detail that it risks becoming, in the minds of its readers, a self-sufficient signified. Similarly, the comparison between *Robinson Crusoe* and *Pamela* can clarify the idea of a formal privatization or internalization by recognizing that allegory remains an element in Defoe's novel, but in vestigial association with a heavily moralized thematic discourse, instead of by providing the sort of overarching allegorical structure that we encounter in *Pilgrim's Progress*. To juxtapose these four narratives allows students not only to see the fundamental formal differences between literal and allegorical narration but also to appreciate that radically different literary forms can be used to articulate similar kinds of content.

NOTE

[1]The modern editions of these texts that I use in teaching are the following: *Pilgrim's Progress* (Oxford World's Classics); *Love-Letters* (Penguin Classics); *Robinson Crusoe* (Oxford World's Classics); *Pamela* (Houghton), but others are suitable so long as they contain all the editorial apparatus that accompanied these narratives.

[2]All citations to *Pamela* are from Eaves and Kimpel's edition.

Pamela: Chastity, Charity, and Moral Reform

Elizabeth Kraft

When I teach *Pamela* to undergraduate English majors over a two-week period, I emphasize its engagement with ethical and moral questions. *Pamela* is centered on the Christian virtues of chastity and charity and argues that these virtues are desirable in every sense of the word. Augustine viewed the distinction between *cupiditas* (lust) and *agape* (love or chastity) as the fundamental choice of life.[1] In *Pamela*, however, Richardson seems to demonstrate that chastity, or what might be called lust unfulfilled, can lay the foundation for a reformed upper class. The creation of a charitable, just society involves not just choosing between two kinds of love but managing a complex love composed of both erotic desire and spiritual longing. Marriages founded on such a love make up a society truly reflective of its Christian virtues. As the conversion of Mr. B. demonstrates, responsive resistance can transform erotic passion into social love or charity, that is, a passion for doing good.

By the time my students encounter Richardson in an upper-division course on the eighteenth-century novel, many of them have already read Aphra Behn's *Oroonoko* and Daniel Defoe's *Robinson Crusoe*, some have read *Moll Flanders*, and a few *Gulliver's Travels*. When I tell students about Samuel Richardson's life and works, they are therefore already accustomed to thinking about issues germane to eighteenth-century life and literature, such as slavery, colonization, and the increasing importance of luxury and pleasure.[2] They are also familiar with the conventions of early narrative such as episodic structure, didacticism, discursive moments, and interest in the forbidden and taboo, expressed in terms that seem to them surprisingly decorous and indirect.[3] The period's intense religiosity has also begun to lose its foreignness for students, and the way Pamela's deep Christian faith plays out in an eighteenth-century English setting seems an extended meditation on earlier preoccupations, particularly those of *Robinson Crusoe*.

The language of mastery and servitude that Pamela uses, as well as the novel's concern with individual autonomy, human worth, and dignity, link *Pamela* stylistically and thematically with Defoe's novel. Both novels seriously address the topic of class difference by highlighting the spiritual superiority of a socially inferior subject. Yet there is a crucial difference in the narrative treatments of Friday and Pamela. In *Robinson Crusoe*, Friday's human dignity, as Charles Gildon pointed out early on, is compromised by his speech.[3] Gildon's Friday complains to Defoe for having "injure me to make me such Blockhead, so much contradiction, as to be able to speak *English tolerably well* in a Month or two, and not to speak it better in twelve Years after" (279). Conversely, although Pamela is only a servant, she is linguistically gifted. Her voice tells her story, but, perhaps as important, she writes poetry to translate her plight into terms universally applicable to the condition of the oppressed. Her letters and her poems become sites of exegesis for Mr. B., whose critical interpretation, both of Pamela's texts and of Pamela as a text, results in personal reform impelling him to social action.

After situating Richardson's first novel in relation to earlier fiction and providing biographical facts to establish the circumstances of its writing and publication, I invite the students to examine moral, ethical, and aesthetic concerns central to eighteenth-century fiction in general and *Pamela* in particular, asking broad questions as well as analyzing specific passages. Although I reveal my opinions in comments and leading questions, I try to create an atmosphere of collaborative learning. I present my views persuasively to show how literary arguments are fashioned and supported, but I also make clear that I am open to contrary views. I have often been convinced by a student's perceptive insight or persuasive logic.

Our first concern is the importance of female chastity. Many of my students are annoyed with Pamela's responses to Mr. B.'s sexual advances, finding her insistence on her virtue as tiresome and perverse as Henry Fielding did. Those who never get over their sardonic, cynical response to Pamela must wait patiently for *Shamela*. Resistant reading is generally a good trait to encourage in young scholars, but I initially discourage it, because I want them to try to empathize with Pamela's point of view. We begin with close reading of two key passages: Mr. B.'s treatment of Pamela in the summerhouse and her response (22–24) and an earlier letter in which Pamela's parents declare that they would rather follow her to the grave than hear that she has lost her virtue (14). I begin by asking whether Pamela makes too much of a few stolen kisses. Mr. B. certainly thinks so: "What a foolish Hussy you are," he says. His next question is pertinent: "Have I done you any Harm?" (23). Has he? I ask the students. Having made a real effort to understand the differences between the twenty-first and the eighteenth century, they are quick to appreciate the dangers of sexual dalliance to an eighteenth-century woman's reputation. Although they understand the risk of unwanted pregnancy in an age of unreliable birth control, they are less attuned to the special circumstances governing the lives of maidservants. I therefore point out the ever-present danger of sexual aggression from masters who considered such indulgence their right, and I mention the difficulty of changing one's situation in a line of work that depended on a "character" from former employers. The text exemplifies eighteenth-century attitudes toward a maidservant's virtue. As Parson Williams finds when he tries to plead Pamela's case to the Darnfords, Mr. B.'s behavior would have been considered perfectly normal: "Why, what is all this my dear," remarks Sir Simon, "but that the Squire our Neighbour has a mind to his Mother's Waiting-Maid? And if he takes care she wants for nothing, I don't see any great Injury will be done her. He hurts no Family by this" (134).

If Sir Simon's attitude is normative, what do we make of Mr. and Mrs. Andrews's earlier remark to their daughter, which seems founded on a completely different notion of family from the Darnfords'?

> If you love *us*, then, if you value *God*'s Blessing, and *your own* future Happiness, we charge you to stand upon your Guard; and, if you find the least Attempt made upon your Virtue, be sure you leave every thing behind you, and come away to us; for we had rather see you all cover'd with Rags, and even follow you to the Church-yard, than have it said, a Child of ours preferred worldly Conveniences to her Virtue.   (14)

The Andrews family, despite being poor and therefore not "family" at all, seem to take themselves very seriously. Why? My students often point to the Christian belief that underpins this parental warning. Concerned for Pamela's soul and believing that Christian morality requires chastity, Pamela's father and mother insist that sexual intercourse outside marriage is wrong.

In that sense, then, Pamela responds morally to Mr. B.'s impropriety in the summerhouse, because his kisses and fondling will surely not stop there. Thus social circumstances and moral codes explain Pamela's near hysteria in this early episode, even if they stop short of convincing students that *Pamela*'s insight into the human condition transcends its own time and place. While it may have been unfashionable for the past twenty years for literary scholars to acknowledge the fact, I believe that undergraduates have always required literature to contribute something to their understanding of the human condition. The best literature, students insist, will tell them something about how to live or think about their lives. Because I agree with the students, I happily allow the discussion to move in that direction. After all, the notion of relevance allows me to shift the conversation from morality to ethics. I explain to students that, although *morality* and *ethics* are commonly used interchangeably, modern ethical theorists distinguish between morality, which consists of codes of conduct, and ethics, which entail a responsive recognition of otherness independent of rules (Buell 14).

While we might rely on codes and social circumstance to explain Pamela's summerhouse hysteria, Pamela does not. Instead, she regards the episode as a quintessentially unethical exchange in which each party—she and Mr. B.—are behaving without the respect they owe to themselves and therefore to each other. In answer to Mr. B.'s question, "Have I done you any Harm?," Pamela insists on the integrity of the self as the basis for erotic and emotional relations with another (or an other):

> "Yes, Sir," said I, "the greatest Harm in the World: You have taught me to forget myself, and what belongs to me; and have lessen'd the Distance that Fortune has made between us, by demeaning yourself, to be so free to a poor Servant. Yet, Sir, I will be bold to say, I am honest, tho' poor: And if you were a Prince, I would not be otherwise."   (24)

Luce Irigaray argues that ethical erotic love is founded on recognition of irreducible alterity and characterized by "double desire," the woman's as well as the man's. Without it, the erotic relationship is one of "possession, consummation, and disgust," leaving no room for the "surprise, astonishment, and wonder" that ideally accompany love. For her, the "forever unknowable" sexual difference between man and woman must be met by each lover with wonder in order to maintain "autonomy within . . . difference," to preserve "a space of freedom and attraction between them, a possibility of separation and alliance." According to Irigaray, the fundamental principle of heterosexual love is that "[o]ne sex is not entirely consumable by the other" (13–14). Thus when Pamela responds to Mr. B. in the summerhouse, she is insisting on what Irigaray would call her essential alterity. Far from being revolted by his physical advances, she is attracted to them, but she will not allow herself to resign what is rightfully hers—autonomy, the right to self-definition. Her goal therefore is not preserving her virtue but retaining a self that she may give freely as soon as she is approached with "surprise, astonishment, and wonder" rather than with a presumed right of possession. Although class, cultural, and historical issues particular to the eighteenth century all contribute to Mr. B.'s conviction that he has such a right, twenty-first-century student readers are not unfamiliar with jealous and possessive love. It can be a powerful classroom moment when the students see that Pamela's forceful self-possession proves her status as an ethical being, her behavior driven not by blind adherence to moral codes but by self-respect as well as by love and respect for Mr. B.[4]

Textual evidence confirms two central arguments: that Mr. B. eventually recognizes and respects Pamela as an autonomous other and that Pamela reciprocates Mr. B.'s erotic feelings. Of course, Mr. B. resists seeing Pamela as an other so long as he attempts to possess, define, and consume her: when he stomps, gropes, and pulls at her (29–33); when he abducts her to Lincolnshire (98–113); when he tricks her by disguising himself as Nan (198–208); when he coerces her, as in the contractual proposal that she become his mistress (188–92). Conversely, the reciprocity of Pamela's feelings for Mr. B. seems clear from her early reluctance to leave his home as well as from her reason for staying—finishing his waistcoat. Other evidence of Pamela's feelings includes her willingness to portray herself as an object of erotic desire, as in the episode in which Mr. B. mistakes her for a country girl (54–59); her displacement of sexual anxiety and frustration into fear of the bull (152–54); and her longing for self-annihilation, which she overcomes only with great difficulty (170–75). Like her "master," however, Pamela resists acknowledging her feelings. Both characters find it equally hard to come to terms with the "surprise, astonishment, and wonder" necessary to bind them together for life. I therefore spend a good deal of time on the scene in which this reciprocated love is achieved (249–59). Here, pointedly and poignantly, the lovers' language emphasizes the mutuality of their love. Mr. B. asks his "generous Pamela" to forgive him (250); and Pamela does, resolving likewise to "trust in his Generosity" (252).

Although my students are certainly right to question, as Pamela does, the forty-eight rules of marriage that she extracts from Mr. B.'s "awful Lecture" about his expectations for his wife (448), it is vital that they accept, again like Pamela, that Mr. B.'s right to these expectations resides in his "generosity," his recognition of his own obligation (448–52). Ultimately, Pamela regards her husband as ethical, his sense of her worth, rather than insistence on his own entitlement, underwriting all his demands. After Mr. B. "hints" that "a Husband, who expects all this, is to be incapable of returning Insult for Obligation, or Evil for Good, and ought not to abridge her of any Privilege of her Sex" (451), Pamela concludes that "a generous Man, and a Man of Sense, cannot be too much obliged" (451). While this ideal of mutual obligation found voice in contemporary conduct books, which treat relations between masters and servants, husbands and wives, and parents and children, *Pamela* acknowledges the difficulty of realizing it in a world that reinforces class and gender privilege. By the end of the novel, however, ethics, not privilege, possession, and dominance, guide Mr. B.'s and Pamela's choices. Gender difference remains not as a marker of masculine control and female subservience but as a source of wonder and awe, prompting mutual respect and responsibility as well as creating the conditions for both ethical obligation and erotic fulfillment.

Pamela argues that this kind of love can bring about reform. Indeed, one of Parson Williams's sermons at the betrothal derives from Proverbs 11.24–25 concerning "Liberality and Generosity, and the Blessing attending the right Use of Riches" (314). The close of the narrative seems to support what Mr. B. observed early on, that Pamela's virtue could change the entire nation. (His actual words are "corrupt a Nation" [162], spoken before his language is informed by the generosity of ethical love.) Mr. B.'s conversion results from reading Pamela's journal, her words, and from observing and learning to interpret her behavior and character as he would a text (249–51). Indeed, that moral or ethical analyses of texts occur frequently in the last third of the book suggests that Richardson is arguing for the reformative power of literature.[5] I ask my class if *Pamela* did change the entire nation? Or, more generally and more broadly, can literature change the world?

To be sure, eighteenth-century reactions to *Pamela* as a text that promoted leveling hierarchical social principles suggest a fear of change. But was that fear unfounded? My students often point out that *Pamela* endorses as much as it challenges the status quo, since patriarchal power and hierarchical social structure seem not only intact but justified at the novel's end. Indeed, as our discussion moves from *Pamela* to the power of literature, we find it difficult to cite a literary work that effected lasting reform. One obvious exception is Upton Sinclair's *The Jungle*, which resulted in the Pure Food and Drug and Meat Inspection Acts of 1906. Sinclair's social conscience informed his entire canon, not just this most famous of his novels. It is therefore significant that in 1950 Sinclair paid homage to Samuel Richardson in *Another Pamela; or, Virtue Still*

Rewarded. As Sinclair says in his foreword, "Who can possibly fail to profit from reading about the possessor of such qualities [virtue, charity, gratitude], no less astonishing in the twentieth century than in the eighteenth" (viii).

Like Richardson's work, *Another Pamela* recounts the story of a poor, young, dependent woman. This Pamela too subscribes to a strict moral code of behavior and falls in love with a profligate, young, wealthy man who behaves in violation of nearly every precept she holds dear. Sinclair's Pamela is a Seventh-Day Adventist whose religion prohibits reading novels, going to movies, and drinking. Like Richardson's heroine, Sinclair's Pamela is self-possessed and serious, but does not adhere blindly to moral codes if ethical behavior demands otherwise. As she tries to come to terms with the ethical and moral predicaments of her love for the dissipated Charles Harries, this Pamela is drawn to the first *Pamela*, stepping around her church's injunction against novel reading to meet her other in the spirit of "surprise, astonishment, and wonder."

Sinclair's heroine justifies reading the novel by declaring, "I am so glad that they are letters, so that it is permitted for me to read them" (145). That is, Sinclair has his Pamela take refuge in the fuzzy generic boundaries and moral ambiguities exploited by Richardson. Sinclair validates his heroine's compromises by pointing to the interrelation between fiction and reality. For her to understand *Pamela*, Mr. Mackenzie, who drew her attention to the novel in the first place, historicizes its events. On one occasion, he explains why Richardson's Pamela cannot simply call the police when Mr. B. mistreats her. On another, in answer to her question, "How can it be possible that a girl would be willing to marry a man who has shown himself so wicked and so treacherous?," Mackenzie lectures Sinclair's heroine about the "rigid" class system of the time (225). In short, as this twentieth-century Pamela explains to her sister, "I am sure this book cannot harm me. It takes me out of one time into another, and is like history; at the same time it does not fail to strengthen my virtue, being full of moral sentiments most uplifting." Her subsequent remark to her sister, "[s]omeday I may persuade you to read some of it and see" (226), suggests that this Pamela's responsiveness to the other Pamela may be a harbinger of a broader reform. Sinclair's Pamela not only feels justified in breaking the rules of her faith but also wants others to do likewise, implying a desire to revise her sect's regulatory precepts. When Pamela finally marries Charles, she reports another "concession": "I have been going to shows with him." She has decided that "the main point" of the Adventist prohibition on movies is "the corrupting of the young," and she deems herself "no longer young in that sense" (311). Besides, she explains, "I have to balance the evil of breaking our church's rule against the evil of managing my husband too strictly and so losing my hold on him" (312).

Can literature change the world? Upton Sinclair thought so, as did Samuel Richardson. Sometimes it succeeds through the kind of legislative social reform that followed *The Jungle*'s revelation of horrors in the meatpacking industry. But literature's more significant effect occurs when the meeting between self and other, reader and text, plays out on ethical grounds like those that define the relationship between Mr. B. and Richardson's Pamela and Charles Harries and Sinclair's Pamela or the intertextuality of Richardson's and Sinclair's narratives. These meetings can be morally confusing because of their blend of sensuality and spirituality, pleasure and purpose, but in that very confusion resides the ethical moment of opening oneself to an other, whether that other is a lover or a text. I urge my students to see such an ethical moment as central to Pamela's story and to their own reading of *Pamela*.

NOTES

[1] This distinction is central to Augustine's thought; see, for example, *Confessions*, book 8.

[2] I use Catherine Gallagher's edition of *Oroonoko* because it contains supporting documents that shed light on both the slave trade and the issue of race. My students are keenly aware of race, but what they do not know is that race was constructed to serve economic and political needs of a specific period.

[3] I draw these categories from Hunter 29–58.

[4] I still find touching and pertinent Florian Stuber's 1989 article "Teaching *Pamela*" about teaching the text at the Fashion Institute of Technology in the 1980s. I often quote for my students a remark of one of his students that reveals a full engagement with the text's moral and ethical dimensions: "I think of Pamela as an example. Now when I have to make an important decision about myself or others, I ask myself, 'What would Pamela do?'" (21).

[5] See, for instance, the reading and commentary on Pamela's version of Psalm 137 (317–22).

Bearing *Clarissa*: Richardson and the Problem of Relevance

Jayne Lewis

> The person who will bear much shall have much to bear
> all the world through.
> —*Clarissa*

To the present-day undergraduate abruptly confronted with the "much" of Richardson's *Clarissa*, Anna Howe's grim maxim will sound, to say the least, entirely relevant. This is not altogether unfortunate, since relevance is one of the great challenges facing today's teacher of eighteenth-century English literature, particularly *Clarissa*. We take what we can get, after all, and if our students somehow find a way into *Clarissa* through the sheer and often physical difficulty of reading its more than a million words, it is hard to be ungrateful. In this essay, I suggest other ways in which *Clarissa* might be made relevant to today's relatively naive and unsuspecting reader. Although my suggestions, like so many of Richardson's, are practical ones, the power of his novel lies in its questioning of the way things are made to seem practical, immediate, and real. So it is important to begin with an attempt to appreciate that power.

   In the last twelve years, I have imposed Richardson's novel on many students, both graduate and undergraduate. I have taught it in abridged form in lecture courses on the early novel and in seminars on epistolary form, and I have set it unabridged before graduate students studying the rhetorics of pain and pleasure from John Wilmot, the Earl of Rochester, to the Marquis de Sade. Twice I have devoted whole senior seminars to *Clarissa*. Each time, but particularly in the undergraduate courses, I have been eager for my students to see how much *Clarissa* has to do with the way we live now. Often, though, its relevance has turned out to be very different from what I imagined. Theoretically, *Clarissa* promises a glimpse of still prevalent psychological, sexual, social, economic, and of course literary paradigms at the catastrophic moment of their formation. But in practice what Richardson's novel offers is what we might call experiential relevance, for it confronts its reader with an arduousness that uncannily replicates the difficulty of the inner lives it represents. In more than one way, it is unbearable.

Clarissa's first readers discovered over the twelve months it took this work to appear in its entirety that there is too much in it to take in, but when the novel is assigned in the classroom over approximately two months, we can appreciate something that Richardson's contemporaries may have found harder to see: a way to conceptualize both the process and the politics of relevance. Although Clarissa and Lovelace might seem at any moment to be engaged in a battle of wills or of epistemologies or of classes or, simply, of the sexes, each is always competing to define what is real, what is relevant to his or her peculiar model of reality. Both aim to ascertain, often through the least endurable of experiments, just how much that model can bear. Thus Richardson perpetually rebuilds in his novel a replica of his reader's interpretive practice, one that makes the ethical dimension of that practice painfully apparent.

In *Clarissa*, real worlds often turn out to be fictions driven by individually legislated standards of relevance and verified at the points where they can no longer be borne. The novel's power to practice and reveal this dynamic speaks to contemporary college students, or at least to those majoring in English literature at my large public institution. I once enticed seventeen of them—sixteen women and one brave or perhaps merely lost young man—into a senior seminar titled Richardson's *Clarissa*: Myth and Meaning. My idea was that over a ten-week term we would read the novel together, reconstructing (on fast-forward) the experience of Richardson's original readers. How could we then fail to discover its many points of relevance to cultural problems that persist today? I assigned the easily available Penguin *Clarissa*, edited by Angus Ross. Although the Penguin edition is based on the first edition (1748–49), I split it into sections corresponding to the eight volumes of the third edition (1751), adding a few snippets from that edition such as Lovelace's infamous fantasy of rape on the way to the Isle of Wight. Each week's reading was framed by student presentations introducing pertinent social history, literary criticism, contemporary correspondence, and literary works known to Richardson.

I wanted my students to see how Richardson's novel either transformed or initiated an array of cultural institutions, literary practices, and socioeconomic arrangements. But I also hoped they would grow intimate with the processes through which we actively assign determinate meaning to this or indeed any text. Because such awareness is easily stimulated through naive engagement with the text—that is, through an imaginative experience of it as if it were real—I launched each meeting with a short writing exercise designed to make my students feel part of the world of the book. Like the presentations, however, this exercise always reflected a myth, institution, or interpretive problem begged by the section of the novel we had read for a given day. Topics ranged from the properties of epistolary writing and the "nature" of family values to the truly unanswerable question of whether or not Richardson was a feminist.

At our first meeting, though, I merely probed my students' expectations, focusing on their associations with the name Clarissa. Many of them thought of Alexander Pope's *Rape of the Lock*, others of the Nickelodeon television series *Clarissa Explains It All*. Neither of these cultural artifacts is irrelevant, since both open up discussion about the fiction of moral instruction and about the often nefarious methods, rooted in the illusion of immediacy, that make such fiction work. I also told my students about Richardson's *Familiar Letters*, his edition of Aesop's fables, and of course the popular craze that erupted around Richardson's earlier novel, *Pamela*. Mention of Virginia Woolf's Clarissa Dalloway placed Clarissa Harlowe at the dawn of a long literary tradition of representing interiority, of creating internal worlds in the act of describing them. *Clarissa*'s complicated history of revision and Richardson's wrangles with his readers also reflect the way in which worlds make themselves through the conscious exclusion of alternatives. Such a process, we saw, was central both to the moral tradition Richardson inherited and to the psychological and aesthetic practices he helped initiate.

By our second meeting, my students had embarked on their own quests for evidence of the novel's relevance. Because we began with *Clarissa*'s first forty-five letters, we concentrated that day on what it means for Richardson to have told his story in letters. At the start of the three-hour class, I asked my students to write a short letter to Clarissa reconstructing her predicament in their own terms and proffering advice on how to deal with it. I then asked two seminar participants to report on Richardson's relation to epistolary style. The first student, who had plowed through Richardson's famous autobiographical letter to Johannes Stinstra, described Richardson's attraction to epistolary form in terms of his precocious ghostwriting of billets-doux and unsolicited moral reprimands. The second student charted the epistolary tradition from which *Clarissa* emerges, using Robert Adams Day's *Told in Letters* for literary history and Janet Gurkin Altman's *Epistolarity: Approaches to a Form* for theoretical ballast.

Our third meeting, covering letters 46–92, took us to the end of Clarissa's trials at Harlowe Place. This class was devoted to social history, particularly that of the family, in the shifting economic context of the mid–eighteenth century. We began by pondering the whole question of what indeed constitutes a family. Did they, I asked my students, see it primarily as a biological, social, economic, symbolic, or emotional unit? What does family mean in *Clarissa*? Does it mean different things to different characters, even those in the same family? A student report based on Christopher Hill's classic "Clarissa Harlowe and Her Times" gave us some historical and sociological perspective on questions that had at first seemed urgent only to us (see also Goody; Stone).

For our fourth discussion, of letters 93–173, we inevitably turned to Lovelace, whose letters come to dominate *Clarissa's* third volume. My students were automatically intrigued by Lovelace's graphic imagination and they imagined him in similar detail. At the outset, I posed several questions about him: What was his relationship to Clarissa? Was he her enemy? Her friend? Her savior? Her true lover? What connotations did his name hold? Finally, I asked my students to read Richard Lovelace's "To Lucasta, Going to the Wars" and to assess its relevance to Richardson's Lovelace. This led us to the issue of Lovelace's originality, contextualized by means of a report on the ambivalent social, sexual, linguistic, and of course literary traditions of English libertinism (see Harris, "Richardson"; Turner). In the fourth volume of the novel (letters 174–231), Lovelace and Clarissa are mainly at Hampstead and then back in Mrs. Sinclair's brothel. Since this section pivots on Lovelace's distortion of Clarissa's world, I wanted my students to see how such a distortion can occur on the cultural level, particularly for women. Our writing exercise showed Richardson constantly representing female lives, bodies, minds, and choices. For instance, Lovelace makes numerous generalizations about "the sex" (female, of course [609]); Anna often tells Clarissa that she shines as an exemplar for all women; and when Clarissa finds herself in a brothel where women are selling their bodies and experiences close physical contact with Lovelace, female sexuality moves to the center of Richardson's plot. Given all this, I asked students what Richardson meant his female readers to think about themselves as women. To what extent does he aim to build the worlds and selves that they experienced? To what extent does his novel reveal that that world is constructed and thus open to renegotiation? Two students then reported on aspects of eighteenth-century women's lives. One used Alice Browne's helpful *The Eighteenth-Century Feminist Mind* to offer an overview of women's social experience in the early eighteenth century, before zeroing in on Rita Goldberg's discussion of contemporary, Puritan-inflected codes of female conduct. The second student turned from female virtue to female vice, drawing on several studies of eighteenth-century prostitution to foreground the questions of female choice that both pave the way for Clarissa's antagonisms toward the women of the Sinclair brothel and suggest her underlying commonality with them.

Our fifth discussion (letters 232–93) centered on the rape of Clarissa. As a social issue, rape needs nothing to make it relevant, but its pertinence to the construction of reality and to fiction making is less obvious. To bring this to the fore, I asked my students to pretend that they were prosecutors attempting to convince a jury that Lovelace had indeed raped Clarissa. After inviting them to suppose that he had pleaded innocent, I pointed out all the circumstantial evidence on his side. Conversely, I asked what arguments, evidence, and witnesses might be summoned to prove Lovelace's guilt. In considering the rape from this admittedly anachronistic perspective, students become conscious of the point often made by feminist critics—and most vivid is Frances Ferguson's influence on discussions of Richardson's novel—that rape is intimately linked to questions of interpretation, authority, and decisions about relevance that finally determine what counts as reality. Many of my students mentioned the drugs used by Lovelace. Here Ferguson's "Rape and the Rise of the Novel" offers not only a valuable conceptual frame but also, in its discussion of ancient Jewish rape law, ballast for a report on Western myths of rape—particularly those of Philomela and Lucretia (see Donaldson). A second report, derived from Judith Wilt's audacious and brilliant argument that, conceptually speaking at least, Clarissa is raped by the Sinclair whores rather than by Lovelace, fascinated my students and allowed us to revisit definitions of masculine and feminine from the previous week. Both presentations exposed connections between what happens to Clarissa and the cultural constructions that work to script her fate.

In the next volume of *Clarissa* (letters 294–419), we witness Clarissa's escape from the brothel, her physical decline, and Belford's acquisition of moral and narrative authority. Because I wanted my students to see how all these events are linked to interpretive authority, I gave them an ambiguous topic to interpret: Clarissa's sickness. Many saw her illness as inherently suicidal, an attempt at self-possession akin to anorexia nervosa. Others speculated that she was actually pregnant, an interpretation that allowed them to explore what the rape had really meant. Then there were other possibilities. One report suggested that because in the eighteenth century it was thought that a woman could only become pregnant if she was sexually responsive, Lovelace's fantasy that Clarissa is pregnant is a willful denial of the fact that he drugged her. A very different report brought out the visual aspects of the novel, paying specific attention to Joseph Highmore's interpretive illustrations as a starting point. The reporter was an enterprising young woman who asked her obliging classmates to draw their own scenes from the novel and then to identify what others had drawn. This surprisingly valuable exercise made us think about what constitutes representable and pertinent moments in the novel, as well as about how those moments become recognizable, meaningful, and therefore relevant to the reader.

Our final engagement with *Clarissa* catapulted us through the equivalent of its last two volumes. Our inevitable theme was death: Clarissa's death, Lovelace's death, eighteenth-century constructions of death, our own sense of death as a commentary on life. A good place to begin (or end) was Belford's description of Clarissa's coffin (1305–06). My students first made a diagram of the lid, then offered interpretations of its various verbal and visual symbols. In the second half of the class, one student interwove part of Jeremy Taylor's *Holy Dying* with Margaret Anne Doody's discussion of *Clarissa*'s deathbed theme (*Passion* 186) to show how modes of death were seen in Richardson's culture as glosses on the lives they concluded, that is, as determinate statements about (and guarantees of) their relevance. A second student returned to Clarissa as a modern Lucretia, focusing on a death that both invokes and rejects the classical myth. Drawing on Ian Donaldson's *The Rapes of Lucretia*, this report foregrounded the conflict between Clarissa's Christian worldview, so different from the Roman plot of revenge, and Morden and Lovelace's determination to fulfill the classical narrative after all. By comparing Lovelace's death with Clarissa's, we were able to discuss not only the violation of Clarissa's will and the circular structure of a novel that begins and ends with duels and wills but also the ways in which the ending of the novel simultaneously opens meanings and seals them off.

For our final class, I asked my students to stand back from *Clarissa* to see how the novel's reception and revisions destabilized the Richardsonian world my students had grown used to inhabiting. I divided the seminar into groups of four or five students, each of which collaborated on some feature of the novel's afterlife. One group read and commented on Lady Echlin's alternative ending to the novel; a second reported on Richardson's revisions to the novel; a third restaged recent contemporary critical debates, as represented by William B. Warner's *Reading Clarissa* and Terry Castle's *Clarissa's Ciphers*. The final group looked up *Clarissa* on the World Wide Web. These exercises allowed my students to examine the novel's many modes of relevance and to think about its relevance to them.

When at the end of the presentations I asked my class what *Clarissa* meant to them, their responses were initially disappointing. My lone male student had decided that he was not the target audience for the novel but remained engaged with it to the end. It had, he felt, given him a deeper understanding of female psychology and made him aware and critical of the libertine aspects of today's male culture. Interestingly, the female students who did recognize themselves as Richardson's target audience were less willing to see its applications to their lives. They certainly did not see as relevant to them Richardson's overt moral lessons about "the undue exertion of [parents'] natural authority" or about the daughterly preference of "a man of pleasure to a man of probity" (36). And while my students could not treat *Clarissa* as a fable with a digestible moral, neither could they profess an unreserved aesthetic appreciation for it. What they eventually found in it was of a different order, something for which they had not been prepared by either the *dulce* or the *utile* of literary experience.

I should note here that although our weekly discussions were always animated and stimulating, most of my students were juggling full-time class schedules with part-time jobs. Some also had families, and of those who had heard of the novel before, several had heard also the campus legend of the lone English student able to finish it, thanks to a fortuitous prison term that left him plenty of time for reading. By the end of the quarter, however, each of my students had found a unique way to possess the novel. One devised a *Clarissa* Web site; one wrote an alternative ending to the novel; another composed and recorded a number of songs based on Clarissa's conflict with Lovelace; another turned

Richardson's story into a cautionary tale for children; still another made a video featuring Hollywood libertines in the Lovelace mode. Several people updated pivotal scenes, setting them in places like the San Fernando Valley and replacing Richardson's series of letters with instant messaging. I also received a few traditional critical papers on such themes as the dreams recorded in the novel, sexual perversion, and female misogyny, but these very topics spotlighted internal dramas of burning interest today. In other words, my students had made *Clarissa* entirely relevant. But to what?

My students discovered that relevance is indeed made, not found. The act of making, not the object made, constitutes the world we experience. The word *world*, with its telling origin in the Old English *woruld*, meaning human existence, appears frequently in *Clarissa*, perhaps most notably in Clarissa's agonized and agonizing outcry, "what a world is this!" Half of "this" world, she notes, is "tormenting the other, and tormented themselves in tormenting" (224). Clarissa's chilling image of the "world" is countered by the jaunty, wanton "one-go-up-the-other-go-down picture of the world vehicle" that Lovelace imagines in his turn (971). Yet the relation between these two perceived worlds is surely as reciprocal as it is oppositional. Indeed, one might argue that Clarissa and Lovelace actually describe the same world. Their different perceptions of the world show that writing can constitute both external objects and the person who describes them. In effect, my students appropriated this descriptive power—a power embodied in Richardson's credo of writing to the moment.

My students were able to use and conceptualize this power because I gave them permission to focus on pieces of the book as opposed to all of it, or even a whole volume. I was often struck by the intensity with which even those who had found the week's reading load all but unbearable were able to pore over specific moments: Lovelace's picture of Clarissa at the garden gate, his terse "I can go no farther" (883), Clarissa's deathbed scene, and several of her mad letters. From short weekly essays in which students related individual extracts to the entire novel as a whole, I came to understand what they had realized about how relevance and therefore reality are constructed, often at the expense of others' realities. While my original vision of this particular seminar had revolved around the relevance of certain themes and structures, my undergraduates grasped the significance of relevance as method—a method as available to them as it was to Richardson. If I can extract any moral from the story of my ten weeks in these students' company, it is that *Clarissa* endures because it forces its reader to find his or her own will—and way—to endure it. So Richardson must have suspected. Certainly his heroine did, as she labored to create the very world she had to bear.

NOTE

Epigraph is quoted from p. 69 of *Clarissa*.

The Antipodean Pleasures of Teaching *Clarissa* in Real Time

Janine Barchas

I taught for five years at the University of Auckland in New Zealand, where I lived near the campus in a suburb aptly named Mount Eden. Even in a post-colonial universe, Aucklanders still frequently compare the dormant volcanoes that mark suburbs such as mine to the seven hills of ancient Rome. But to me, even after years in their presence, these volcanic cones—clad year-round in the iridescent greens of local vegetation—do not evoke memories of my European youth. Instead these curious peaks remind me of the imaginary landscapes of Dr. Seuss. In these wondrous surroundings, I twice taught *Clarissa* as a yearlong seminar for master's-level students in the Department of English. Because of the peculiar calendric dimensions of the teaching year in New Zealand, February to November, the seminar allowed us to read *Clarissa* in something approximating real time—a fortuitous synchronicity between our present and the one lived in the fiction. In this essay I share what it is like to devote an entire year to the study of this single and singular text. Although a Northern Hemisphere location may prohibit the duplication of the New Zealand academic year that enabled our real-time exploration of *Clarissa*, some of the fruits yielded by- a yearlong study of this novel may, I suggest, be harvested in the north—outside Eden.

That the academic year in the Southern Hemisphere corresponds, roughly, to the generic calendar year that organizes the novel (the letters date from 10 January to 18 December during an unspecified year) not only provided me with an organizing principle for the class—reading *Clarissa* in real time—but also accommodated a novel whose sheer bulk had never allowed me to squeeze it into other busy eighteenth-century offerings. Whenever I wish to use the Richardson-Fielding rivalry as a means of illustrating the double-helix structure of the eighteenth-century novel's DNA, I find myself opting to teach all of *Pamela* instead of parts of *Clarissa*. Yet *Pamela* has never been a satisfying substitute. In lectures I find that I compare it unfavorably with *Clarissa* and beg students to take it on faith that the tentative features of Richardson's debut novel acquired gravitas and complexity in his later masterpiece. Eighteenth-century colleagues elsewhere (many of them ambitious and enthusiastic teachers) seem prone to make the same compromise with the same feelings of dissatisfaction, if banter at conferences is proof. A yearlong graduate seminar offered a unique chance to concentrate on *Clarissa* without distractions.

Compromises, however, still remained: our reading was always an approximation of a real-time commitment, rather than a strict adherence to it. The dates of the fiction did not correspond *exactly* with the start and end of the February-to-November academic year. In the first weekly meeting, I provided some general background information on Richardson, eighteenth-century print culture, and the epistolary form. The second week was devoted wholly to *Pamela*. Thus it was not until the middle of March that we officially turned to *Clarissa*. Yet because relatively few of the novel's letters are "authored" between 10 January and 1 March, we soon found ourselves reading about events in parallel with our own calendric present (unfortunately the days of the week for the dates did not match those in the novel).[1] Because the dates of the letters, rather than a set number of pages, guided our reading, some weeks had a heavier reading load than others. I tried to structure the assignments accordingly, asking for essays and projects in weeks with comparatively lighter reading loads. Toward the end of an academic year that ends with examinations throughout November, the reading assignments again broke away from real time by forcing us to read ahead of our calendric present. So from start to finish, even our unique yearlong commitment demanded that the real-time concept be somewhat fudged.

Still, our slow calendric progress through the book had a number of effects that I organize under four rubrics: magnification; reenactment; space of time and graphic design; and real time is more time. I devote most of this essay to graphic design—a topic that, being suited to both graduate and undergraduate teaching, does not require a year to harvest.

Magnification

Our slow progress through the book seemed to magnify the intensity of student response. Although students occasionally confessed to having been unable to ration their reading (some read ahead, a few lagged behind), the conscious attention to the dates that organized the text made students acutely aware of the slow, drawn-out plotting of the initial months; the overwhelming rapidity of action mid-year; and the deliberate austerity of events in the closing volumes. Students often used their observations about the dearth or cacophony of actions and voices during a specific period to contextualize a character's response to an event that had occurred then. The students noted how the flurry of letters around a certain date would effect a character's emotional response to an event or letter. A busy week would exert a tax on the characters, just as it taxed the students in their attempts to keep up with the reading. In weeks with light reading, students agreed with Austen's Anne Elliot that the relative quiet saw, to borrow Jane Austen's phrase, "our feelings prey upon us," heightening sensitivity in both characters and readers (*Persuasion* 241).

Reenacting the First-Edition Experience

Richardson once confessed to having played "the Rogue" with his readers, "intending them to think now one way, now another, of the very same Characters" (Richardson, *Selected Letters* 248). Our slow progress seemed to generate just such oscillation of feeling in students, who championed and vilified the same character by turns in different weeks. Interestingly, since Richardson originally published the novel in three installments over the twelve-month period from December 1747 to December 1748, our class had just about the same amount of time to process *Clarissa* as did its first-edition audience. I tried to reinforce this additional synchronicity between our experience and the experience of the eighteenth-century reader by having students read the marginalia in Lady Bradshaigh's first-edition copy side by side with their Penguin text (Barchas); their reactions to specific passages were unsurprisingly distinct from hers.[2] Yet students felt as free as Lady Bradshaigh did to pronounce, renounce, restate, and readopt positions over the course of the year. Although I would never claim that authorial intention anticipated all such oscillations of feeling, Richardson may have been aware that the length of time spent with a text influences interpretation. If he was, the class was actually re-creating the temporal experience originally designed by Richardson.

Space of Time and Graphic Design

Richardson was acutely aware of the temporal dimension of his fiction. Writing to Aaron Hill during the composition of *Clarissa*, Richardson describes the struggle to reconcile his prolixity with the novel's commitment to realism:

> Length is my principal Disgust, at present. . . . The fixing of Dates has been a Task to me. I am afraid I make the Writers do too much in the Time. If Lazy Ladies that is to say, Ladies, who love not Writing, were to be Judges, they would think so: especially if not Early Risers.
>
> (*Selected Letters* 63)

Despite Richardson's self-conscious "fixing of Dates," many readers find the temporal plausibility of the epistolary form problematic. His precise specification of clock time and calendar time—those hours, days, and dates to which our own reading in Auckland was so committed—troubles George Sherburn, who observes that "during the period from 6 A.M. to midnight of June 10, Lovelace along with normal activities of the day is supposed to write something like 14,000 words" (Sherburn xii). Mark Kinkead-Weekes briskly dismisses such computations as overreading: "it is silly to calculate how many hours a day characters must have had to spend scribbling" (*Samuel Richardson* 421), whereas Terry Castle counters that "the fact that we invariably do (even if secretly or intermittently) points to the unresolved difficulty in the form itself—one that ultimately undermines the mimetic contract with the reader" (*Clarissa's Ciphers* 154). Although these two critics differently assess the relative importance of accurate timekeeping in *Clarissa*, they each acknowledge that the epistolary novel distorts temporal realism and plausibility. These critics do not debate the manner in which Richardson, who acted as printer, author, and publisher of *Clarissa*, turns to graphic design and layout to augment the passing of time in, as well as between, the letters. Richardson's innovations in the use of printer's ornaments as temporal markers are something that I have explored in my research.[3]

The letters written by the main characters of *Clarissa* are, in all editions printed on Richardson's press, marked by small printer's ornaments, or fleurons, at moments when a character is interrupted at his or her writing desk.[4] These frequent interruptions are necessitated by the novel's generic commitment to realism. Given the amount of time that the main characters spend writing, interruption is a realistic by-product of their closeted surroundings. Anna Howe, for example, disparages the little domestic intrusions that are marked in her letters by small groupings of fleurons. These graphic markers stand in for an offstage announcement, presumably from a household servant:

> A little interruption. What is breakfaſt to the ſubjeſt I am upon!
>
> ❦ ❦
>
> LONDON, I am told, is the beſt hiding-place in the world. I have written nothing but what I will

([1st ed.] 2: 232)

Richardson thus highlights both the offstage event, here a seemingly trivial invitation to partake of the morning meal, and the "mimetic contract" with the reader, as Castle terms it. Breakfast and its well-preserved etymology of the break in fasting is significant in a story filled with problematic instances of ritualized fasting and emotionally fraught refusals to partake of communal meals, as Donnalee Frega shows in *Speaking in Hunger*. But not all these graphic interruptions, of which several hundred occur in the first edition, mark rejected invitations to meals. By means of these constant interruptions Richardson flags the tension between the idealized self and the messy facts of social living, thus assuring us of the novel's mimetic fidelity. As a result, when other events violate the novel's glassy realism, we are more prone to be disturbed by the ripple of implausibility set off by such events. In later volumes, the ornaments, which the reader now understands to signify temporal breaks, increasingly appear on the novel's pages without explanation in the accompanying text. As unglossed stops, or periods of contemplation unacknowledged by the characters, the ornaments may mark hesitations imposed by the letter writer that reflect unease. Ironically enough, then, an ornament may expose an area where the "*instantaneous*" veracity of the novel's famous to-the-moment style is compromised (Preface [1st ed.] 1: viii).

These tiny, ubiquitous graphics beg to be compared with Richardson's creative use of type elsewhere in the novel. In original editions, *Clarissa* periodically strays from its visual uniformity as a printed book to imitate the appearance of the letters: for instance, Clarissa's musical composition, rendered as an engraved folding plate; the pointing hands drawn by Lovelace in the margins of an intercepted letter by Anna; the arrangement of the heroine's disjointed thoughts in the tenth mad paper; and the cursive script of Clarissa's signatures found in her last letter to Anna and on her "Last Will and Testament" ([1st ed.] 7: 297). In each of these moments the novel breaks the printed form of typographic regularity in the service of mimesis.[5] In fact, compared with these moments, the printer's ornaments scarcely look mimetic at all. It would be silly to suppose that, like Lovelace's hand-drawn indices, such marks reproduce sketches made in the supposed original holograph of the letters. While Lovelace actually admits to having annotated Anna's intercepted letters with marginal pointing hands, the characters nowhere admit to drawing fancy ornamental flowers or curlicues on their pages to document a temporal interval. Thus, although the ornaments perform a mimetic temporal function, they remain telltale signs of the printing press. As such, they betray the fact that the reader engages with a printed book rather than a collection of original letters. A class discussion that asks students to consider the interpretive impact of each graphic design can help them determine the extent to which Richardson's creative application of the printing press contradicts the epistolary form he uses. In the absence of a rare-books room with early editions of *Clarissa* such as at the University of Texas, Austin, the AMS facsimile of the third edition was indispensable. Now the *Eighteenth-Century Collections Online* (*ECCO*) has made classroom examinations of Richardson's original citations even easier.

In the third edition of *Clarissa* (1751), Richardson enlarges the role of the printer's ornaments when he assigns the principal characters in the fiction specific ornaments that mark temporal interruption in their letters throughout the edition's eight volumes. Such graphic consistency does not exist in earlier editions of *Clarissa*, in which the same fleurons almost indiscriminately interrupt letters penned by Anna, Clarissa, Lovelace, and others. Because the assigning of specific fleurons to individual characters is stable in the 1751 text, however, the third edition allows for a sustained association between graphic symbol and letter writer. Like Wagnerian motifs, the unique ornaments that interrupt each character's letters proffer themselves as recurrent hallmarks of the protagonist. Clarissa, that "flower and ornament" of the Harlowe family, is assigned a rosette that looks like a small petaled bloom:

([3rd ed.] 2: 199)

Breaks in Lovelace's writing, meanwhile, are now marked exclusively by an ominous astrological constellation of asterisks:

> determined not to go off with ?— *The Sex ! The Sex,*
> *all over !*—Charming contradiction!—Hah, hah, hah,
> hah !—I muſt here—I muſt here, lay down my pen,
> to hold my ſides ; for I muſt have my laugh out now
> the fit is upon me.
>
> ** *   * **
> **   **
>
> I BELIEVE—I believe—Hah, hah, hah !—I believe,
> Jack, my dogs conclude me mad : For here has one

([3rd ed.] 3: 30)

The starlight of Lovelace's ornaments in the third edition adds new significance to the villain's references to Clarissa as his "lucky Star" ([3rd. ed.] 3: 283) or to his declared intention to prevent Clarissa from "soaring to her native Skies" by keeping her with "us Subluniaries" ([3rd ed.] 3: 276).[6] When paired with the iconography of the printer's ornaments, Richardson's metaphors now reinforce the importance of his visual marks on the printed page. Like "the primitive symbolic alphabet of the coffin emblems," which some critics, as Doody notes, have read "graphemically," Richardson's printer's ornaments interlineate the text of the novel with emblematic signs and symbols (Castle, *Clarissa's Ciphers* 142–43; Doody, *Passion* 186n1).

By focusing on the graphic elements of *Clarissa*'s design, the students discovered for themselves Richardson's obsessive control over the printings of his fictions from edition to edition. When we compared the printed appearance of key passages in various editions by consulting slides, handouts, microfilm, some rare books, and the AMS Press facsimile of the third edition, the students generated animated questions about interpretation that were based on a text's physical appearance as a printed book. These queries prompted discussion of editorial theory, bibliographic "accidentals" (the standard, though misleading, term for ornaments and punctuation), as well as the problematics of selecting which edition to quote in the study of Richardson. That none of the printer's ornaments and only some of Richardson's other and more obvious graphic designs are reproduced in modern editions of *Clarissa* gave concrete shape to editorial theory.

Real Time Is More Time

Very simply, when a class devotes an entire year to the study of *Clarissa*, plenty of time remains to add other things. For example, I asked students to rewrite their essays. Consequently, I was able to annotate and evaluate the same project twice, at different stages of maturity, and track the success and failure of my initial comments. Through this exercise I learned as much about my own modus operandi as I did about that of my students. While devoting twice as much time to a single essay, we considered time-saving strategies in a session devoted to Richardson resources online, including *Literature Online*'s searchable edition of *Clarissa*. Although the search function was useful in some ways, having students search electronic texts yielded far too many essays that were essentially glorified lists of examples rather than expository argument. Unlike *ECCO*'s searchable facsimile-like digital scans of the early editions, the *Literature Online* texts of *Clarissa* do not reproduce layout or graphic design.

The extra time enabled a new close-reading routine. At the start of each session we opened our books randomly to a page in the calendric confines of our reading for the week. Our communal reading of this randomly chosen passage, intended as a fifteen-minute icebreaker, was frequently so animated that I allowed it to go on longer. My sense was that the students engaged more readily in close reading once they were assured that the instructor's observations were not carefully scripted. Although this experiment involved an element of risk, since some passages are less rich or pliable than others, I was surprised to find that many of the issues that I had tagged for that week, whether narrative reliability, heroism, or conduct literature, might still be reached by means of a passage chosen at random. I've tried this approach with other texts and classes since then, but never with as much success. Time pressures in a survey course usually foreclose the luxury of lingering on a passage, and selecting a passage at random can generate anxiety in students who are still trying to master the plot.

Class time was closely structured in other ways. Students were each assigned an oral presentation on one critical work devoted to Richardson. Since only the student assigned to the work was allowed to check this book out from the library, the arrangement solved resource problems (students did not recall each other's books) and forced cooperation among the students (during a set week they had to make their book available to others for consultation). As a result, some class time was used for presentations on critical works that everyone would otherwise not be able to read. Another unexpected bonus was that, by virtue of their being assigned to a specific critic or critical approach, students became instant experts on a given topic or theoretical approach. Our deference to their expertise built up students' confidence—even the confidence of those who were initially reticent or intimidated by undertaking an oral assignment in front of their colleagues.

Finally, every student chose to read one modern novel consciously written in *Clarissa*'s wake. This exercise was intended to track some of the characteristics we'd come, by the end of the year, to associate with Richardson's prose. Choices ranged from a local Auckland novel called *Safe Sex: An E-Mail Romance,* by Linda Burgess and Stephen Stratford, to the more well known of Richardson's legacies, such as Jane Austen's *Persuasion* and Anne Brontë's *The Tenant of Wildfell Hall*. In our final reckonings about the genre, we did not arrive at any definitive assessment of Richardson's influence on the modern novel, but, rather, we found a way of resisting the inevitable close of the year. Our *Clarissa* experience, we decided, might be rediscovered, at least in part, in the books we read in the future.

NOTES

[1] In his introduction to the 1985 Penguin edition of *Clarissa*, Angus Ross suggests that 1732 is "the most likely year" for the temporal setting of the novel, as the particulars of that calendar year correspond neatly to the scarce mentions of specific days and months in the letters (23).

[2] As editor of the ELS edition of *The Annotations* I was extremely eager to give this a try. The edition includes the corresponding Penguin page numbers in precisely to facilitate such use.

[3] My argument on printer's ornaments in this essay is adapted from my book *Graphic Design, Print Culture, and the Eighteenth-Century Novel* (Cambridge UP, 2003). This adaptation appears with permission from the Cambridge University Press.

[4] For a detailed bibliographic account of the editions of *Clarissa* printed by Richardson, see Sale, *Bibliographical Record* 45–63.

[5] It pays to compare the modern Penguin edition's rendition of these moments with the first- and third-edition texts. The Penguin page numbers are 1534 (the musical engraving is reproduced as an appendix), 743, 893, 1349, and 1420. The corresponding page numbers in the seven-volume first edition (available on microfilm and on *ECCO*) are 2: 50; 4: 328; 5: 239; 7: 198, 309. Compare the eight-volume third-edition text (available through AMS Press as a facsimile and also on *ECCO*): 2: 54, 5: 30, 5: 308, 7: 408, and 8: 113.

[6] For a discussion of comets and stars in the novel, see Harris, *Samuel Richardson* 51.

Is *Clarissa* a Woman's Narrative?

Judith Moore

I have taught *Clarissa* several times in a master's-level eighteenth-century literature course called Studies in Neoclassical Literature. So far, so good, but the syllabus subtitle under which I have included *Clarissa* is Women's Narratives. On the syllabus, I tell students:

> The eighteenth century is commonly considered the point of origin of the novel as we know it. It is also the first point in Western literature when women began to contribute in volume to literary production. Traditionally, we might read various works labeled good and analyze their structural components, and we will do some of that, but the primary focus of this course is on what constitutes a woman's narrative as such. Is it written by a woman, about women, both? How, if at all, is it differentiated from a man's narrative, and how are fictional and nonfictional narratives distinguishable from each other—if they are? What elements in the society in which these works were written help to shape them?

In the class as a whole, I emphasize a cultural studies perspective that asks the students to see the texts they are reading primarily as products of a particular time and society, but my intent is holistic rather than political. The focus of the course's subtitle is on gender, but the goal is to historicize and problematize rather than define the term. Since both male and female students regularly enroll in this course, making a male writer, Richardson, central to it is part of a strategy to address two questions: How is a male novelist telling a woman's story from multiple points of view, including her own, perceived in a context of women writing women's stories? Will men's and women's reading reveal gender at the heart of reading itself? My goal here is not to lead students to a right formulation in response to these questions but to induce them to explore what asking such questions means. Should they simply assume—as many of them initially do—that women's stories can be told only by women or that only women will find them compelling? Since I ask them to read *Clarissa* in parallel with Frances Burney's *Cecilia*, we discuss not only Richardson's choices in telling his story but also Burney's. Why don't we get Mortimer's perspective as we do Lovelace's? Whose narrative asserts more authorial control, or are Burney's and Richardson's techniques simply incommensurable? Why does Clarissa die? is a good question, but so is Why does Cecilia live?

In some institutions, though not in mine, similarly specialized courses are offered at the undergraduate level in both English and women's studies, so such a specialized course is not necessarily only for graduate students. There might

be a somewhat lower total volume of reading in an undergraduate version, however, and the writing assignments would almost certainly be different. Those
who teach a novel the length of *Clarissa* to students at any level should address
some practical considerations before the more philosophical and theoretical
ones. I use Angus Ross's Penguin edition of the first edition of the novel. The
price is reasonable and the type not unbearably small. The worst thing about
this edition is that the back cover reveals that Clarissa dies—but most students,
I find, do not read that and do actually experience the novel sequentially.

I give the novel ten hour-and-a-quarter class sessions in a semester, during
which the class meets twenty-eight times. These classes take place over nine of
the fourteen weeks, so that the reading of *Clarissa* is interspersed with other
reading assignments. The most significant assignment in relation to *Clarissa*
is *Cecilia*, which we read over five weeks, alternating with assignments in *Clarissa*. But the class begins with a selection of shorter tales by Aphra Behn, Delarivier Manley, Jane Barker, and Eliza Haywood in Paula Backscheider and John
Richetti's anthology, *Popular Fiction by Women, 1660–1730*. These readings
give the class time to cohere and to develop a reading context for the longer
works to follow. *Cecilia* and *Clarissa* not only differ in narrative technique from
these breathlessly narrated texts but also provide examples of strikingly long
novels focused on exemplary heroines whose merits are insufficient to ensure
their triumph; Cecilia does not die, but her experience of madness and loss of
fortune brings her close to both literal and symbolic death. After completing
the last assignment in *Clarissa*, the class reads Frances Vane's "Memoirs of a
Lady of Quality," from Tobias Smollett's *Peregrine Pickle*. The contrast of our
tragic heroines with this insensitive but apparently indestructible demimon-
daine deters students from overgeneralizing the fictional paradigm. The class
ends with another discrepant comparison, Mary Wollstonecraft's *Mary* and *The
Wrongs of Woman* with Jane Austen's *Sense and Sensibility*.

The most obvious problem in teaching the full text of *Clarissa* in a course
at any level is how long it takes to read. This is a practical but also a literary
consideration, because *Clarissa* treats time very differently from most of the
novels my students have previously read. Thus they need to think not only of
their customary reading schedules but also of the effects that the sequen-
tiality of the letters and the alternation of first-person perspectives in epistolary
fiction have on their expectations about pace and point of view. The level of
detail in *Clarissa* inevitably draws in student readers and occasions a good deal
of discussion on questions of mimesis. The drawing out of suspense elicits real-
life emotions even while the length and detail of the letters together with the
complicated procedures for writing and transmitting them strain credulity.
Since the time required for such a volume of detail to be assimilated never
ceases to be a challenge, even after the initial fear of the book's length is overcome, I begin the class with an encouraging talk about the length and intensity

of *Clarissa*, offering practical advice from a colleague on speed-reading techniques. As students read, they become increasingly engaged in Clarissa's story and the parallel story of their own reading experience. Speed-reading has an ominous ring to most literature specialists, but the simple technique of holding a blank three-by-five card above the line one is reading and moving it gradually down the page in fact improves comprehension as well as speed. My other suggestion, that students take breaks in their reading when they find their attention wandering, may seem counterintuitive but is effective in practice. Graduate students find these adjustments surprisingly productive; undergraduates might benefit by the additional encouragement of very brief quizzes over the content of each assigned reading before the day's discussion begins.

Beginning with the second meeting of the fourth week of the class, the reading schedule proceeds as follows, with the Burney assignments included to show how the pairing of these texts works:

Fourth week
Assignment 1: *Clarissa*, preface, letters 1–45

Fifth week
Assignment 2: *Clarissa*, letters 46–92
Assignment 3: *Cecilia*, volume 1

Sixth week
Assignment 4: *Clarissa*, letters 93–162
Assignment 5: *Cecilia*, volume 2

Seventh week
Assignment 6: *Clarissa*, letters 163–217
Assignment 7: *Cecilia*, volume 3

Eighth week
Assignment 8: *Clarissa*, letters 218–45
Assignment 9: *Cecilia*, volume 4

Ninth week
Assignment 10: *Clarissa*, letters 246–94
Assignment 11: *Cecilia*, volume 5

Tenth week
Assignment 12: *Clarissa*, letters 295–347
Assignment 13: *Clarissa*, letters 348–421

Eleventh week
Assignment 14: *Clarissa*, letters 422–92
Assignment 15: *Clarissa*, letters 493–537

In both novels, I use textual divisions rather than page numbers to de-emphasize the sheer length of the assignment and foreground the structure of the work. In fact, not all the *Clarissa* assignments are equal in length: the earlier ones are the longest, the first three averaging 170 pages and the last six 130. My reason for this perhaps chancy decision is that, since students need to be engaged with the novel early, the first assignments have to give them Lovelace's voice as well as Clarissa's. By the end of the second assignment, which the class has had a long weekend to read, Clarissa is writing from St. Alban's and the students are caught up in her situation. A week of class time has elapsed since they began, significantly less than the fraught two and a half months that have passed at Harlowe Place but enough to suggest the tension of stasis and action that characterizes the novel as a whole. *Clarissa* can only be experienced, however, as a simultaneous delaying and unfolding. I alert the class early to the Web site *Reading* Clarissa *in Real Time*, which records observations from a group of readers who read the text on the dates corresponding to those of the letters and exchanged their reactions online. The experience of reading this Web site reinforces the intense temporality of the novel while demonstrating the passions it can arouse in readers.

I routinely reread the novel at the same pace as the students. My personal copy of the text is heavily annotated by now, but I keep a running index of passages I want to highlight in discussion as I read. I urge students to do the same. In a text of *Clarissa's* density, it is inevitable that someone will remember some pertinent passage that he or she neglected to make a note of, but the less this happens the less class time will be spent hunting for references.

The loquacious Lovelace's terse report of Clarissa's rape—"And now, Belford, I can go no farther. The affair is over. Clarissa lives"—occurs in letter 257 (883), in the sixth reading assignment from the novel. It is followed by the last assignment in *Cecilia*, a juxtaposition that raises significant questions about the theme of the course, including the horror with which Richardson treats the forcible violation of Clarissa's virginity and Burney presents Cecilia's concealed marriage and its consequences. Both heroines suffer madness, but the end of Cecilia's sufferings is visibly at hand. Whereas Burney's conclusion is muted but not long delayed, the students must wait until the following week's assignment in Richardson to read Clarissa's account of what has happened to her. Much more is still to come, as the heft of the volume and the sequence of the assignments both attest.

Lovelace's pursuit of the escaped Clarissa and her own resolute descent to death complete Richardson's capture of contemporary students. Students at first disagree with one another over Clarissa's determination not to marry Lovelace and continue to disagree that her death is necessary, whether medically or aesthetically. None of them, however, denies the almost intolerable effect of the enactment of the process in their reading, unrelieved by any alternative texts during the last four assignments. Here as throughout the reading of the novel, male and female students tend to occupy the same range of positions. Their resistance to the death of a character of Clarissa's verisimilitude and moral stature is initially intense—the more so, I believe, because Clarissa is dying in a novel. Students simply do not perceive the novel as a tragic genre but, having just completed *Cecilia* and been told of Burney's resistance to the pressure to supply a more conventional happy ending, are furnished with an enlightening comparison. Scornful as they tend to be of the sort of conventional conclusion described by Henry James as "a distribution at the last of prizes, pensions, husbands, wives, babies, millions, appended paragraphs, and cheerful remarks" (438), students are appalled that Clarissa receives no such rewards—and are not satisfied that Cecilia is left with only a flawed husband. The intensity of their reaction returns the class to genre questions: is it the novel form that limits what stories can be told in it, or are readers' expectations required to enforce those apparent prohibitions? Do those expectations come from the forms readers police or from the culture that gives rise to those forms? My students are for the most part in agreement that in their own world it is unnecessary, perhaps positively wrong, to die as the result of undeserved abuse. But they hesitate to declare Clarissa at fault, especially since they know that eighteenth-century readers also found the end of the novel shocking.

At this point, they begin fully to perceive that *Clarissa*'s designation as a "woman's narrative" is genuinely difficult and not just tricky. Writing from a Foucauldian perspective, Sue Warrick Doederlein argued in 1983:

> If we . . . uncritically view "femininity" as a natural (albeit culturally charged) category to which Richardson gave compelling voice, we miss the crucial opportunity to see what this male novelist adds to the complex network of power/knowledge relationships that shaped this then inarticulate "femininity" into words and gestures. (403)

Students almost invariably agree, but they tend to feel at the same time that their own apparent critical sophistication seems to give them no intellectual edge over Richardson and thus no enhanced ability to come to a comfortable conclusion.

However inchoate eighteenth-century definitions of femininity may be from our perspective, they are already complex in Richardson's practice. As D. C. Rain put it in a review of Terry Castle's *Clarissa's Ciphers:*

> The issue of putting constructions on things is fundamental in *Clarissa*. The first thing we learn about the heroine is that she has "become the subject of public talk.". . . As characters within the novel strive to impose on others what they regard as the correct reading of their experience, so the novel's critical interpreters, whatever their particular points of view, attempt to convince other readers of what they consider to be the truth about the novel's characters and events. (521)

Clarissa concludes decisively. The principal characters not only are dead and buried but also have been shown to readers in the light of the Final Judgment.

The characters and their story, however, are still "the subject of public talk," and that talk, impassioned as it often is, fails to conclude. Richardson—obviously and proudly a moralist—remains an evasive author. Students see the need to define all terms carefully here, and words such as *woman, feminist*, and *feminine* almost cease to appear in their discourse without qualification. But the question whether *Clarissa* is a "woman's narrative" remains hard to answer. Clarissa tells her own story, but so do Lovelace and a host of other figures, and the stories challenge and qualify and contradict one another. But the stories of individual characters are also internally incoherent. It begins to seem at last that such a narrative as *Clarissa* can never belong to a single figure, however commanding that figure's moral excellence. If narrative is defined with an emphasis on process, *Clarissa* certainly qualifies, but insofar as narrative also implies resolution, *Clarissa* refuses compliance. Students now sympathize more fully with Samuel Johnson's dictum that "if you were to read Richardson for the story, your impatience would be so much fretted that you would hang yourself" (qtd. in Boswell 480).

I assign a take-home exam at the end of the course to give students an opportunity to address these issues of narrative definition in a final essay, distanced from the charged dialogue of the classroom. Their answers naturally vary, but I have yet to encounter anyone who regrets having read *Clarissa*. Indeed, many students express an intention to read it again in a hope that a second, more knowledgeable reading will bring them closer to answering the course's questions. At the last, during the three-hour time slot allocated for the traditional in-class final, I show the BBC adaptation of *Clarissa*—now available for purchase from a variety of Web sites. Pictures and a description of the project are also accessible on the Web at *The Compleat Sean Bean* homepage. I show the adaptation primarily for fun, and students who are by now experts on the text enjoy critiquing it. They also enjoy the acting, sets, and costumes but come to agree on one point that would have amazed them at the beginning of the semester: three hours is simply too little time in which to tell Clarissa's story.

Richardson, *Clarissa*, Hypertext

Mark James Morreale

Over the last decade, a growing body of material has demonstrated the potential uses of hypertext in the classroom.[1] Such works suggest that hypertext encourages students to think of audiences greater than their instructor, that it graphically illustrates how texts might be decentralized from the critical focus. That is, hypertext not only creates new modes of discourse but also encourages active versus passive reading. Moreover, hypertext allows students to become self-directed reader-authors and fosters collaborative writing. Finally, hypertext empowers students to think independently as scholars by encouraging them to become responsible for their own education. It also decenters instructors, making them facilitators or co-collaborators. My project demonstrates the reality of these claims by creating a collaborative academic Web site that annotates and illuminates a small portion of *Clarissa*.[2] Along the way, students familiarize themselves with basic text-editing skills, HTML encoding, critical controversies surrounding *Clarissa*, and the textual and critical history of Richardson's novel. In this way, they learn not only to transcribe accurately but also to edit and write about literary texts.

Richardson's *Clarissa* works especially well with hypertext, given its frequent use of cross-referencing, allusive character, and complex structure.[3] If Terry Eagleton's twenty-year-old claim in the preface to *The Rape of Clarissa* is true, "that we may now once again be able to read Samuel Richardson" because of "certain new ways of reading developed in our own time" (vii, viii), I suggest that hypertext gives us a fourth way to read Richardson's masterpiece that Eagleton at the time could not have anticipated.[4]

Where to Begin: Learning the Basics of HTML

First, students should be introduced to hypertext. Instructors might distribute a handout that includes examples of basic HTML code as well as the HTML template, such as that provided by *HTML-Kit*. (For the assignment given to students and for selected results of that assignment, see Morreale, Assignment; Results.) The experience of students already familiar with HTML can be advantageous as the project proceeds. This introduction to HTML should also include a hands-on experiment with HTML, using one of the readily available HTML editors on the Web. Adventuresome students and faculty members may try HTML encoding using *NotePad* or *WordPad*, simple ASCII word editors available on many desktops. I encourage students, however, to use the freeware version of *CoffeeCup* (http://coffeecup.com) or *HTML-Kit* (http://www.chami.com/html-kit). Both provide the students with the HTML template and have excellent shortcut features so that students need not remember everything, such as the code for making a table. They need to understand how a table works to execute it properly, however.[5] It has been my experience that diligent students learn how to create an HTML document in about a week. I strongly discourage students from simply saving a document in a word processing program as an HTML file because such a procedure often adds proprietary code to the document, which will later have to be deleted if the document is to be properly read by a variety of browsers. Also, if students let the word processing program do the code, they will not learn it.

The Project

For the second step, create groups of no more than four students and ask them to develop strategies for annotating a sequence of *Clarissa* letters. Each sequence chosen should be between three or four letters in length, for example, letters 7–10 (58–71), concerning Clarissa's initial rejection of Mr. Solmes, or letters 56–59 (237–52), with their lively debates about marriage and other matters relevant to the Solmes issue. A class of twenty students might digitize and then annotate twenty or more letters. Each student might be responsible for one letter in the sequence, although some tasks might require students to work with several letters located beyond the chosen sequence. Groups then decide on how best to enhance their chosen letter sequence with graphics; links (both internal and external); student and critical commentary; literary, historical, and cultural contexts; and even an annotated bibliography of Richardson criticism. Students' commentaries and annotations provide an important way to gauge their analytical skill through close reading.

In the third step, each group scans its interrelated set of letters from a clean text of the novel. Since this step depends greatly on the technological capabilities of the campus, instructors might need to consult with their institution's information technology department. Students save the scanned files in ASCII or plain HTML format and then determine the accuracy of the digitized version they have created.

Finally, the class decides on the look of the Web site. What font should be used? What size should headings be? Should a background color be used, and, if so, which one? How will the site's navigation work? Will frames be used? Will a cascading style sheet be necessary?[6] Once the letters have been formatted and linked to one another and once all internal links, glosses, images, and scholarly annotations have been established, students will complete the project by writing an introduction to the site. I suggest that each group prepare its own introduction and then combine the best ideas into a final draft.

Clarissa and Hypertext: An Example

Even a cursory glance at Angus Ross's "Table of Letter Numbers in Other Editions" reveals the complexity of *Clarissa*'s textual history (1512). Ross's edition, for example, follows the seven-volume first edition (1747–48) by omitting letters 43, 66–67, 122, 208, 249, 468–69, and 537, all of which are included in the eight-volume third edition of the novel republished by Oxford between 1925 and 1934. Many students will probably not have access to the complete third edition because it is only available as an expensive hardcover. The conflated Everyman Library version is widely available, as are George Sherburn's abridged—and at times truly imperfect—Riverside Editions text[7] and the Penguin text edited by Ross, which reprints the first edition. If students have access to multiple versions of *Clarissa*, they may wish to make a hypertext that compares various versions of the text, linking alternative versions to each other, for instance. I recommend a somewhat less ambitious task for undergraduates.

Students interested in a particular letter sequence that includes letter 194 (617–20), for example, can link Lovelace's reference to Thomas Otway's *Venice Preserv'd* to a digitized version of Otway's play to deepen appreciation for the significance of Richardson's allusion. From this reference can emerge a short hypertext paper, which, when linked to the letter, explicates the connection in greater depth. What might the play's subtitle—*or a Plot Discover'd*—suggest about Lovelace's letter and his ongoing plot against Clarissa? Or, given Janet Aikins's subtle exploration of the connections between Otway's play and Richardson's novel in her "A Plot Discover'd; or, The Uses of *Venice Preserv'd* within *Clarissa*," students may try their hand at a psychoanalytic or psychosexual reading of "the failure of Lovelace's 'key'" (Aikins 228) and its relation to Clarissa's theatrical outing.[8] Students could even cross-reference several of the allusions to the play together—Aikins points out that these allusions are spread out over some 166 pages (221)—and discuss their relation to one another. Similarly, students can explore additional dramatic allusions in Richardson's novel, using Otway as a springboard.[9] Alternatively, students can develop a cultural glossary for the text that explores Richardson's references to money, the law, religion, clothing, eighteenth-century artifacts, transportation, etiquette, class, politics, sexuality, disease, and so on. Such references may be linked where appropriate to other relevant sections of the larger class project. The effect of such cultural annotations may actually tend to decenter the novel when connections get further and further afield, but this is not necessarily a bad thing.[10]

Again, letter 194 provides a number of examples. Many undergraduates will be unfamiliar with Lovelace's French expressions (e.g., *couteau* or *dishabille*) and may have no clear understanding of Lovelace's reference to "Nat. Lee's left-handed gods at work, to dash our bowl of joy with wormwood" (620). Students who struggle to understand what Lovelace means might profitably annotate such references as "wormwood," even if those references are minor. Annotations might consider what the references suggest about Richardson's original readers or about Lovelace's aristocratic education.

References to other characters, such as Mrs. Sinclair or Singleton, can be linked to an annotated character list, generated by students, that describes the roles played by these characters. Students could even make a hypertext link to a student discussion about particular themes, such as Lovelace's references to feeling: "I had too much *feeling*, I said. There was enough in the world to make our hearts sad, without carrying grief into our diversions, and making distresses of others our own" (618). Students with opposing views could present a lively discussion about whether Lovelace is disingenuous here, as he often is, or whether something else has managed to slip through, such as genuine sentiment or vulnerability?

So far I have explained how hypertext can help illuminate *Clarissa* in more or less traditional ways: through careful annotation, through close readings of various types, through historical and cultural contextualization. But what are the implications of these activities? Hypertext, when seen as a kind of narrative theory, sheds light on *Clarissa* in ways only hinted at above. As Jerome McGann observes, "Unlike a traditional book or set of books, the hypertext never need be 'complete'—though of course one could choose to shut the structure down if one wanted, close its covers as it were" (71). Each link, each annotation, adds yet another piece to an ever-growing web of connection.

Imagine *Clarissa* existing as a hypertext surrounded by all the commentary ever produced about it, as well as commentary about that commentary, creating a web of metacommentary. The original *Clarissa* scan would become protean, ever changing, ever evolving semester after semester as more and more students added to the original project. Its organizational structure would also evolve, thereby altering how future classes would read this text as they alter and augment the commentary of previous semesters. The reader of a hypertext *Clarissa*, as McGann, speaking generally, puts it, would be "encouraged not so much to find as to make order——and then to make it again and again, as established orderings expose their limits" (71). In other words, readers of hypertext can enter the hypertext at any point and can browse in any direction they choose.

Imagine further that our hypertext *Clarissa* belongs to a larger archive, an archive of eighteenth-century texts; or, larger still, an archive of British literature; or define the archive as you will. Hypertexted student commentary on and about *Clarissa* would become part of a context far beyond the confines of a given semester. The theoretical implications of hypertext profoundly illustrate the viability of reader-response and psychoanalytic theory just as they illuminate certain tenets of deconstruction, reception theory, new historicism, and cultural materialism. It becomes, in this light, a kind of metanarrative theory that students can not only discuss but also put into practice.

Some Important Technical Considerations

Most undergraduate literature majors—and frankly most undergraduate literature professors—generally do not have the requisite experience or training with

TEI (text-encoding initiative), a tag set for the humanities of SGML (standard generalized markup language), the "mother tongue" of text encoding, or with XML (extensible markup language), a subset of SGML—to create a technologically sophisticated scholarly electronic edition. Because students need to walk before they can run, I have not suggested that they take valuable time away from their literature experience to learn complex encoding tools in a content-heavy literature class. In my experience, such tools require at least a semester's worth of training to learn and much longer than that to master. In spring 2003, I taught an upper-level English course at Marist College entitled Writing for the Web: From Text to Hypertext that introduced literature students to some of the complexities and theories of creating and using electronic editions, but even after having taken such a class, students need more experience to successfully negotiate a sophisticated electronic edition. However, the HTML versions of students' files, once converted to XML or SGML, could be extremely valuable to any truly scholarly electronic edition at a later date.[11]

NOTES

[1]See, e.g., Landow, *Hypertext 2.0* and *Hyper/Text/Theory*; Joyce; Finneran; Sutherland; Murray; Galin and Latchaw; and McGann.

[2]After I began this project in the fall of 2002, Project Gutenberg produced a plain text version of *Clarissa* divided into nine volumes. Since the third edition of the novel consists of eight volumes, it is clear to me that the Project Gutenberg edition was scanned from an edition not printed in Richardson's lifetime. *Blackmask.com* has produced a seven-volume Web version of the novel as well, which I assume comes from the first edition. Both may be located conveniently at *Online Books* (http://onlinebooks.library .upenn.edu).

For a selection of Web sites devoted to Richardson, see my Richardson page located at http://library.marist.edu/diglib/english/englishliterature/17th-18thc-authors/richardson-samuel.htm.

[3]Note Richardson's use of footnotes in the first edition to the novel. I notice several types: explanatory (e.g., pp. 142, 865, and 927); cross-references, the most numerous type (206, 1149); expansive (933); directive, more frequent in the later editions (744, 1425); encyclopedic (863); and proleptic (414). Numerous notes serve more than one function. I would argue that Richardson anticipates reading hypertextually with a number of these notes.

[4]Eagleton suggests three ways of reading *Clarissa* that were unavailable to previous generations of Richardson scholars: poststructuralist, feminist and psychoanalytic, and historical materialist (viii).

[5]Another popular HTML editor available as a free download: AOLPress, available at www.aolpress.com.

[6]A cascading style sheet (CSS) is a simple file attached to a document's header—usually just after the title code—that handles most formatting features. It would be attached using the following nomenclature: link rel="stylesheet" href="the location/file name

of the CSS" type="text/css." I recommend using a CSS because if a project has many files with similar formatting instructions, one only has to change the attached CSS to change all files associated with it rather than change each individual file. Here is an example of a CSS:

BODY {background-color: #FEFFE1}

P {font-family: Goudy Old Style; font-style: normal; font-size: 14pt; text-indent: 0in}

H1 {font-family: Goudy Old Style; font-style: normal; font-size: 24pt}

H2 {font-family: Goudy Old Style; font-style: normal; font-size: 18pt; color: #F7200A}

A:link {color: #F7200A}

A:visited {color: #666699}

[7] I find it necessary to teach from Sherburn's abridged text, given the length of the novel and the time constraints of the semester, although I require students to read additional passages Sherburn has omitted. However, for this project, I require students to use the complete Penguin edition, since it is the most accessible complete paperback edition.

[8] I wish to thank Lisa Zunshine and Jocelyn Harris for suggesting Aikins's essay to me. I would expect students to consult the rich critical history concerning Lovelace's potency or lack thereof to do such an assignment justice. A recent example of this fascinating debate appears in Helene Moglen's "*Clarissa* and the Pornographic Imagination."

[9] Again Aikins's article would assist students in this matter. Students should pay special attention to the references she lists in her first footnote ("Plot" 230n1).

[10] For example, should students begin exploring the significance of fashion or transportation in the eighteenth-century world of *Clarissa*, either topic would lead students to a deeper examination of class issues or the mechanics and conditions of eighteenth-century manufacturing or manufacturing's connections to colonialism and empire. All these topics would be viable, since they would help historicize the novel for the students, existing as it does in a historical moment most modern readers have lost touch with (Aikins, "Plot" 219).

[11] Here is a select list of useful Web sites for the instructor: *A Guide to Creating Web Sites with HTML, CGI, Java, JavaScript, Graphics* (http://www.wdvl.com/Authoring/) and *The World Wide Web Consortium* (W3C) (http://www.w3.org/), the place to go for the latest in HTML and many other Web-related issues. Instructors interested in SGML and its relation to XML may wish to consult Pfaffenberger; Harold; Eckstein; and M. Young. Those interested in TEI should consult *Guidelines for Electronic Text Encoding and Interchange* (TEI P3), available on the University of Virginia's Electronic Text Center Web site.

Clarissa Lives! Reading Richardson through Rewritings

Jocelyn Harris

At the University of Otago, in Dunedin, New Zealand, I enjoy the luxury of teaching *Clarissa* for two hours a week throughout a thirteen-week semester. Classes have ranged from ten to eighteen fourth-year students. Our objectives are to check our own reading of the novel against the readings of a range of critics and to discover how later writers have re-visioned Richardson's masterpiece, to use Adrienne Rich's terminology (see "When We Dead Awaken").

I advise students to read *Clarissa* over the summer vacation (December to February), but they don't all manage to. In the first session we talk about the way that *Clarissa* develops out of *Pamela*, which most have studied in their third year. We discuss Richardson's writing career and the social and political background of the work. The first hour of the next four sessions is devoted to close reading of passages from each quarter of the book. Students have a long list of passages to choose from, each of which opens up issues of a more general nature, such as family relations; love, seduction, and rape; whether Clarissa's death is suicide, self-starvation, anorexia, or a hunger strike; the construction of masculinity; advantages and disadvantages of the epistolary method; and the whole hermeneutic endeavor of the book.

The second hour is spent watching a modern re-visioning, the adaptation of *Clarissa* by David Nokes and Janet Barron in four episodes for BBC Television. We discuss how effective it is as a "translation," how faithful or unfaithful, whether more or less powerful, and why.[1] All this gets students through the book in four big chunks and familiarizes them with key passages. Most have read the whole book by the end of the fifth week.

The next five sessions are occupied by student presentations either on critical texts about *Clarissa* or later re-visionings. Students who take the first option choose from a list provided by me, identify the critic's theoretical position, explain the theory, summarize the argument, and assess how well that particular reading works for the text. This process serves several functions: students work with a wide range of critical stances and test them against their own readings; they learn that everybody works from a critical position derived from his or her experience, historical moment, beliefs, and training; they see that no one position can be definitive or authoritative; and they learn to trust their own judgments. After discussion and feedback from their colleagues, they write up their analysis as a five-thousand-word essay.

Students who choose the second option submit their essay about a re-visioned version of *Clarissa* from the following list:

> the revised ending suggested by Lady Bradshaigh, together with her annotations and Richardson's on her personal copy (see Eaves and Kimpel, *Samuel Richardson* 221–25; Barchas, *Annotations*)
>
> the alternative ending written by her sister Lady Echlin
>
> one of the *Clarissa* novels of the late 1760s and early 1770s, as identified by Perry ("Clarissa's Daughters")
>
> Choderlos de Laclos, *Les liaisons dangereuses* (1782)
>
> Jane Austen, *Sense and Sensibility* (1811)
>
> Virginia Woolf, *Mrs. Dalloway* (1925)
>
> Michael Cunningham, *The Hours* (1999)
>
> Kingsley Amis, *Take a Girl Like You* (1960)
>
> *Take a Girl Like You*, dir. Jonathan Miller (1970); *Take a Girl Like You*, dir. Nick Hurran (2000)
>
> John Fowles, *The French Lieutenant's Woman* (1969)
>
> Harold Pinter, *The Screenplay of* The French Lieutenant's Woman (1981)
>
> Margaret Doody and Florian Stuber, screenplay (1984) and video of "Dramatizing *Clarissa*" (1986)
>
> Jane Campion's film *Holy Smoke* (1999)
>
> Ian McEwan, *Atonement* (2001)

All these works provide meditations or variations on Richardson's original text. I ask students to note similarities and differences, particularly divergences that suggest that the re-visioning author is in fact an imitator, who, as John Dryden put it, endeavors to

> write like one who has written before him on the same subject: that is, not to Translate his words, or to be Confin'd to his Sense, but only to set him as a Pattern, and to write, as he supposes, that Author would have done, had he liv'd in our Age, and in our Country.   (184)

I also ask them to observe signs of radical disagreement with the original text, that is, to note where the rewriting becomes itself a resisting critique rather than a validation. These discussions lead naturally into issues of plagiarism, influence, imitation, allusion, intertextuality, and creativity, especially in a context of postmodernism where books are assumed to be made out of other books.

Critiquing the critics is a self-explanatory exercise, and it is exciting to watch students gain confidence as they confront critical "authorities." But those who choose a re-visionist reading are startled to discover that the only author brave enough to press on to a tragic conclusion is the original progenitor of the story, Samuel Richardson. Everybody else wants Clarissa to marry Lovelace. Nobody wants them to die. That is, later writers read Richardson just like those first resisting readers of the manuscript, proofs, printed volumes, reviews, and presentation copies signed by the author.[2] So eager are they to erase his tragedy that they write whole new books to wrench his authorial authority away. Considering why this might be so opens up larger discussions among the students about tragedy and comedy, the authority of the author, reader response, and differing horizons of expectation over time.

Lady Bradshaigh told her friend Richardson that she had "shed a Pint of Tears" over the ending of *Clarissa*, and there they remain to this day, splashed on the page, making the ink run (Eaves and Kimpel, *Samuel Richardson* 224). She was only in the vanguard of those who ever since have refused to accept Richardson's tragic ending (with the notable exception of Sarah Fielding in her *Remarks on* Clarissa 47–50, 55–56). Even Laclos lets two of his protaganists live. I have therefore found it necessary to provide students with some background material explaining Richardson's choice of tragedy.

Even in his own time, the difference between Richardson and his contemporaries was starkly exposed when he begged David Garrick to produce *Lear* in Shakespeare's version instead of Nahum Tate's revised one, in which Lear survives to see Cordelia marry Edgar. Garrick ignored his plea, and various versions of Tate's play remained popular over the next one hundred and fifty years. But Richardson follows Aristotle in his unflinching belief that tragedy alone causes the pity and fear that moves spectators to their necessary reform. He spells out these views particularly in his prefaces and postscripts to *Clarissa* (see Harris, Introduction xxiii–xxiv). Also, after Pamela's critics had accused her of self-interest and materialism when her virtue was rewarded on earth, Richardson seems to have heeded the suggestion of his friend John Dennis about postponing his Christianized poetic justice to eternity (Dennis 49). And if *Pamela's* happy ending had obscured the real seriousness of rape, Richardson demonstrates in *Clarissa* what could happen if that threat was actually fulfilled—such a radical destruction of self that the heroine wills herself to die. He certainly remembered Lucretia, the Roman matron who killed herself in public after being raped by Tarquin (see Donaldson), and perhaps, he also remembered Sophocles's *Antigone*, in which a woman dies when the laws of man run counter to the laws of heaven. In *A Room of One's Own*, Virginia Woolf lists Antigone and Clarissa among women "who have burnt like beacons in all the works of all the poets from the beginning of time" (42). Many on her list are suicides. But when Woolf came to write *Mrs. Dalloway*, she swerved from her initial impulse to kill off the heroine she named so pointedly after Richardson's. In fact, the fifty-one-year-old Clarissa Dalloway lives on to a moment of possible reconciliation with her returned and repentant Lovelace, Peter Walsh.

Clarissa is also a tragedy for Lovelace, and many readers have wanted to see him live. But I ask students to think about the way that Richardson draws on powerful stereotypes such as the medieval Vice, Milton's Satan, Shakespeare's Proteus and Richard III, the real as well as the imagined Earl of Rochester, and especially Molière's and Thomas Shadwell's Don Juan, all of which lock the character into a fatal pattern of defiant evil doing, crises of conscience, renewed transgression, and death.[3] As Ovid put it, they see the better but follow the worse (bk. 7, ll. 20–21).[4] Given that Richardson based Lovelace on such important avatars of darkness, how could he give in to sentimental pleading? Again, students might contemplate how more recent and more secular authors re-vision Lovelace and what their alterations say about Richardson's time compared with theirs.

Richardson drew on not only Greek, Roman, and English traditions and Rochester, a real-life morality Vice, but also his bleak Judeo-Christian heritage when Clarissa compares herself explicitly to Job and implicitly to Christ. In so doing, he confronts the difficult fact that God inflicts pain on those who do not deserve it. In developing the character of Clarissa, Richardson appropriates Job's suffering, his alienation from society, and his wish for his story to be told, but he omits Job's restoration to family, health, and wealth. Instead, Clarissa follows Christ's path to death and a heavenly reward. The strenuous resistance of Richardson's contemporaries to his tragic ending is therefore remarkable. When these professed Christians begged that she should live, they denied a basic tenet of their faith, the existence of an afterlife superior to this one. Under the sway of Richardson's persuasive and affective realism, they essentially declared themselves unbelievers.

Tate's rejection of tragedy in his rewritten *Lear* was understandable in an Enlightenment context of economic development, imperial expansion, and optimistic rationalism. But Richardson justifies his choice by looking back to older and darker modes of thinking. Twenty-first-century students might like to consider just why a character drawn from Lucretia, Antigone, Job, and Christ is anathema to the enlightened and modern world. Is a principle, especially a sexual one, no longer something to die for? And why did later writers such as Austen, Woolf, Amis, and Campion turn Richardson's tragedy into comedy, or at least provide alternative endings, as did John Fowles and Ian McEwan?

Here are a couple of examples to show what can be done. One student (John Forde) was inspired by Lady Echlin's rewritten ending to rewrite *Clarissa* for himself by means of a video, using a Barbie doll to illuminate issues of being a female hero and inserting clips about responses to seduction and rape in works ranging from *Les liaisons dangereuses* to *Thelma and Louise*. Such rewriting can be a marvellous way for students to appropriate the text through play, thus relativizing it in different times and cultures.

Virginia Woolf's rewriting of Richardson in *Mrs. Dalloway* is of course more thoroughgoing. Clarissa Dalloway has rejected Peter Walsh, her Lovelace, and survived to the age of fifty-one. She has married a Hickman, or even a Solmes grown agreeable as well as rich. On the day recorded in the novel, she is giving a party, and Peter, the man whom she might have married, visits her on his return from India. Sally Seton, with whom she was once very close, also appears. The news of Septimus Smith's suicide is told at her party. The story proceeds in linear time, but memories overlay the present, with flashbacks filling out the Richardsonian scheme. Peter's arrival at the party marks the end of the book.

The critical moment of Woolf's divergence is when she makes Clarissa Dalloway's father not a tyrannical patriarch, but a "querulous, weak-kneed old man" (47). At one stroke Woolf spirits away the intolerable pressure that made Clarissa Harlowe turn to a rake for help. Richardson's Clarissa yearns to live with Anna in a Protestant nunnery; Woolf's Clarissa represses emotion to the point that she feels "like a nun" (33). Mrs. Dalloway, though a mother, still cherishes her sense of virginity (36), like Clarissa Harlowe after the rape. If Peter thinks, "There was always something cold in Clarissa" (55), Lovelace calls Miss Harlowe cold.

In *Mrs. Dalloway*, the only possible response to the Great War is Job's stoicism, just as Clarissa Harlowe found a mirror for her misery in the Book of Job. The party restores not only Mrs. Dalloway's powers but also her sense of mediocrity, waste, and death. If she feels simultaneously young and unspeakably aged (10), Peter first imagines her dead and then, Lovelace-like, denies it (56). In fact, Clarissa Dalloway does not die, but through her empathy with her double, Septimus Smith—his sense of his mind being essentially raped (163), his madness, his suicide—she links herself imaginatively with Clarissa Harlowe. It is particularly significant that Smith's Italian wife is named Lucrezia. When Richardson represents Clarissa Harlowe as Lucretia, her penknife at her breast, he suggests that she too dies essentially by suicide (900).

Peter Walsh resembles Lovelace in being fascinating, witty, energetic, and full of gaiety. Lovelace is relentlessly allusive, seeing himself as the hero of every reference; Peter is "bookish" (172) and especially well read in the eighteenth century (140). But Lovelace's flaws are also Peter's: extravagantly altering moods, jealousy, a self-deceiving fondness for playacting and inventing, and a lack of empathy that leads to battles with Clarissa. Peter's desire for variety makes him antagonistic toward marriage, like Lovelace. The "other thing," Peter thinks, comes so much more "naturally" (172). It is Lovelace's constant cry that natural law should prevail and partners change on Valentine's Day, like the birds (872). Lovelace is elated by the changes and metamorphoses of the chase, and Peter is similarly exhilarated by his pursuit of a young woman. But his fun is "half made up . . . invented . . . making oneself up; making her up, creating an exquisite amusement, and something more" (61). Here Woolf catches perfectly Lovelace's self-aggrandizement; his delight in playacting and invention; his lack, really, of a core.

Peter, unlike Lovelace, does not rape his Clarissa; he simply goes away to India. How do Clarissa and Peter feel, having lived for thirty years longer than their predecessors? Peter had asked Clarissa to meet him by the fountain, as

Lovelace made an assignation with Clarissa by the garden gate, but Woolf's Clarissa had been unyielding. When Peter returns, years later, Woolf anticipates the survival, even the improvement, of love. It is almost as though Woolf has turned back the clock when she ushers the "trembling" Peter into Clarissa's drawing room "at eleven o'clock on the morning of the day she [is] giving a party" (45).

Clarissa Dalloway's relationship with Sally Seton similarly represents Woolf's "reading" of Clarissa Harlowe's relationship with Anna Howe. If Anna is lively and unconventional, Sally is daring and exuberant. Like Anna, she stands up for the rights of women, fights with her family, becomes engaged, and falls out with her friend's father. Critics debate the exact nature of the affection between Clarissa and Anna Howe, but Woolf, who loved women herself, certainly interprets Clarissa Harlowe's solidarity with Anna as love. In Woolf's novel, Clarissa and Sally's kiss is interrupted by Peter, making Clarissa feel that marriage is a catastrophe designed to separate female friends, much as Anna and Clarissa had felt. And yet like Anna's encouraging Clarissa to admit that Lovelace attracts her, Sally implores Peter to "carry off" Clarissa, to save her from the perfect gentlemen who would stifle her soul, make a mere hostess of her, and encourage her worldliness (84). That "carry off" is a sharp reminder of the first Clarissa.

Woolf picks up Richardson's hints at Anna's sympathy for Lovelace—for instance, at the ball, when Clarissa is dying (1132–39, letter 367). But Sally has been diminished by marriage and by motherhood. An Anna married to her Hickman, she has lost her luster (182). The wild, the daring, the romantic Sally boasts of five enormous boys (190) and a large house near Manchester. Woolf seems to say that Sally is worldly like Anna, who urged Clarissa to marry after the rape.

Richardson constantly represents Clarissa's power over Lovelace in imagery of light, and Woolf too describes her Clarissa as brilliant, radiant, sparkling. In fact, Mrs. Dalloway has already enacted Clarissa Harlowe's "play," even if conditionally: "Take me with you, Clarissa thought impulsively," for "it was as if the five acts of a play that had been very exciting and moving were now over and she had lived a lifetime in them and had run away, had lived with Peter, and it was now over" (53). Woolf's book ends at the same point as that moment in *Clarissa* when the story could have gone either way, when she bursts upon Lovelace at the gate, "all at once in a flood of brightness" (399–402). So too Peter stands dazzled by the beauty, power, and control of Clarissa Dalloway. The book ends merely with Peter's words:

> What is this terror? What is this ecstasy? . . . What is it that fills me with extraordinary excitement?
> It is Clarissa, he said.
> For there she was.

But the sense of merciful replay, even the restoration of a fallen world, is overwhelming. Like almost every reader of Richardson, Woolf did not want Clarissa to die and wrote for her Clarissa a future where she need not.

Woolf reads Richardson perceptively when she makes Clarissa Dalloway dwindle into a wife, when she lets her sympathize with the sense of violation that leads Septimus Smith to suicide, when she represents Peter as charming but invasive, when she enlarges on the love between Clarissa and Anna to make Clarissa Dalloway and Sally Seton actually kiss. Students enjoy pursuing analogies and differences—one of them pointed out gleefully that Mrs. Dalloway's dog is called Rob (67), like Robert Lovelace. But remarkably, though Woolf knew well why Clarissa Harlowe killed herself, she allowed her own Clarissa to live.

Richardson has a trick of turning up all over the place—when the class and I attended Christopher Hampton's play of *Les liaisons dangereuses*, Mme de Tourvel said she had been reading *Clarissa*; we all gasped, startling the actress, who had presumably never had a response to that line before. I urge classes to be always on the lookout for more versions, believing that Richardson will inevitably continue to inspire new writers. Clarissa lives indeed!

NOTES

[1]Lois Chaber ("'Fatal Attraction'?") provides a lively analysis of the series.

[2]See Eaves and Kimpel, "Revisions"; Harris, *Samuel Richardson*; and Barchas *Annotations*.

[3]See Harris, *Samuel Richardson* 68–71, 131; "Richardson: Original or Learned Genius?" 196–201; and "Protean Lovelace."

[4]This is said of the mad Medea. Adam and Eve make a similar choice in the Garden of Eden.

Richardson's Revisions in the Third Edition of *Clarissa*: For Better or Worse?

John Richetti

Until 1985, when Angus Ross's Penguin paperback of the first edition of *Clarissa* (1747–48) appeared, only abridged versions of the novel, notably George Sherburn's Riverside paperback, were available for classroom use. But when I first assigned Ross's unwieldy volume to a graduate class, I was dismayed to find that the edition ruled out my best instructional gambit, which depended on a long sequence added in the third edition, on which Sherburn had based his abridgment (161–72). Using Ross's first edition in the classroom rendered some of my old teaching notes irrelevant and dramatized for me what I had always known about *Clarissa* but never fully appreciated or integrated into my class presentations: that from the first drafting of his text, Richardson wrote in response to his readers' reactions. More than any other eighteenth-century English novel, *Clarissa* is a dynamic or even fluid text, its alterations reflecting Richardson's continual dialogue first with readers of his manuscript and then with the wider audience for his printed texts.

This fact was brought home to me with clarity five years later by the publication, as part of The *Clarissa* Project, of a facsimile edition in eight volumes of the third edition of the novel (1751), featuring Richardson's final substantive revisions, with major additions marked in the margins with bullets. In his introduction to this edition, Florian Stuber makes a good case for the superiority of Richardson's more or less final version, since it records what he justly calls the dynamic essence of the book as virtually an extended collaboration between Richardson and his readers (2). Stuber describes Richardson as essentially a rewriter and *Clarissa* as "an intimate engagement between writer and reader that is reflected and presented in the text of the Third Edition" (2). As Stuber explains, this edition of the novel contains over two hundred pages of additions, including the restoration of materials cut from earlier editions (15).[1]

The *Clarissa* Project edition, always unaffordable for students, is now in any case out of print. Since then, however, Chadwyck-Healey has included in its *Eighteenth-Century Fiction Full Text Database*—part of its *Literature Online*, or *LION*, database, to which most college and university libraries subscribe—copies of both the first and the third editions of *Clarissa*, featuring hyperlinks that allow easy and instant comparison of each letter in each edition. But the online third edition does not retain the marginal bullets by which Richardson marked his substantial additions. I am not so sure as Stuber is that the third edition is superior to the first, but, because of Richardson's additions, revisions, and possible restorations from his original manuscript, it is certainly more interesting to teach. Because of the availability of Ross's Penguin paperback and of the online availability of both these editions, I can invite students to discuss the significance and the merits of Richardson's revisions in the face of readers' responses by focusing on the largest set of those additions in the third edition: volume 3, letters 25 (131–41), 26 (141–46), 27 (146–52), and 31 (160–69), the first three from Clarissa to Anna Howe and the last from Lovelace to Belford. (In the first edition, these are letters 28 [155–59], 29 [159–63], 30 [163–66], and 32 [171–72].)[2] Before turning to these additions, I talk in general terms about *Clarissa*'s initial reception, which provoked Richardson's obsessive revisions—those thousands of small changes as well as substantial additions and explanatory footnotes. Broadly speaking, his revisions marked his anxiety over the moral ambiguity and even the controversy and scandal created by the first edition. It can also be argued that he tried to move in the direction of more fully justifying Clarissa's character and actions as well as modifying the power and subversively magnetic charm that readers of the first edition tended to find in Lovelace.[3]

The critical issue underlying classroom discussion is the unstable nature of novelistic imagining as Richardson uniquely managed it. Once characters such as Clarissa and Lovelace have been fully evoked and set in motion, they may be said to acquire an expressive life of their own that eludes precise authorial control, passing into an interpretive arena where readers are free to perform their own imaginative moves. Are Richardson's additions to the third edition an attempt at didactic damage control, an effort to restrict or at least to influence his readers' interpretive freedom? Since the issue is complex, the sequence of letters describing Clarissa's experience with Lovelace at St. Albans is rich in possibilities. If Stuber is right to argue that Richardson's revisions are signs of his instinctively profound grasp of textual instability as well as testimony to his intellectual and moral engagement with his readers, comparing the two versions of this particular scene provides perhaps the best occasion for evaluating Stuber's claim.

The context for these letters is as follows: Clarissa has just been tricked into running away from her father's house and is in lodgings arranged by Lovelace in St. Albans, where she hardly knows what to expect or do. Lovelace is secretly ecstatic, bragging with sinister bravado to Belford that she is entirely in his power:

> [A]s I have ordered it, the flight will appear to the Implacables to be altogether with her own consent: And that if I doubt her Love, I can put her to trials as mortifying to her Niceness, as glorious to my Pride. —For, let me tell thee, dearly as I love her, if I thought there was but the shadow of a doubt in her mind, whether she preferred me to any man living, I would shew her no mercy.   (3rd. ed. 3: 4)[4]

In these early days just after her escape, Clarissa is still unaware of Lovelace's machinations. Her letters to Anna therefore portray primarily a self-confidence upset by the enormity of her act in leaving her father's house with a man, though troubled as well by her suspicions of Lovelace's moral unsoundness.

In the first edition, letter 28 (155–59) is almost pure epistolary exposition, Clarissa, on the Saturday evening marked in the letter, reacts to Anna's warnings in letter 26 (149–51) about Lovelace, a notorious seducer, and to her advice that Clarissa marry him nonetheless, "as soon as possible" (150). She describes her feelings after reading Anna's letter: it so affected her, she says, "that the moment I saw him, I beheld with indignation the seducer, who had been the cause of all the evils I suffer, and have suffered." She then narrates how Lovelace mollified her slightly by hinting that he has received letters from his relations, the Miss Montagues, which at first give her pause and then cause for more concern as she wonders whether those ladies "may hold me unworthy of their alliance, if they may think my flight a voluntary one?" (156).

The third edition shifts the narrative method from Clarissa's epistolary self-expression to her exchanges with Lovelace the following Sunday morning, rendered in dramatic dialogue and recorded in the same letter (number 25) as "warmer dialogues than ever yet we have had" (132). In place of the first edition's brief epistolary paraphrase of conversations with Lovelace and its account of her thoughts and feelings—that is, her confused uncertainty about what Lovelace may be up to and what she herself should do—the third edition has Clarissa sending Anna many pages of extended quotation, which turn the scene into a tremendous row between Clarissa and Lovelace. Their debate includes exact notation of both characters' speeches and of their emphases and gestures, reported at first by Clarissa but later verified by Lovelace when he describes the same scene much more briefly. This crucial expansion of Clarissa's hints in the first edition about their interchanges that Sunday morning represents a fundamental although not unique alteration in narrative method. The third edition sequence moves from the more or less plausible epistolary mode into a fantastically precise stenographic reproduction of dialogue and dramatic action.[5]

What is remarkable in this totally new section, marked with bullets, is Richardson's attempt to develop his fearful, faltering, deeply insecure Clarissa into a confident and supremely articulate heroine who in a rhetorical battle of speech and gesture may be said momentarily to defeat Lovelace by literally rendering him speechless. To be sure, because Clarissa has already displayed her considerable rhetorical powers in her encounters with her mother, her brother, and her sister, this addition arguably builds on that key aspect of her character. But I suggest to my students that this sequence, being more than a debate or heated conversation in its extent and intensity, has no exact precedent in earlier editions. We might want to call it in effect a flyting, an exchange of witty insults that shifts the balance of rhetorical power temporarily from Lovelace to Clarissa. To bring things up to date, it resembles a lengthy eighteenth-century version of the dozens, or dissing.

Here are some of Clarissa's remarks in letter 28 of the first edition, before they are expanded by Richardson in letter 30 of the third edition:

Sunday Morning.

What an additional concern must I have in my reflections upon Mr. Lovelace's hatred of all my relations? —He calls some of them implacable; but I am afraid that he is as implacable himself; as the most inveterate of them.

I could not forbear, with great earnestness, to express my wishes for a reconciliation with them; and, in order to begin a treaty for that purpose, to re-urge his departure from me: He gave himself high airs upon the occasion, not doubting, he said, that he was to be the preliminary sacrifice; and then he reflected in a very free manner upon my brother; nor spared my father himself.   (156)

. . . .

He said many things in his own defence; but not one, as I told him, that could justify a daughter to *hear,* or a man to *say,* who pretended what he pretended to that daughter.

And then, seeing me very sincerely angry, he begg'd my pardon, tho' not in a very humble manner. But, to change the subject, he took notice of the two letters he had received, one from Lady Betty Lawrance, the other from Miss Montague; and read me passages out of both.   (157)

In the third edition, just before Lovelace's characterization of the Harlowes as "implacable," Richardson inserts a prelude in which Clarissa drives Lovelace into a corner and even provokes his extreme language after he suggests that she litigate for her estate: "I suppose, Sir, that if my Father propose my return, and engage never to mention Solmes to me, nor any other man, but by *my consent*, and I agree upon that condition to think no more of *you*, you will acquiesce." By Clarissa's account, Lovelace is so deeply "struck all of a heap" by her cogent demands that he is reduced to hemming "twice or thrice" before "rising from his seat with petulance." As if driven into a defensive and self-pitying mode of speech, into displaying visible and vulnerable emotions in which his clever volubility is subordinate to her analysis of the situation, he complains, "At *last* I am to be a sacrifice to your Reconciliation with your implacable family." Clarissa answers him with "Sir, when you call *others* implacable, see that you deserve not the same censure *yourself*" (134).

This exchange sets the pattern for subsequent pages in which Clarissa mockingly echoes Lovelace's key terms of self-justification and self-dramatization, egging Lovelace on to defend himself and his version of events in what she successfully exposes as his self-serving and self-dramatizing manner. In these pages, where represented and dramatic speech erases the epistolary mode of the first edition, dramatic objectivity seems to drive out subjective uncertainty, at least for the moment. Clarissa goes out of her way to add stage directions and italics, where appropriate, to underline her tone and emphasis. For instance, after she says that she now doubts that her father meant to force her to marry Solmes, Lovelace objects, saying, "Everybody living, Madam, is obliged to you for your kind thoughts but I." She responds in kind: "Excuse me, good Mr. Lovelace [waving my hand, and bowing] that I am willing to think the best of my Father" (136). All these pages expand on just one sentence, Clarissa's paraphrase of an exchange in the first edition's version of the scene: "He said many things in his own defence; but not one, as I told him, that could justify a daughter to *hear*, or a man to *say*, who pretended what he pretended to that daughter" (157).

Lovelace, at least as Clarissa depicts him in the third edition, tries to answer her mockery in kind, moving from whining self-pity, "I think, Madam, my sufferings for your sake might have entitled me to some favour" to "assuming a drolling air" (136) to launching into a heavily charged and anaphoric summary of events that occupies several paragraphs. Recounting her story up to now, he punctuates his ironic summary of her persecution with the mock concession that she has

> been *only* made a prisoner in your Father's house . . . *only* had an insolent Brother take upon him to treat you like a slave . . . *only* been persecuted, in order to oblige you to have a sordid fellow. . . . And the man, who, at the hazard of his life, has delivered you from all these mortifications, is the only person you *cannot* forgive!   (136–37)

Goaded by Clarissa, who remarks at the end of this tirade, "Can't you go on, Sir? You see I have patience to hear you. Can't you go on, Sir?," Lovelace returns to what he calls his own "suffering" (137), but Clarissa brings him up wonderfully short when he recounts what he has undergone for her: "Forced to creep about in disguises—and to watch all hours." She catches him repeating himself, "And in *all weathers*, I suppose, Sir—That I remember was once your grievance!—*In all weathers*, Sir" (138). In a new footnote, Richardson inserts a cross-reference to Lovelace's earlier self-dramatizing letter, written as he claimed from the ivy coppice, "On one knee, kneeling with the other, I write!—My feet benumbed with midnight wanderings thro' the heaviest dews, that ever fell: My wig and my linen dripping with the hoar frost dissolving on them!" (122, letter 19). Here Richardson grants Clarissa a retrospective awareness of Lovelace's false posturing and stagy self-dramatizing that she previously lacked.

Clarissa's final riposte in these exchanges is a rhetorical tour de force in which she gathers up all Lovelace's self-serving terms, his "only's" and his "sufferings," and turns them back on him. In this remarkable speech, she skewers him with the ultimate demeaning and wickedly knowing epithet for a master of language and wit such as he fancies himself—"voluble Sir." She, of course, is voluble in the extreme, except that she has the last word when she caps the debate with a devastating analytic exposé of his language and version of events. Always worth reading aloud in class, her oration needs to be quoted in full:

> O Sir, Sir! What sufferings have yours been! And all for my sake, I warrant!–I can never reward you for them!–Never think of me more, I beseech you–How can you have patience with me?–Nothing has been owing to your own behaviour, I presume: Nothing to your defiances for defiances: Nothing to your resolution declared more than once, that you *would* be related to a family, which, nevertheless, you would not stoop to ask a Relation of: Nothing, in short, to courses which every-body blamed you for, you not thinking it worth your while to justify yourself. Had I not thought you used in an ungentlemanly manner, as I have heretofore told you, you had not had my notice by pen and ink. That notice gave you a supposed security, and you generously defied my friends the more for it: And this brought upon me (perhaps not undeservedly) my Father's displeasure; without which my Brother's private pique, and selfish views, would have wanted a foundation to build upon: So that for all that followed of my treatment, and your redundant *Only's*, I might thank you principally, as you may yourself for all your sufferings, your *mighty* sufferings!—And if, voluble Sir, you have founded any merit upon them, be so good as to revoke it: And look upon *me*, with my forfeited reputation, as the only sufferer—For what—Pray hear me out, Sir [for he was going to speak] have you suffered in, but your pride? Your reputation *could not* suffer: That it was beneath you to be solicitous about. And had you not been an unmanageable man, I should not have been driven to the extremity I now every hour, as the hour passes, deplore—With this additional reflection upon myself, that I ought not to have *begun*, or having begun, not *continued* a correspondence with one, who thought it not worth his while to clear his own character for *my sake*, or to submit to my Father for *his own*, in a point wherein every Father ought to have an option.   (138–39)

As I have argued, in leaving her father's house, Clarissa has been tricked into playing a role in a dramatic enactment of Lovelace's devising. His subversive and specifically aristocratic comedy of seduction and stratagem replaces the essentially novelistic sense of reality that characterizes Clarissa's good-faith negotiations with her family in the opening volumes of the novel, when she seeks to evade the marital and economic destiny planned for her and to develop her own sense of integrity and self-determination.[6] Ensnared as she is in that comedy of seduction, Clarissa rises to the generic occasion engineered by Lovelace, thanks to Richardson's revisions in the third edition, where she acquires a full sense of agency in playing by the rules of sex comedy. She becomes, as it were, Millamant to Lovelace's bewildered Mirabel. In this astonishing comic moment,

Richardson's stitching arguably becomes visible. In a desperate response to Clarissa's rhetorical and analytic attack, Lovelace admits defeat but tries to save the situation by shifting the discourse into the dramatic register of amatory melodrama, as we might call it, in place of the witty argumentation preceding it:

> Darkness, light; Light, darkness; by my Soul!—Just as you please to have it. O Charmer of my heart! snatching my hand, and pressing it between both his, to his lips, in a strange wild way, Take me, take me to yourself: Mould me as you please: I am wax in your hands: Give me your own impression; and seal me for ever yours—We were born for each other!— You to make me happy, and save a soul—I am all error, all crime. I see what I ought to have done. But do you think, Madam, I can willingly consent to be sacrificed to a partial Reconciliation, in which I shall be so great, so irreparable a sufferer!—Any-thing but that—Include me in your terms: Prescribe to me: Promise for me as you please—Put a halter about my neck, and lead me by it, upon condition of forgiveness on that disgraceful penance, and of a prostration as servile, to your Father's presence (your Brother absent); and I will beg his consent at his feet, and bear any-thing but spurning from him, because he is your Father. But to give you up upon *cold* conditions, D—n me [said the shocking wretch] if I either will, or can!   (139–40)

The argument and analysis highlighted in Clarissa's speech give way to pure and desperately incoherent expressivity in Lovelace's response: note the dashes and the conventional melodramatic ranting, as well as Clarissa's comment, "These were his words, as near as I can remember them; for his behaviour was so strangely wild and fervent that I was perfectly frighted." Clarissa understands, to paraphrase Desdemona, a fury in Lovelace's words but not the words themselves. Indeed, in her next letter in the third edition (141–46, letter 26), Clarissa stresses Lovelace's impenetrability or elusiveness, in another bulleted passage, calling him "a perfect Proteus . . . a perfect chameleon; or rather more variable. . . . And tho' *black* seems to be his natural colour, yet has he taken great pains to make me think him nothing but *white*" (141–42). Lovelace himself, however, when reporting this scene to Belford in letter 31 of the third edition, stresses the involuntary nature of his reaction: "I could hardly forbear taking her into my arms," he writes (162). In recording part of his "Darkness and light" speech, he admits that "there was, I believe a kind of phrensy in my manner" (163). Thus Clarissa not only wins the logical and rhetorical battle of the moment but also triumphs emotionally. She provokes Lovelace into expressing a psychosexual truth behind the melodramatic idiom, extracts feelings that up to now he has managed to control and manipulate, and negates the comedy of sexual stereotypes that he has constructed. To be sure, in his report to Belford, Lovelace resorts to his old tricks as a self-dramatizer, grandiosely comparing Clarissa's panic to nothing less than Semele's, "when the Thunderer, in all his majesty, surrounded with ten thousand celestial burning-glasses, was about to scorch her into a cinder" (163). And yet in the very next sentence, likewise new in the third edition, Lovelace concedes to the novelistic contextualizing of their situation when he admits that Clarissa has for the moment the upper hand—he allows that "she was not so much in my power, but that she might abandon me at her pleasure, having more friends in that house than I had." "Had not my heart misgiven me," he adds, he "should at that moment have made offers" (163). Lovelace reads the scene as a close call, a near defeat by those circumstances outlined in Clarissa's discourse. Richardson clearly meant his revision to level the playing field, at least temporarily, between these well-matched antagonists.

In one sense, these additions represent a weakness in Richardson's revisions, in that they simplify Lovelace's character. They also set up a more melodramatic opposition between Richardson's characters, which transforms this sequence into dueling operatic arias—at this point an opera buffa, later very much an opera seria—with no exact precedent in the first edition. Clarissa and Lovelace continue their verbal battles, of course, and Lovelace recovers his dominance by what may be called trickery of the foulest sort. Just before and after the rape, Richardson will offer readers much more dramatic dialogue as well as pure epistolarity, but in such sequences Clarissa is forced to adopt her own form of melodramatic utterance. Richardson was attempting in this particular revised sequence to stabilize and simplify the complex effusions of his original imaginative constructions and to prolong, even to perfect, Clarissa's rhetorical power. Or it can be argued that the sequence establishes a short-lived balance of power between the two characters in which Clarissa manages to shift the discourse from sex comedy to intellectual and moral debate, from the abstractness of amatory fiction to the deep contexualizing of the new novel, in which characters fully possess themselves. At the very least, this fascinating sequence provides opportunities to discuss the meaning and the effectiveness of Richardson's revisions.

NOTES

[1]Richardson claimed that many of the additions to the third edition were restorations from the original manuscript of *Clarissa*, but Mark Kinkead-Weekes argues that most were in fact written in response to what Richardson considered dangerous misinterpretations (see "Clarissa Restored?"). See also Kinkead-Weekes's *Samuel Richardson: Dramatic Novelist*, where Richardson's revisions are seen as a clumsy didactic response to his readers (151). Tom Keymer finds evidence to suggest that Richardson both added and restored material to the third edition, but he admits that in the absence of documentary proof the two strands can never be disentangled ("Richardson's *Clarissa*" 51n147). See on this question Peter Sabor, Introduction xi. For a thorough discussion of Richardson's revisions, see Shirley Van Marter, "Third and Fourth Editions."

[2]In his one-volume reprint of the first edition, Ross chose to number the letters consecutively. So these letters in his edition of *Clarissa* are 121, 123, 124, 125, 126, and 127 (454–65).

[3]Students will presumably catch Lovelace's subversive charms without much trouble, but they may wonder how Clarissa can be taken as less than a paragon. Keymer offers a particularly persuasive case for Clarissa being seen negatively by many eighteenth-century readers. "Her letters," he suggests, "seem determined not by 'reality' but by the self-image she prefers to project, and they are based on a model of daughterly exemplariness that is increasingly at odds with her actual state" ("Richardsons *Clarissa*" 135).

[4]Throughout this essay I refer to the online versions of both the first and third editions.

[5]Sabor calls this addition an advance in subtlety and complexity on the first edition reading, "as flat reportage gives way to dramatic presentation" (Introduction xviii).

[6]See my "Richardson's Dramatic Art in *Clarissa*," Numerous critics have commented on the dramatic and theatrical sources and affinities of *Clarissa*. For instance, Jocelyn Harris makes an elaborate and convincing case that Richardson's "entire method [was] essentially dramatic" (Introduction xxxv).

Kinship in *Clarissa*

Ruth Perry

My most interesting experiences teaching *Clarissa* were in graduate classes taught with an anthropologist (in 1994 and 1995) called Narratives of Kinship in Industrializing Societies. Offered by the innovative Graduate Consortium in Women's Studies at Radcliffe, these classes were developed as interdisciplinary explorations of subjects outside the ordinary purview of any standard discipline. We were interested in how industrialization and capitalism altered kin relations in different periods and different national contexts. Eighteenth-century England provided our fullest case study of an industrializing society, and *Clarissa* without comparison was our most significant text; but we also read materials from other cultural contexts such as nineteenth-century Tonga and twentieth-century Africa. Buchi Emecheta's *The Joys of Motherhood* (1979), for example, a late- twentieth-century Nigerian novel, provided another perspective on the impact of industrialization on women from another country and another century. It was in the context of this course that my coteacher, who had never read *Clarissa* before, interrogated Richardson's novel as an anthropologist might, asking about Clarissa as a member of her generational cohort, as a food producer, as a link in a female lineage, as the reproducer of the next generation, and so on. She queried the implicit system of kinship in the novel to understand the power relations among characters, posing questions that I had never thought to ask before. These questions led me to new observations about this profound book and revealed new areas of coherence and resonance.

At the most basic level, the opening volume depicts a family determined to marry its daughter to a suitor she despises. From the insistent pressure brought to bear on her, despite her reiterated resistance, it appears that females in this society were not altogether powerless—at least not in ideology—for Clarissa says, "[A]lthough I am to be treated by my brother and, through his instigations, by my papa, as a slave in this point, and not as a daughter, yet my mind is not that of a slave" (111). To be a "daughter," according to this rhetoric, was not to be a "slave"—and vice versa. Yet in the terms of the novel, and certainly to Clarissa's obedient mind, this daughter *was* understood to be the property of her father. "I will be obeyed" (64), thunders Mr. Harlowe again and again in his "big voice," his "terrible voice" (60).[1] And Clarissa pays the ultimate price for disobeying him.

In traditional societies, according to Claude Lévi-Strauss, among others, the exchange of women was meant to forestall violence, whether by guaranteeing military protection, cementing peace treaties, or creating alliances between clans. Giving one's daughter in marriage was a political pledge of good faith; she became a hostage to one's peaceful intentions. It was precisely because she carried the clan's blood in her veins that a daughter could function as a kind of voucher in such exchanges. Not that the acquisitive Harlowes urge Clarissa to marry Solmes for this reason. Their motivation, in addition to placating her brother's and sister's envy and spite, comes from what Solmes has offered to give the Harlowe family in the marriage settlements if there are no children: his considerable property, contiguous to the Harlowe estate.

But Clarissa does function as a propitiatory offering—the kind of offering that Lévi-Strauss had in mind—when Mrs. Harlowe asks her to maintain her correspondence with Lovelace for the sake of family peace, to pacify him and to prevent him from responding with physical force to the provocative gestures of James Harlowe, Jr. Clarissa begins her correspondence with Lovelace "with general approbation" (47), but she continues it to keep the peace, to maintain the balance of power between the two families, and to ensure that their individual male representatives will not fight a duel and spill blood. It is important to remember that Mrs. Harlowe reads these letters fairly late in the game and approves Clarissa's replies to Lovelace's letters even though she hides the fact of the correspondence from Mr. Harlowe.

Fathers and paternal relatives matter in this kin universe more than mothers or maternal relatives. Both of Clarissa's paternal uncles side with her father and brother, with the lineal males rather than with Clarissa, although their styles are very different as Stuber has pointed out ("Clarissa"). Like other "sea-prospered" men, Uncle Antony, who made his fortune in shipping, is violent (291). As Clarissa observes, they are "not used to any but elemental controul, and even ready to buffet that; [they] bluster often as violently as the Winds they are accustomed to be angry at" (291). Uncle John, on the other hand, whose wealth comes from mining, uses guileful affection to dig deep into Clarissa's heart and soften her up for her interview with Solmes. Clarissa explains that these uncles have determined to remain single and to funnel their wealth to her brother, James, who, it is hoped, will stand for Parliament as a large landowner and someday earn a peerage. The bachelor uncles do not procreate; the relatively new capitalist enterprises in which they make their fortunes—merchant ships and coal mines—are represented as sterile. Only the precapitalist form of wealth—the landed estate of Mr. Harlowe—is fruitful; only he among his brothers has children.

Clarissa's maternal relatives—the kin most responsible for protecting female offspring in many traditional societies—sympathize with Clarissa, although they seem unable to do anything to help her. Mrs. Harlowe has almost no leverage with Mrs. Harlowe, despite the considerable fortune that she brought to him. Mr. Harlowe's unyielding disposition is explained by the constant pain his gout causes him. Mrs. Harlowe's legal existence as a *feme covert* is represented by her extreme ineffectuality in the face of her son and husband's determination to appropriate Clarissa's inheritance and to make her marry whom they will. Richardson invents a financial obligation to explain the powerlessness of Mrs. Harlowe's relatives, although the diminished rights of mothers and of maternal relatives over the persons and property of children is a fact of legal history that needs no objective correlative.[2] Clarissa's brother, James, has paid off a mortgage on part of Mr. Hervey's estate (Clarissa's mother's sister's husband), which has put the Herveys in debt to him. Anna Howe observes that this is "a small favour . . . from kindred to kindred: but such a one, it is plain, as has laid the whole family of the Herveys under obligation to the ungenerous lender, who has treated him, and her aunt too (as Miss Dolly Hervey has privately complained) with less ceremony ever since" (212). Like Mr. Harlowe's gout, that constant irritation that keeps his wife cowed and obedient, this debt is a plot device to explain changed family dynamics in a society affected by the drive to accumulate.

It is no coincidence that Cousin Morden, Clarissa's ultimate defender and trustee of her grandfather's will, a maternal relative, is sojourning in Italy, a country coded female in much eighteenth-century English fiction. Everyone expects Cousin Morden to save Clarissa from the greed of her paternal relatives on his return. Indeed, their pressure to marry her is geared to his imminent arrival. As Clarissa tells Anna, her brother is "continually buzzing in my father's ears that my cousin Morden would soon arrive, and then would insist upon giving me possession of my grandfather's estate, in pursuance of the will, which would render me independent of my father" (167–68).

In a cognatic, bilateral kinship system such as had always been practiced in English society, inheritance and derivation are traced through both maternal and paternal lines. One consequence of this kin system is that siblings often have a special closeness because they alone share identical relatives through both the mother and the father. Analyzing kin relations in the Harlowe family reveals a number of distortions of this traditional English bilateral system caused, in part, by the (relatively) new family strategies to accumulate and concentrate capital and property in the male line. To begin with, the sibling identity of this traditional kin system has been undermined by competition for family resources. Clarissa's brother, James, resents Clarissa's inheritance of their grandfather's estate, which, as she puts it, "lopped off one branch of my brother's expectations" (77). He had expected to inherit all the Harlowe property—and with reason. For although female offspring could still technically inherit property in England, and certainly had in the past, by the time Richardson wrote *Clarissa* it was increasingly common to leave land to sons and a single lump sum to daughters, either to be used as a dowry or to be invested for a maintenance if they did not marry. Although grandfather Harlowe's will clearly stipulated that his estate was to go to Clarissa and requested expressly that no one impugn or contest that bequest, her uncle Antony warned her that "the will *could* be set aside, and *should*" (60) if she tried to claim her inheritance. That is, leaving such an estate to a female in a family with a son was unusual enough to ensure that law courts would be ready to find the anomaly illegal.

The above-mentioned powerlessness of Clarissa's mother and of maternal relatives is another example of the distortion of bilateral cognatic kinship by the relatively new forces of capital accumulation. That Richardson invents an intra-familial debt, as well as Mr. Harlowe's gout, to explain this powerlessness shows the residual expectation that mothers and maternal relatives could—and often did—weigh in on decisions concerning daughters. But in this family focused on enlarging their estate and settling it on their son, the mother and her family count for very little.

The most telling distortion of traditional bilateral kin relations in *Clarissa*, however, is the importance of James Harlowe, Jr., relative to his two sisters and even his father. The superiority of the older sister, Arabella, to the younger one, Clarissa, reasonably enough determined by age, is almost entirely overshadowed by this extreme gender preference. As early as her fourth letter to Anna Howe, Clarissa remarks on her brother's unprecedented power in the family hierarchy. On returning from inspecting his estates in Scotland and Yorkshire (property left to him by a generous godmother), James thanks his father for waiting to consult him about Lovelace's suit "as a superior would do when he commended an inferior for having well performed his duty in his absence" (48). This distortion of intergenerational relations as well as cross-gender relations is caused by the combined effects of primogeniture and strict settlement, whose result was to settle the family wealth on the firstborn son when he reached his majority and to reduce the father's claims to a life tenancy in the estate. As Clarissa explains her brother to Anna Howe, "Possessing everything, he has the vice of age mingled with the ambition of youth" (55). Many estate owners in the late seventeenth and early eighteenth centuries did object to the way this legal arrangement skewed father-son relations and refused to succumb to the fashion—but not the Harlowes. Clarissa reports James's smug remark "[t]hat his grandfather and uncles were his stewards: that no man ever had better; that daughters were but encumbrances and drawbacks upon a family" (77). She observes resentfully to Anna Howe that, "previous to every resolution taken by his superiors, whose will ought to be his," they ask, "How will my *son*, how will my *nephew*, take this or that measure? What will *he* say to it? Let us "consult" *him* about it" (54). Clarissa tries repeatedly to reassert an earlier, more natural family dynamic, to return family relations to what they were before perverted by acquisitiveness and her brother's will to power. She reminds her parents of their moral authority over their firstborn son and insists to her brother that he is her sibling and peer and not her superior. He has "no more right to control me than I have to control him" (307), she writes to Anna. "[Y]ou are *only* my brother," she keeps telling him (57).

Richardson was born about the time that the strict settlement was first invented; he was nine years old when the Bank of England was established. In his lifetime he saw the beginnings of institutionalized capitalism in England and its effects on human relations. Comparing a traditional bilateral cognatic kin system with relations in the Harlowe family—a comparison made by parsing maternal and paternal lineages; gendered inheritance patterns; and relationships between siblings, parents and children, uncles and aunts (brothers and sisters of the previous generation)—reveals one possible configuration of these effects. Although Clarissa claims that "never was there a family more united in its different branches than ours" (56), the fissures are there, right beneath the surface, waiting to crack open as soon as anyone resists the family's redefined raison d'être: not to share resources among its members but to hoard an ever greater estate for the next male heir in order to guarantee this nouveau riche family a higher position in the new dispensation based on class rather than status. Richardson, a man who was born to an earlier time and whose identification with women was unusually strong, must have felt the tragedy of these changes, and represented them in, among other things, the kin relations of his great novel.

Students taking graduate consortium courses are drawn from the graduate programs of six institutions in the Boston area and specialize in a variety of subjects. They thus approach the materials of a course like Narratives of Kinship in Industrializing Society from the perspectives of students working in subjects such as history or political science or Latin American literature or nineteenth-century French art. In spring 1994 a South African graduate student named Shamim Meer from MIT's Department of Urban Studies and Planning had enrolled in the course. It was May 1994, and the African National Congress (ANC) had just been elected by a landslide to jubilant international applause in the first free and equal election ever to be held in South Africa. Meer, a longtime activist, was about to return to her country to work with the newly elected ANC on land redistribution policies; she was concerned about ensuring rural women's access to land for subsistence food production. Her final paper, presented in the last week of class, was an analysis of the place of gender and the role of women in industrializing economies—complete with policy recommendations for distributing land among rural women in South Africa. It was an electrifying moment because we all felt that our grasp of social anthropology and our literary critical capacities were contributing to the world in a way that was not merely academic. *Clarissa* had helped us all to understand how existing land redistribution policies might not protect rural African women in the new economy.

Meer explained that under the then existing South African legal system, only married African women could own land. They could not pass on land to their unmarried daughters if their husbands predeceased them; if they were widowed, their land reverted to tribal ownership, which was in reality ownership by tribal chiefs. These modern legalisms were embedded in a traditional kinship system that protected, rather than curtailed, women's access to subsistence agriculture. That is, tribal ownership had been a system that protected the use rights of lineage women. Our class had studied the impact of commercial agriculture on developing economies and in particular on women. Even in *Clarissa* we had seen trace elements of gendered land-based subsistence economies in the references to the "dairy house" (66) and the poultry that Clarissa inherits from her grandfather (56). These subsistence economies, occasionally extended for local markets, had been in Richardson's time traditionally female domains, predating the eighteenth-century parliamentary acts that enclosed common land for private ownership. Symbolically, the female substances produced by these particular economies on common land—milk and eggs—reinforced the historical reality that dairying and raising poultry had traditionally been women's activities.[3]

In her presentation Meer emphasized the need to safeguard rural African women's use rights in whatever land redistribution policy evolved in South Africa. She wanted to try to reproduce the inalienable use rights of lineage wives and children in tribal lands that had operated in many traditional African societies. So long as women could grow food on commonly owned land, no one would starve. Everyone in that room was thrilled to extrapolate the historical lessons we had learned about gender, ownership, and commercial economies to a new and idealistic political situation. Nearly two hundred and fifty years later, *Clarissa* was deeply relevant to a political situation halfway around the world.

One final note about pedagogy: to fully appreciate Richardson's masterpiece, one has to live with *Clarissa* for a long time. That is one effect of its length: we come to empathize with Clarissa because we share her consciousness, her vocabulary, her plight long enough for them to really sink in. Even students from other disciplines, unused to reading eighteenth-century fiction, came to feel her dilemma most poignantly by immersing themselves in the unabridged text. A graduate student in sociology told us that she became so involved in Clarissa's tragedy while reading the book that she did not get out of bed for two days. Our students—not to mention our world—need that kind of practice with the empathetic imagination; they need the experience of giving over to another's sorrows. Reading the unabridged *Clarissa* can be, in that sense, an education all by itself.

NOTES

[1]This observation about Mr. Harlowe's loud "voice of authority" comes from Florian Stuber's unpublished typescript "Clarissa and Her World." Stuber, a brilliant reader of Richardson, died 11 September 1997, to our continuing loss. Terry Castle's *Clarissa's Ciphers* also observes the way Clarissa's speech is stymied, interrupted, and overpowered by her family. See the chapter "Interrupting 'Miss Clary'" (57–80).

[2]See ch. 8, "The Importance of Aunts," in Perry, *Novel Relations*.

[3]See Perry, *Novel Relations*, ch. 1, "The Great Disinheritance."

Teaching Space in *Sir Charles Grandison*

Cynthia Wall

My recent experience teaching *Sir Charles Grandison* in a graduate seminar on space and description in eighteenth-century poetry and prose was—I'll have to admit—unexpectedly successful. The seminar was called The Poetics of Space, and a general knowledge of eighteenth-century literature was presumed. We looked at (rather than read closely) a wide range of texts—the poetry of Alexander Pope and Mary Leapor, Jonathan Swift and Anna Seward, James Thomson and Ann Yearsley, as well as the prose fiction of John Bunyan, Eliza Haywood, Daniel Defoe, Samuel Richardson, Ann Radcliffe, and Walter Scott—to see how the genres of poetry and novels developed their attention to interior space and domestic detail over the course of the century. (I could imagine using the same teaching approaches with far fewer texts in a less-specialized or lower-level course.) *Sir Charles Grandison* was central, both in the course and for understanding the changing attitudes toward spatial detail in the eighteenth century, as I argue here. And one thing I discovered with delight was that this experience with the least-known, least-taught of Richardson's novels suggested new ways of teaching Richardson in particular and the eighteenth-century novel more generally—in any kind or level of course. The emphasis on spatial detail helped crucially; as Samuel Johnson said about *Clarissa*, if you read for the "story" you would hang yourself (qtd. in Boswell 480), and I always prefer to think in terms of immersion rather than progress or linearity when teaching Richardson. We move down into his worlds and stay there awhile. As one student put it, "The story slips by like scenery on the banks as I drift down a slow-moving river."[1] But the "scenery" is for the most part—and most distinctively—indoors.

Sir Charles Grandison (1753–54) is one of the first English novels that describes at length and with particular detail the interiors of houses. Harriet Byron's (and Lucy Selby's) description of Grandison Hall is the most prominent example, late as it is (in Richardson's vol. 7, letters 5 and 6 in particular), and seems to be lifted primarily[2] from the traditions of the country-house poems, guides, and architectural treatises, which see (or want to see) the master emblematized: "The gardens and lawn seem from the windows of this spacious house to be as boundless as the mind of the owner, and as free and open as his countenance" (3: 272).[3] But more interesting—and more innovative—is Harriet as describer and Sir Charles as spatial negotiator. Harriet is always profoundly interested in her own spaces, and no space gets described until she possesses it (and defines herself by it) in some way or another. Sir Charles, however, *manages* space. He moves himself and others into specific places and positions within rooms and thus creates different social orders, different axes of power. In the particular textual space of this essay I look briefly at the history of spatial description to contextualize its remarkable presence in *Sir Charles Grandison*. I assemble a variety of the students' weekly interpretive commentaries on the functions of description and kinds of spaces in *Sir Charles Grandison*, which I hope will be useful for thinking about Richardson and the eighteenth-century novel more generally.

When Harriet Byron, as Lady Grandison, first arrives in great triumph at Grandison Hall, she promptly informs her grandmamma and extended family exactly what it looks like in almost every detail, adding (as if to share the responsibility for her descriptiveness):

> It is no news to you, madam, that Sir Charles shews a great regard to every thing, place, and disposition, that was his father's; and not absolutely inconvenient, and inconsistent with the alterations he has thought necessary to make: And which Dr. Bartlett praises highly, and promises to *particularize* to me. (3: 271–72; my emphasis)

And great particularization ensues: the drawing room, called "the Lady's," is "elegantly furnished. It is hung with a light green velvet, delicately ornamented; the chairs of the same; the frames of them gilt; as is the frame of a noble cabinet in it" (3: 269). She continues, entranced, with details about the fabrics in the dining room, the chairs in the bedchamber, the portraits and furniture (272). But Harriet's extended descriptions have not been a favorite item with readers and critics. Malcolm Kelsall, in *The Great Good Place*, remarks:

> The meticulous particularity of [Richardson's] description of his "good man's house" in a long series of letters in his seventh volume provides a veritable checklist of desirable features given local habitation and a name. It runs the risk, however, of making the ideal ridiculous by too much detail. Richardson rarely knows when to stop. (94)

Kelsall's criticism falls tidily into a long historical tradition of description—in particular, minute spatial description—as aesthetic anathema.

One of the problems is that description historically behaved as a sort of hired hand; it was not genteel. It was not even "hired," according to Gérard Genette; description was

> quite naturally *ancilla narrationis,* the ever-necessary, ever-submissive, never-emancipated slave. There are narrative genres, such as the epic, the tale, the novella, the novel, in which description can occupy a very large place, even in terms of sheer quantity the larger place, without ceasing to be, by its very vocation, a mere auxiliary of the narrative.   (134)

Description focused on surfaces—Aristotelian accidentals rather than universals, Johnsonian tulip streaks rather than tulipness. Until the middle of the eighteenth century, spatial description primarily served nonliterary (social, economic, military, historical, scientific) ends and was on par with lists and other useful things. And in an aristocratically centered world, what is useful is rarely genteel. Jean François Marmontel had complained, "What we call today, in Poetry, the descriptive genre was not known by the Ancients. It is a modern invention, of which, it seems to me, neither reason nor taste approve" (qtd. in Hamon 8).

By the end of the eighteenth century, however, the arguments changed. As Thomas Gray insisted, "Circumstance ever was, and ever will be, the life and the essence both of nature and of poetry" (qtd. in Clutton-Brock 96). Hugh Blair thought that the greatest art of description lay in the selection of circumstances and the particularization of the object: "No description, that rests in Generals, can be good. For we can conceive nothing clearly in the abstract; all distinct ideas are formed upon particulars" (Blair 174). By the nineteenth century, vivid, detailed description is everywhere in novels—space is fully filled in, *bursting,* in Benjamin Disraeli and Charles Dickens. Rather than ancillary, it becomes essential, expected, inwoven.

Richardson's three novels conveniently encapsulate this conceptual and rhetorical shift—this gentrification of description. The spatial rhetoric of *Pamela* is much like that of Bunyan, Defoe, and Haywood: specific interior details appear precisely—and more or less in isolation—when they are needed, instead of being presented as connected visual wholes. Windows, closets, and wainscottings emerge when jumped out of, hidden in, or fainted against, and not a moment sooner. Pamela's first impressions of Mr. B.'s Lincolnshire estate are vaguely Popean—and vague: "About eight at night we entered the court-yard of this handsome, large, old, lonely mansion, that looked to me then, with all its brown nodding horrors of lofty elms and pines about it, as if built for solitude and mischief" (*Pamela* [ed. Sabor] 146). Space is intermittently perceptible. *Clarissa* is a bit different. Both at Harlowe Place and in London Clarissa's perspective is imprisoned, and she imperfectly apprehends spaces beyond her immediate boundaries; thus she needs to interpret motives, events, and possibilities by deciphering the sounds that human beings make in architectural spaces. In different ways each of the characters moves in spaces that seem clearly defined and understood—the father and brother issuing orders from *below stairs*, the lover plotting in the *next room*, the best friend reading helplessly *at home*, the aunt and mother shrinking into the *window*—but the spaces are all oriented toward the location of Clarissa, their boundaries converge on hers, she defines theirs.[4]

In *Sir Charles Grandison*, the boundaries—Harriet's, at least—become very clear; implicit spaces become articulated. Harriet gives us detailed, guidebook-like descriptions of many architectural interiors—but they are always her own: "At our alighting [at Grandison Hall], Sir Charles clasping me in his arms, I congratulate you, my dearest life, said he, on your entrance into *your own* house" (3: 269). When they enter the drawing room, "called, The Lady's" (Sir Charles's mother's), Sir Charles announces: "The whole house, my dear, said he, and every person and thing belonging to it, is yours: But this apartment is more particularly so. Let what is amiss in it, be altered as you would have it." Harriet responds, "O Sir! grasping his presenting hand between both mine, was all I could say" (269). But of course that's not all she could say; this is precisely where she launches in. We still witness a hierarchy of description here; Cousin Lucy describes the gardens and Harriet takes over the interior. But this is an inverted hierarchy: Harriet's depiction of interior space is in fact an act of gentrification, appropriating the tradition of landscape poetry by bringing description more fully and visibly inside the house, inside the novel.

In this graduate seminar, everyone was required to submit at least ten one-page analytical commentaries on texts—close readings of a passage, a phenomenon, an oddity. Students were allowed to develop themes throughout the commentaries, to write more than one commentary on a single text, and in general to use the commentaries to focus their thinking around their own conceptual or research interests. Neil Hultgren, for example, developed some remarkable observations on *Sir Charles Grandison*; from him I learned that Sir Charles, perhaps because of his rank and gender, but certainly because of his nature, has a relation to space that's different from Harriet's. He doesn't describe it; he creates and defines it. Hultgren focused on the scene in which Sir Charles invites Mrs. Oldham, his sisters' former governess and their father's mistress, to be present for the breaking of the seals of Sir Thomas's estate in Essex. To emphasize Sir Charles's "proxemic politeness," Richardson contrasts Sir Charles's actions with those of his sister through the details of the room and Sir Charles's organization of its spaces. Mrs. Oldham was a lady (or at least a woman of "fine qualities") and an "œconomist," adept at managing the house and its funds (3: 366). She was therefore presumably the mistress in many senses of the rooms she occupied. Nonetheless, before Sir Charles enters the scene, his sisters manage very effectively to alienate her from her own space: Mrs. Oldham "stood, as well as she could stand" and "leaned against the tapestry-hung wall" after entering the room with the sisters (3: 362). Although, as Jocelyn Harris's note implies, a tapestry-hung wall probably indicates a damp wall (3: 487n), Charlotte and Caroline "asked her not to sit down, tho' they saw the terror she was in: And that she had the modesty to forbear sitting in their presence" (3: 363). But as Hultgren notes:

> Sir Charles's arrival ends Mrs. Oldham's domestic torture: the best of men both leads the woman to a "chair not distant" from the sisters (the use of "not distant" rather than "close" reflects the corrective aspect of his action) and seats himself between the two parties [3: 364]. He places Mrs. Oldham at the eye level of the women and within a comfortable range. When she bursts into tears, Sir Charles uses the picture on the wall not as a torture device (like the tapestry), but as a tactful gesture [364]. His motion for chocolate, while still "employment" that will have Mrs. Oldham "direct the maid," actually restores Mrs. Oldham to her domestic space, acknowledging that she knew "best where every-thing was" and temporarily relieving her from the stressful scene [365]. Although Sir Charles selectively regards Mrs. Oldham as an oeconomist (it was "the only light in which this pious son was then willing to consider her"), he does everything in his power to restore her to harmony with the home for which she is responsible [365].

Sir Charles's small acts of spatialized courtesy in this room prefigure his larger generosity in securing Mrs. Oldham's rights to her money and possessions and confirm his heroism in Harriet's eyes in yet another dimension—as Hultgren says, "when he is simply asking someone to take a seat."

Discussing description and space in *Sir Charles Grandison* proved remarkably profitable.[5] Issues of public and private space get interestingly entangled in this text. As Hallie Smith commented:

> Within London, the Reeves's residence would seem to be a private space, but Harriet feels encroached upon in nearly every room; she attempts to overcome and rectify moral ambiguities and inappropriate encounters in public and semi-public space by constantly creating miniature versions of a more private space, the family.[6]

Smith goes on to identify Harriet's predilection for appointing acquaintances to be her new family members as one instance of redefining boundaries and her inconsistencies about her public appearances as another:

> Why has she come all the way to London only to stay in her room writing letters? It seems she's overwhelmed by the "publicity" she receives. The Arcadian princess dress turns out to be exactly what Harriet had dreaded;

because it is silver and spangled and very conspicuous, wearing it removes her sense of privacy and modesty. She closes the curtains to her chair on the way home because of the dress—and her need for privacy partially enables her captors. She's constantly concerned with the impression the dress creates, even in the midst of her kidnaping. She never fails to quote her complimenters even as they torment her.

As Harriet's elaborate description (publication, in a way) of her very conspicuous costume suggests, she is deeply, if ambivalently, attracted to the public life of London, confessing to Lucy that her "present reluctance to go [out] so very often, must not be overcome, as it possibly would be too easily done, were I to give way to temptation" (3: 91).

Other descriptions by and of Harriet occupy suggestive positions in this novel. In general, people as well as places were becoming more textually visible to the reader by the middle of the eighteenth century. We studied Greville's many-paragraphed description of Harriet's person (shape, complexion, forehead, face, neck, cheek, mouth, nose, eyes, hair, neck again, arm, hands, fingers [1: 10–13]) not only in terms of the traditional blazon but also as a rhetorical strategy that, like the descriptions by other characters of Clarissa, would seem to allow Harriet modestly to escape the problems of Pamela, who had to record all praises of her by herself. Yet Harriet doesn't catch the ball: she invents descriptions of herself by other people (1: 68–72) and admits she has a tendency to repeat praises of herself (1: 239). She also manages to describe other women to her own distinct advantage (1: 42, 59). Physical descriptions, whether of self or others, are themselves descriptive acts, revealing to the reader through the choices of word and tone and topic as much perhaps about the descriptor as about the described.

Where people stand or sit in various rooms in literature can supply a way of reading relations of power or vulnerability, incoherence or expressiveness. Narrative description creates the spaces and highlights the implications of narrative action. I outline a graduate seminar in this essay, but the issues are equally appropriate to and exciting for undergraduate courses. Asking students to describe descriptions—to pay attention to how authors construct rooms and position their characters in them—opens up galleries of conceptual space, so to speak. And historically, Richardson's novels in general—and *Sir Charles Grandison* in particular—let us watch up close the now familiar feature of detailed spatial description move slowly but steadily inside the home, settle in, and make itself a cup of tea.

NOTES

[1]Kristin Jensen, commentary on 2 April 2001 for the course Poetics of Space, Prose of Things at the University of Virginia.

[2]Although, as Jocelyn Harris notes of the description of the gardens and orchards laid out by Sir Thomas, who had "a poetical, and, consequently, a fanciful taste" (3: 273), the design was "a significantly close copy of God's landscaping in Eden (*Paradise Lost*, 4: 139–49)" (3: 509).

[3]Harris's, Oxford edition divides the novel into three "parts." Citations in this essay refer to Harris's part numbers, not to Richardson's original volume numbers.

[4]I have dwelt on the spatial implications of *Clarissa* more generally in "The Spaces of *Clarissa* in Text and Film," from which this paragraph is adapted.

[5]Other students considered the textual space of Harriet's letters, the description of Sir Charles's treatment of animals, and the gothic aspects of the spaces produced and occupied by the Italians.

[6]Hallie Smith, 5 April 2001.

Students in the Cedar Parlor: How and Why to Teach *Sir Charles Grandison* in the Undergraduate Classroom

Teri Ann Doerksen

I began my career at a small liberal arts college that allowed a great deal of leeway in developing syllabi and course materials. This freedom encouraged classroom innovation and the inclusion of texts not always found in an undergraduate curriculum. A professor with a particular enthusiasm could therefore try to inspire similar enthusiasm in his or her students. I introduced Richardson's novels successfully at several levels in my courses: *Clarissa*, in either George Sherburne's abridgment or my own redactions from the Penguin edition, became a key text in the *Beowulf*-to-Samuel Johnson survey for freshmen and sophomores, and *Pamela* was soon a mainstay of The Eighteenth-Century Novel, an upper-division course for majors. Students responded positively and inquired about other works by Richardson. When I was asked to design and teach an eighteenth-century literature course, I considered it an ideal environment to teach *Sir Charles Grandison*, or at least extended selections from it. Still, I hesitated. How would students respond to the internal struggles of the "Good Man" with a divided heart (3: 462), so much more subtle than the external struggles of Richardson's heroines? Would they care about the delicate negotiations between the Protestant and the Catholic, the continental and the insular, that characterize Sir Charles's courtships at home and abroad? How would they react to Richardson's fascination with moral discussion and modeling, which places *Sir Charles Grandison* on the knife's edge between a novel and a conduct book? I find these aspects of the text both absorbing and crucial to my understanding of the eighteenth century and its literature but feared that the students, many of them first- and second-year undergraduates and nonmajors, would find them tedious and inexplicable.

Within the first weeks of the course, it became obvious that *Sir Charles Grandison* would take center stage. I had originally decided to work with *Grandison* in a limited way, using passages from the novel to introduce some general concepts about literature in the eighteenth century. The students were then to read some relatively brief excerpts (totaling 200–300 pages) later in the term. But when I outlined the course, students who had read *Clarissa* with me the previous semester asked if we could read more than I had assigned. Their enthusiasm was contagious, and others in the class backed them up. At their request, I rewrote the syllabus to enlarge the *Grandison* selections and reconfigured early assignments around Grandisonian premises. Assigned reading was roughly chronological, which meant that the main reading of *Grandison*, a text originally published at midpoint of the century, came roughly halfway through the course. I expanded the reading to about 1,000 pages. We read a 700-page abridgment of the Oxford text, edited by Jocelyn Harris, during weeks 7 and 8. The other 300 pages consisted of selections that connected thematically with other assigned texts. We read and discussed at least one of these brief selections almost daily throughout the first half of the term. Since students read a passage from *Grandison* together with another primary text outside class, discussion focused on questions and on comments and connections students made between the texts. After we had read and discussed this substantial portion of *Grandison* mid-semester, the students took over the job of selecting passages and preparing questions for discussion.

As a class, we worked to develop a "cedar-parlor" atmosphere (3: 52), so-called after the intimate space in Harriet Byron's childhood home where important and life-changing conversations often take place. We created a classroom where I read aloud regularly from *Grandison*; where students memorized and recited poetry; and where, eventually, students felt comfortable analyzing and extending the conversations that they had read in Richardson's text. They were enthralled by the debates between characters about women's education, proper moral behavior, and filial responsibility. They often continued their discussions after class was officially over or at lunch. They wanted to understand the relation between Richardson's representation of these debates and the way that Richardson's contemporaries might have understood them. Technically, we were scheduled to discuss *Grandison* for six one-hour class periods, but in essence it became the subtext of almost every class.

Granted, this was not a typical class. I recount this experience not to inspire envy or incredulity but to explain what the experience made possible in less exemplary classes. It helped me reimagine my approach to teaching eighteenth-century literature to undergraduates and had a profound impact on my course planning. I now use *Sir Charles Grandison*, with its models of social and cultural interactions, as a central text, a lens through which students can examine different aspects of literature written in the period. Its model of intelligent conversation, translated into the classroom, allows students both to play a role and to feel that they are a part of the century they are studying. It also offers them an entrée into thoughtful argumentation and careful discussion. At the same time, the wide-ranging discussions in the novel connect with almost every text I have placed on a syllabus and strike sparks that frequently take fire. Even a brief passage, such as Mr. Greville's declaration to Lady Frampton early in the novel that he is now convinced that "women *have* Souls" (1: 13) can inspire a discussion about authorial choice, characterization, culture, and gender that colors an entire term of readings, from *Moll Flanders* to *The Monk*.

Although not all groups of students are as enthusiastic about massive quantities of Richardsonian prose as that first class was (or as I am), students become more and more intrigued as the semester progresses. Many of the pedagogical approaches I use in my classroom, especially early in the term, are designed to lead students to understand some of the ways in which eighteenth-century literature differs from what they have come in contact with. There is no question that students find reading Richardson engaging, but they also find his work to be challenging and occasionally frustrating. In my experience, students find the de-emphasis of plot-based narrative to be the most difficult hurdle to face, followed by the unfamiliar tone and diction of Richardson's writing. I address these difficulties directly, articulating for the students some of the challenges they are likely to face, giving a name to their frustrations, and at the same time suggesting ways to ameliorate those challenges. I address the lack of plot-based narrative, for example, by sharing with them Samuel Johnson's (in)famous claim, as cited in James Boswell's *Life of Johnson*, that "if you were to read Richardson for the story, your impatience would be so much fretted that you would hang yourself" (480). This usually gets a laugh, but it also validates students' frustration with the text and suggests that there is something worthwhile to be gained by reading Richardson for other reasons than the plot.

Next, I draw an analogy between narrative convention and film convention, an area where students are often much more adept. Most students have seen early film or television, where every step in a process had to be reproduced on screen (man puts on hat, opens door, walks down hall, presses button, steps on elevator, stands in elevator, exits elevator, walks out door, enters taxi . . .). They are able to see that current conventions, which skip the intermediary steps (man puts on hat, then is seen in taxi), are less transparent and obvious than they had originally imagined. In short, I ask them to entertain the idea that their expectations about plot-based narrative are no more objectively transparent than film conventions are and that Richardson, like many other authors (and not only in the eighteenth century), requires them to become familiar with a different set of conventions that may eventually seem just as transparent. Tone and diction then become subsets of a larger idea, that as students they have gaps in their understanding for which they are responsible. This small realization has far-reaching ramifications, because if students imagine that the problem lies with Richardson, they perceive themselves as helpless before the text. Conversely, if the problem is a gap in their own experience, they have the power to fill that gap, to learn to be excited by the text and to engage with it.

These exercises provide a starting point for involvement in Richardson's text. As students read, I ask them to take notes. When they become frustrated, they are required to try to solve the problem. Don't understand the word? Look it up and define it in your notes. Don't understand a reference? Look for footnotes; look at context; and, if still in doubt, mark the passage for class discussion. I ask them to pay particular attention to moments where they become bored or itchy because "nothing is happening" and to narrate, in their notes, what is being illuminated in the text at that moment. In general, once they are motivated to become aware of their responses and once they are responsible for attributing their responses to their training rather than to the book, they are able to start talking positively about Richardson's accomplishment. I am very careful when I talk about this process, so that the students never see this assignment as justifying their impulse to kvetch. As a part of the same exercise, I ask students to note moments that spur them to think, infuriate them, strike an emotional or intellectual chord, or remind them of another text we have read. As the semester progresses, students are able to chart their growing expertise by looking at the changing ratio between notes of frustration and notes of engagement.

Classroom discussion mirrors this developing confidence. Students who once relied on me for pearls of wisdom begin to take responsibility for their own intellectual positions and to share them in a thoughtful, considered, but enthusiastic way. Some even role-play, asking themselves how a Richardsonian character would respond to an issue or text. Many are inspired by Charlotte Grandison's witty defiance of convention as well as by the calmly measured tones of Sir Charles or the self-deprecating ingenuity of Harriet Byron. I encourage the identification. Charlotte's rebelliousness makes her popular with undergraduates. Her quickness and willingness to challenge received wisdom make her a good model for scholarly thought.

I also try to model eighteenth-century didactic conversation from the start. The first issue I address in any eighteenth-century literature course is the definition of literature. How did readers and writers understand the term then, and how do we understand it now? I begin with an analogy, comparing eighteenth-century literature (defined then more broadly than today as letters or the written word) to an extended conversation carried out through a range of media, from plays, novels, and poetry to sermons, political pamphlets, and conduct books. Like *Grandison*, I explain, eighteenth-century literature is a collection of "letters" written "to the moment" but in dialogue with one another (*Grandison* 1: 4). To illustrate such conversations, I give the students passages spanning the eighteenth century that debate the issue of Protestant convents, including, in chronological order, sections from Mary Astell's *A Serious Proposal to the Ladies*, Alexander Pope's "Eloisa to Abelard," Susanna Centlivre's play *A Bold Stroke for a Wife*, a Swiftian satire of Astell from the *Tatler*, *Sir Charles Grandison* (2: 355), Sarah Scott's *Millenium Hall*, Mary Wollstonecraft's *Vindication of the Rights of Woman*, and Ann Radcliffe's *The Romance of the Forest* and *The Italian*. Students are quick to note that the handout looks like a conversation in a computer chat room, though written from differing viewpoints and using different literary media. Some authors address each other directly. For instance, Swift is in conversation with Astell (even if the conversation is a bit one-sided), and Scott is clearly following up arguments in Richardson. This exercise works well to introduce the material and provides a foundation for later discussion.

With this activity as an entrance point, I ask students to imagine the classroom as a place where they will be in conversation with one another, using the excerpts they have read as one potential model for their conversation and, as another, the characters in *Grandison*. Many aspects of the course help facilitate a sense of the cedar parlor in the classroom. At least once a week I schedule a "fireplace reading," where the group gathers around to hear me read passages from *Grandison* that comment on or counterbalance issues from the other literary works we discuss. As the course progresses, the students again take over the responsibility for finding and introducing passages. They then engage in conversation about the connections between the texts. As they become familiar with longer texts about similar issues, they quickly see the connections. They then find themselves revisiting the positions of Richardson's characters as a way of constructing their own informed critical responses. For example, the class sets Jonathan Swift's *The Battle of the Books* alongside Harriet Byron's account of a lengthy discussion with several learned men, in which she declares a position on the education appropriate to men and women. She also addresses what one of her companions calls the "competition set on foot between the learning of the an[c]ients and the moderns, [which] has been the subject of debate among the learned in the latter end of the last century" (1: 53). When pressed, Miss Byron admits that she has read *The Battle of the Books*. Suddenly, students start asking questions, trying to figure out what aspects of Swift's work show up in the discussion and what Miss Byron's take on his work might be. This juxtaposition of Richardson and Swift also introduces a discussion of historicity, because students want to know how much time has passed between the writing of the two texts and what other kinds of writings or events might affect the way that Richardson, through the character of Harriet Byron, sees Swift's work. As students entertain such comparisons, *Grandison* moves to the center of the syllabus. Grandisonian didactic conversation becomes a guiding metaphor in the course.

Other assignments are similarly designed to make the classroom into a community of discussion, debate, and shared scholarship. Building from an awakening student interest in eighteenth-century history and culture, I assign brief research presentations to contextualize our materials. Twice during the term I schedule recitations for which students have to entertain the class by memorizing and reciting a poem. They then initiate a discussion about it in the light of our shared understanding of the eighteenth century. Toward the end of the term, I require each student to read a full-length critical text on eighteenth-century literature; to summarize it both in writing and in an oral presentation; to apply its ideas to a book on our reading list not addressed in the text itself; and, finally, to cite their own text and at least two discussed by other class members in a seminar paper. The goal of the assignment is to give students a general understanding of eighteenth-century literary criticism and to enable them as a class to understand broad outlines of critical thought. It also immerses them in a situation where they learn from and debate with one another, just like the characters in *Grandison*.

Classroom discussions further the atmosphere of didactic conversation. My pedagogical methodology is a modified Socratic dialogue, since I intersperse questions, student responses, and occasional five-to-ten-minute prompted minilectures in response to student interest or confusion. This methodology meshes so well with *Grandison* that students often bring up the similarities between our classroom conversations and the debates described by Harriet early in the novel. By the time we begin to read *Grandison* formally, about halfway through the semester, the class has a sense not only of the text but also of its moral debates, the logic behind the detailed conversations, and some of the conventions of its century. With this understanding comes an enthusiasm for Richardson that often surprises us all. By the end of the term, students learn to feel comfortable about extending Richardson's moral and cultural conversations. They feel at home in the cedar parlor.

To return to my original question: how would students respond to the subtle and complex aspects of the text? Sir Charles's struggles with his divided heart have prompted analysis of gender representation in the eighteenth century; cultural research into the origins of the idea that a person should only love once; and some fairly inspired comparisons with Pope's "Eloisa to Abelard," Henry Fielding's *Tom Jones*, and Charlotte Smith's *Emmeline*. The marriage negotiations between Sir Charles and the della Porretta family have spurred students to look for connections between personal narrative and politics in other eighteenth-century texts from Restoration drama to the gothic novel. In addition, they have sparked many productive class discussions about the ways in which British authors before and after Richardson wrote about national and religious identity. The mode of moral discussion at the heart of the novel is often a mystery to my undergraduates, but because they know that eighteenth-century readers found it fascinating, they try to trace connections to the moral didacticism of Daniel Defoe's *Moll Flanders*, the utopian vision of Sarah Scott's *Millenium Hall*, and the conduct-book elements of Frances Burney's *Evelina*.

Thus, placing *Grandison* at the center of the classroom experience has deepened and enriched my students' understanding of the entire century. Any student who understands the intricacies of Sir Charles's and Clementina's varied rationales for marrying or not marrying will understand cultural expectations of gender, political ramifications of religious identity, and eighteenth-century moral impulses. Such an understanding will help the student comprehend Pope's "Essay on Man," Burney's *Cecilia*, or Radcliffe's *Romance of the Forest*, whether by comparison or by contrast. Even a brief discussion of why Richardson's "good women" are physically threatened with acts such as rape and his "good man" faces emotional consequences such as a divided heart illuminates eighteenth-century cultural assumptions in the works of authors from Aphra Behn to Ann Radcliffe.

I offer these suggestions to illustrate the usefulness of Richardson's work, and of *Grandison* in particular, for helping students make the connections among a single, well-crafted, and didactically motivated text; the literature with which it was in conversation; and the literary culture in which it was produced. Whether taught in its entirety or in excerpted form, *Sir Charles Grandison* can be practical and invigorating when assigned as the key text of an undergraduate course in eighteenth-century literature or the eighteenth-century novel. In short, I would argue, a student who is at home in the cedar parlor is in a very important sense at home in eighteenth-century literature.

Sir Charles Grandison, Literary History, and the Philosophy of Enlightenment

David C. Hensley

Terry Eagleton remarked in the early 1980s that "we may now once again be able to read Samuel Richardson" (vii). This insight, however, did not alter the practice of treating Richardson as the author of only *Pamela I* and *Clarissa*. Few scholars had read his third novel, *Sir Charles Grandison*, and fewer still had studied it. Although Eagleton noted *Grandison*'s ideological importance, he did not suggest that it belonged in the curriculum. In fact, like most other critics, he confirmed the nineteenth-century prejudice that the novel was an insufferable bore.

Intrigued by this critical contradiction and prompted by the availability of Jocelyn Harris's edition of *Grandison*, I decided to test the renewal of Richardson's relevance by teaching his most notoriously tedious work. A highly rewarding series of graduate seminars and supervisions beginning in 1989 at McGill University has been the surprising result. My students and I have found *Sir Charles Grandison* not only readable but also eminently teachable.

Richardson often claimed to have written *Grandison* "on purpose to provoke friendly Debate" (*Selected Letters* 315). Declaring that he "designedly" made readers "think now one way, now another, of the very same Characters" (*Selected Letters* 248), he specified various episodes that would complicate and test the reader's appraisal of Charlotte, Clementina, and Harriet. He carried out "Trials of the Readers Judgment, Manners, Taste, Capacity" (*Selected Letters* 315) not only in his personal correspondence but also in social gatherings such as the one depicted in Susanna Highmore's drawing of 1751, reproduced on the cover of the volume, that shows Richardson reading the manuscript of *Grandison* to six friends at his North End house. His apparently disengaged curiosity is enviable. "I have often sat by in Company," he writes, "and been silently pleased with the Opportunity given me, by different Arguers, of looking into the Hearts of some of them, through Windows that at other times have been close shut up" (*Selected Letters* 315–16). Richardson, however, was first and most importantly an animator of argument and only intermittently an auditor and spectator. I would expect today's academic instructors as well as their students to debate *Grandison* as interlocutors and learners, just as my students and I have enjoyed the sociable self-disclosure of this intellectually stimulating process.

I begin where the classroom experience ends by recounting students' final assessments of the courses in which they read *Grandison*. I then outline two different approaches to teaching the novel.

The *"Debate"* in Overview: We Love to Hate Sir Charles

McGill's evaluation forms invited my students to comment on the positive and negative aspects of the *Grandison* seminars. On the positive side, they express decided praise: the *Grandison* courses, they write, were "very interesting"; more specifically, our "interesting reading" was "excellent in class discussion." In these groups of ten to twelve students, as one of them puts it, "everyone was verbal and contributed actively." Such a statement exaggerates only slightly. Most participants seemed pleased to study materials that were culturally remote yet oddly close to their own concerns. Looking back, they express satisfaction with having completed educationally significant work in a communicative setting that some see as echoing the conversational forms and the controversial issues of *Grandison* itself; indeed, they feel they were invited "to investigate areas of study that were of interest to them personally." But their personal interest is inseparable from the ways of talking about the text that they learned from reading it. Although emotional participation is a well-known effect of Richardson's fiction, I had not expected the much-disparaged *Grandison* to be quite so effective as a pedagogical tool.

Even my students' negative comments indicate a real curiosity about unfamiliar features of eighteenth-century life. For example, in reflecting self-consciously on learning and teaching, students request greater clarity of historical explanation while mentioning the benefit of encountering "obscure" learned traditions in a modern context, itself a key pedagogical issue in *Grandison*. Even their most emphatically disapproving response shows them attracted to unfamiliar forms of Enlightenment thought and feeling. To the question, "What do you consider to be the negative aspects of the course?" several of them answered simply, "Sir Charles Grandison!!!" Yet as one of them writes, Richardson's exemplary hero is nothing less than "the good man we love to hate."

My students are well aware that their paradoxical reactions reflect traditional ambivalence about Richardson's last novel. *Grandison* is "very interesting" partly *because* it is "boring," they say. Sir Charles himself epitomizes this paradox. It is clear that Richardson does not chiefly aim to please a reading public of thrill-seeking consumers. Who else, then, could novel readers be, and what is the novel for? At first, the students responded with predictable complaints about "too much reading," and they regarded reading the seven-volume work as an oppressively "voluminous" and "painful" task. But they gradually came to recognize in *Grandison* a fascinating historical and philosophical challenge, "an enriching experience" that required them to make sense of "a social climate" less different from our own world than they had initially imagined. One student expressed a typical sentiment: "I do feel somewhat proud to have completed the most infamously boring novel in English letters (of course, all of us who have read it know this judgment to be false!)." Such an ambivalent tribute and sense of triumph reveal historical as well as aesthetic puzzlement, but students' praise that the process of reading and discussing *Grandison* had intellectual "depth" was theoretically astute.

Ever since the eighteenth century, Richardson has been regarded as the most European and philosophical of British novelists. As the students wrestled with the rhetoric, logic, and conceptual presuppositions of *Grandison*, they rediscovered this effect for themselves. "I am continually impressed by the richness of its formulations," writes one. As a group, they admired Richardson's "intellectually formidable" articulation of issues in "a difficult and profoundly contradictory period." I was delighted by their alertness to "evidence" of intellectual and cultural history and by their readiness to consider Richardson's "reevaluation" of post-Miltonic sentimentalism and post-Lockean philosophy. These two emphases shaped two versions of my seminar, one focused on contextualizing *Grandison* in its literary tradition and the other exploring Richardson's philosophical coordinates.

Two Approaches to Grandison: Milton and Sentimentalism, Locke and Sensibility

"A good Character," remarked Richardson, "is a Gauntlet thrown out" (*Selected Letters* 315). In telling the story of his "good man" Sir Charles, Richardson challenged readers to engage in controversy about everyday feelings and behavior, moral attitudes and social customs.[1] Debate, he believed, becomes instructive if *Grandison* induces readers to judge the motives, views, and conduct of the fictional characters; to refine these judgments through conversation or letter writing; and to use such procedures in interpreting their own experience. But what principles of judgment are the best or most enlightening? Richardson continually poses this question by inviting us to apply Sir Charles's "sentiments" to the consequences of his actions and to compare his criteria of judgment with those of the other figures around him. Richardson certainly supported his hero's views, and yet his third novel also tries to provoke discussion by incorporating statements that run counter to those of his exemplar.

In teaching *Grandison*, I have tried to do justice to the often underestimated dialogism of the text's conceptual and affective alternatives. Thus my two approaches highlight Richardson's built-in conflict of beliefs and styles by emphasizing either literary history or Enlightenment philosophy. These approaches are not mutually exclusive but mutually enhancing. Nevertheless, in a one-semester seminar with only thirteen to fifteen meetings, at least half of them on *Grandison*, I have found it practical to select only one orientation.

Whichever approach I choose, I represent *Grandison* as a valuable literary work as well as an encyclopedic register of historical and theoretical problems. In both versions of the seminar, my agenda is essentially the same in the final seven or eight weeks. However, for the first six or seven weeks I select readings

that promote one or the other of my sets of intellectual-historical contexts, ana-
logues, and concepts as tools for exploring the main text. Of course, *Grandison*
is always on the table, and participants refer to it from the start. But a gradual
buildup to the novel has advantages. One practical suggestion from the course
evaluations was that students should be urged to begin reading *Grandison* before the term commences. Those students who decide to take the course in the
first week of classes, however, should be allowed time for substantial reading
before the detailed in-class analysis of the novel gets under way. As Richardson
repeatedly insisted, every "Episode" in *Grandison* should be understood as part
of the edifying "Design" of "the Whole" (*Grandison* 1: 4). Students will learn
more from one another if they have read as much as possible of the novel before we focus directly on it.

To contextualize *Grandison* in either the literary history or the philosophy of
the period is to expose the ideological roots of eighteenth-century "sensibility."
During the initial six or seven weeks of either version of the seminar, therefore,
while students are reading as far as they can into Richardson's sixteen-hundred-
page narrative, I like to spend at least two sessions asking how *Grandison*, which
is often treated as the founding novel of manners, could have developed out of
the religious, ethical, and representational traditions of the Renaissance and
the seventeenth-century baroque. In both my literary-historical and my philosophical approaches, I introduce the emblems of George Wither and Francis
Quarles as models for John Bunyan's novelistic didacticism in *The Pilgrim's
Progress* (1678), which I ask students to compare with Richardson's revision of
Roger L'Estrange's version of *Aesop's Fables.*[1] To what extent, I ask, do the intent and form of the emblem book anticipate Richardson's challenging decision
to exhibit exemplary exhortation and argument through scenic construction? In
comparing some illustrations for *Pamela* with those for *Grandison*, I invite students to consider how the static conventions of an ancient theological symbol-
ism are related to the representation of motion and emotion. We discuss how
situation and gesture in the illustrations attest to the increasingly secularized
function of the novel. I also ask how Richardson's *Sentiments* (1755), the collection of moral observations and maxims drawn from his three novels, relates to
the usual understanding of sentimentalism in the history of European literature
and philosophy. In what sense could Richardson be seen as "the first sentimen-
talist" (as Leslie Stephen called him [59]) or indeed as sentimental at all?

The next stage in my literary-historical approach is to consider the didactic
model of the conduct book. Through short selections, we look back to Thomas
à Kempis's *Imitation of Christ* (1418) and Baldassare Castiglione's *The Book of
the Courtier* (1528). We also compare Sir Thomas Overbury's Theophrastian
Characters (1614) with the salty secular collection *The Mysteries of Love and
Eloquence* (1658) and contrast these works to Richard Allestree's pious manu-
als *The Whole Duty of Man* (1658) and *The Ladies Calling* (1673) as well as
John Norris's *A Collection of Miscellanies* (1687). The maxims of worldly prudence and Christian civility in the Marquis of Halifax's *The Lady's New-Years*

Gift (1688) afford an apt transition to conduct literature closer to the period of *Grandison's* composition. Among later conduct books I assign passages from Daniel Defoe's *Religious Courtship* (1722) and *A New Family Instructor* (1727), both of which Richardson printed (Sale, *Master Printer* 162–63). I also refer to the didactic portraits in William Law's *A Serious Call to Devout and Holy Life* (1728).

In my opinion, Richardson's single most important literary precursor is John Milton. That most of my students at McGill University are acquainted in advance with *Paradise Lost* means that summaries of *The Doctrine and Discipline of Divorce* (1643) and of relevant passages in *Paradise Lost* (e.g., 3.80–134; 4.1–113; 5.234–45, 520–43; 7.165–73; 9.760–62) can remind them of what is at stake and of Milton's influential role in the construction of moral and affective individualism and the sentimental understanding of gender.

Milton's intellectual contribution to the emergence of sensibility can be highlighted by comparison with Caroline theology, which anchored the practice of casuistry and the theory of love, as Milton's faith also did, in ancient metaphysics, but without his sociopolitical and emotional radicalism. We discuss the claims and metaphors of a dialectical tradition that descends through Neoplatonic Christianity to the seventeenth century, as one can see in the indebtedness of Jeremy Taylor's *The Rule of Conscience* (1660) to the rational method of Platonic dialogue. Likewise, Plato's myth of the Androgyne (22–27) and his ladder of love (44–49) in the *Symposium*, together with Plotinus's influential mystic parable of the two Aphrodites in the *Enneads* (191–201, 622–23), underpin John Norris's "Concerning Platonic Love" (1687) and *The Theory and Regulation of Love* (1688). The words of John Tillotson, cited at the end of the "Concluding Note" to *Grandison* (3: 466), may also be compared with Richardson's adaptation of the idea that divine perfection is the true pattern of "Wedded Love" (*Selected Letters* 208).

My literary-historical lead-up to *Grandison* ends with two seminar sessions on Restoration and early-eighteenth-century drama. I assign two plays for each session and ask the participants to read at least one play a week. To ensure that all the plays are discussed, I divide the seminar into two groups, each of which must report to the other about the play they have read in relation to the other materials assigned. In the first week we read William Wycherley's *The Country Wife* (1675) alongside part of Jeremy Collier's indignant antitheatrical reaction in *A Short View of the Immorality and Profaneness of the English Stage* (1698). We then read William Congreve's suave response to Collier in *The Way of the World* (1700). I schedule two extra hours for screening videotaped performances of both plays. Our second week's work on drama addresses the post-Collier sentimental revision of English theater typified by Colley Cibber's *The Careless Husband* (1705) and Richard Steele's *The Conscious Lovers* (1722). We compare their revisionist attitudes with Joseph Addison on masquerades in the *Spectator* (1: 35–38 [1710]) and the *Guardian* (50–04 [no. 154; 1713]), on dueling in the *Spectator* (1: 416–19 [1710]), and on gender roles in the *Specta-*

tor (4: 24–26; 4: 27–30 [1711]). The contrast between these two weeks' readings points up an ideological shift away from the identification of masculinity with libertinism and femininity with virtue.

The alternative version of my course stresses sentimental philosophy. After two or three weeks of readings in Renaissance and seventeenth-century didacticism, I insert three or four sessions on the Lockean legacy. Selections from John Locke's *Essay concerning Human Understanding* (1690) and *The Reasonableness of Christianity* (1695) help define modern problems of knowledge that destabilize religious certainties. The ensuing sentimentalism of such inquiries as the third Earl of Shaftesbury's *Characteristics* (1711–14) and Adam Smith's *Theory of Moral Sentiments* (1759) forms a project of strenuously optimistic wish fulfillment. It looks back to Neoplatonism in its quasi-magical claims for a sympathy that tries to preserve the "divine analogy" against the internal contradictions and doubts that disrupt its secularized program of reconciliation. Such disruption, typified by the corrosive skepticism of Bernard Mandeville's *The Fable of the Bees* (1705–24), acknowledges the pervasiveness of evil, against which sentimentalism asserts our fortunate Fall. If *Grandison* is considered an allegory of sentimental philosophy, as it often is, then Richardson, like the sentimental philosophers, never succeeds in vindicating the potential purity of the moral will in action. Thus his fiction of post-Lockean sensibility remains a discourse of wish fulfillment that inadvertently undermines any attempt to harmonize public interest with self-interest on behalf of human perfectibility. Either before or after reading Locke, Shaftesbury, Mandeville, and Smith, I would again recommend spending a couple of sessions on drama, which even in its sentimentalized eighteenth-century forms is still haunted by Hobbesian or Mandevillean libertinism, a threat that sentimental philosophy fails to overcome.

"Different Ways of Thinking" about Grandison's *Characters as Interpretive Problems*

Richardson, who wrote that *Grandison* was intended to elicit "different ways of thinking" about "delicate Situations" (*Selected Letters* 311, 283), rightly pointed out that the novel "abounds" with problems for interpretation (*Selected Letters* 296, 311). In keeping with Richardson's theory of the text, the second half of my course proposes problems to explore through the analysis of character.

To open up discussion of Richardson's theory of fiction in *Grandison*, I draw on the novel's preface and "Concluding Note" and his personal correspondence. In the first of two sessions we talk about letter writing as a form of friendship, contextualizing Richardson in intellectual history through definitions of friendship in Cicero, Michel de Montaigne, Francis Bacon, Jeremy Taylor, John Norris, and Joseph Addison. We then examine both the overt and the implicit claims of his epistolary theory of writing "to the *Moment*" (*Grandison* 1: 4). In the second session, we attend to the criterion of candor in relation to the ongoing sincerity crisis epitomized by the Bangorian controversy of 1717–18. The ethical uncertainty of "Bangorian sincerity" permeates all forms of first-person secular narrative as the problem of autobiographical self-justification, to which sentimental sympathy is an inadequate solution, as Harriet Byron's early letters suggest.

Next we track Richardson's reappraisal of the Restoration stage rake as a figure of drastically reduced power and authority, comparing John Greville, Sir Hargrave Pollexfen, and Sir Charles's father Sir Thomas Grandison with their theatrical prototypes. Since all are overshadowed by Richardson's sentimental protagonists, we ask what, in the world of Richardson's "good man," has become of evil, so potently symbolized by Milton's Satan.

Conversely, making Sir Charles a persuasive exemplar of virtue is Richardson's hardest artistic task, and I therefore devote a session to the paradoxes of the "moderate rake" (*Selected Letters* 171), with reference to Steele's *The Christian Hero* (1710). Grandison's "divided Heart," the result of his "supposed double Love" for Harriet and Clementina (*Selected Letters* 254, 264), is a formal problem of Richardson's dramatic narrative, but readers' perennial doubts on this point reflect the intellectual vulnerability of his secular sentimental rewriting of Milton's Christian epic.

Because Harriet Byron is far more interesting than Sir Charles, I devote two further sessions to her. The true subject of the dialectic of love in courtship, she, like Sir Charles, is shaped by Richardson's strained effort to reconcile sentimentalism and evil, to prevent the defeat of pleasure by virtue. Her candor, however, unlike Sir Charles's honorable conscience, cannot save her from the ambivalence of a divided mind. Despite her resolution not to divide heart from hand, this ethical conflict between will and desire proves an emotional ordeal. To enrich this interpretation of Richardson's moral critique of romantic love, I pursue his allusions to Ovid's stories of Tiresias, Narcissus and Echo, and Pygmalion and review Milton's account of the creation of Eve from Eve's and Adam's divergent perspectives (4.449–91, 8.437–559). In a second session about Harriet, I underscore Richardson's Collierite spiritual polemics against the theater. After reading antitheatrical statements from Richardson's *The Apprentice's Vade Mecum* (1733), *A Seasonable Examination of . . . Play-houses* (1735), and *Familiar Letters* (1741), I summarize antitheatrical elements in *Pamela* and *Clarissa* to show that Richardson, like Milton, not only condemns the idolatry of romantic love but also censures the popular discourses of contemplative beauty and the sublime that inform the spectacular logic of theatricality. Harriet's continual embarrassment represents the scandal of bourgeois manners deprived of a morally acceptable aesthetic in the quest for happiness. Her suffering through love cannot sanitize the sentimental project of wish fulfillment. For, despite Richardson's supposed reconciliation of virtue and pleasure, seeking happiness remains uneasily selfish in *Grandison*.

In a class on all the other women in *Grandison*, we discuss Richardson's preoccupation with their excesses. Whether excessively rational, like Miss

Barnevelt; or excessively emotional, like Charlotte Grandison, Emily Jervois, and Lady Olivia; or even more dangerously transgressive through the pathetic "enthusiasm of the Lady Clementina della Porretta," (*Grandison* 2: 220), all the women except Harriet typically lack balance, measure, and harmony. Our discussion of these characters benefits from study of contemporaneous proto-feminist statements produced by the Richardson circle, such as Jane Collier's *Essay on the Art of Ingeniously Tormenting* (1753) and John Duncombe's *The Feminiad* (1754), together with essays from Samuel Johnson's *Rambler* by Richardson (4: 153–59) and by his female friends Hester Mulso (3: 50–56), Catherine Talbot (3: 163–67), and Elizabeth Carter (3: 237–42 and 4: 169–73).

We start our last session by analyzing the novel's final scenes, in which Richardson proposes an affective community of "a family of love" as the sentimental solution to impasses of social experience in both domestic and public life (*Grandison* 1: 133). Considering his censure of the sentimental *"happiness"* (*Grandison* 3: 466)endorsed by Henry Fielding's *Tom Jones* (1749) and his warnings in *Grandison* (as in *Pamela* and *Clarissa*) that "the *best* performances of human creatures will be imperfect" (*Grandison* 3: 466), this ostensible cancellation of *Grandison's* contradictions seems artistically as well as theoretically inconsistent. Still, the contrived synthesis of the novel's ending is a parting provocation to debate, which I try to enliven by assigning Francis Plummer's *A Candid Examination of the History of Sir Charles Grandison* (1754).

When Richardson wrote that he "intended more" in *Grandison* "than what, at first sight, may be thought of, on a cursory reading" (*Selected Letters* 275), he demanded of his contemporaries the meditative attention that would catch the imagination of Jane Austen. Even though such an expectation may seem unrealistic today, I have found that teaching this text can still convince students to take seriously the challenge of evaluating Richardson's characters' psychological and moral nuances. Too few people since the eighteenth century have been able to share this pleasure with other readers of his last and most sociable novel. But the pleasure and instruction can be renewed in the classroom.

NOTE

[1]See Wither's *Collection of Emblemes* (1968 or 1989) and Quarles's *Emblemes* (1991) and *Hieroglyphikes* (1969) for facsimile reproductions that are useful in the classroom. For information on Richardson's edition of *Aesop's Fables*, see Sale (*Bibliographical Record* 3–4 and *Master Printer* 147).

Teaching *Sir Charles Grandison* instead of *Pamela* to Undergraduates

Lisa Zunshine

Having taught the first two volumes of *The History of Sir Charles Grandison* in an upper-division undergraduate seminar on the eighteenth-century novel, I am convinced that *Grandison* is the novel of choice for an instructor who feels that *Clarissa* is too long to tackle in a course alongside a fair selection of other works but believes that the post-*Clarissa* Richardson makes for a more interesting classroom presence than the Richardson of *Pamela*. In what follows, I discuss my experience teaching Richardson's last novel at the University of Kentucky, Lexington, and make a case for *Grandison* as both a viable and exciting alternative to *Pamela* and a default undergraduate offering.

Because throughout my essay I refer to the first two volumes of the novel (or the 465 pages that compose the first part of Jocelyn Harris's three-part Oxford University Press edition of 1972) as "the" *Grandison*, I should start by discussing the pros and cons of the decision not to teach the whole book. First, I have no doubt that reading the novel in its 1,600-page entirety would have left my students with a very different—and richer—view of Richardson's achievement, providing them with a more satisfying sense of closure than would any synopsis of the remaining five volumes (or parts two and three of Harris's edition). At the same time, something should be said for the gratification of having one's students read the remaining 1,135 pages on their own, as several of them did. One student borrowed the rest of *Grandison* and, on finishing it in a week, moved on to reading the unabridged *Clarissa*. Another asked her mother for the whole *Grandison* as a Christmas present. Several students contacted me after the grades were in (at which point they had presumably no reason to impress me with their zeal) and asked me how to order the remaining parts.

I have to pause here and explain that I ordered only the first part of Harris's edition for my class, which also meant that my students paid only one-third of the overall price. Those interested in acquiring the unassigned second and third parts could later contact the printer themselves (steve.williams@stonebow.otago .ac.nz). Indeed, the present situation with the availability of *Grandison* is uniquely favorable for such selective ordering because the novel is being re- produced under license from the Oxford University Press by Otago University Print, which is willing to sell the parts separately. In the hope that that this ar- rangement will last, I appreciate both the prescience of Harris and her original publisher who decided to bring out *Grandison* in three separate volumes, and the flexibility of the Otago UP manager, Steve Williams.

But aside from the satisfaction of having one's students want to finish the novel on their own, is there something particular about the structure of *Gran- dison* that renders the idea of assigning only the first two volumes somehow less pernicious than the idea of assigning the curtailed *Clarissa*? Having successfully taught the unabridged *Clarissa* to Kentucky undergraduates, I shrink from the thought of withholding any part of *Clarissa* from my students. However, the end of the second volume of *Grandison* impresses me as a logical stopping point for an instructor wishing to whet his or her charges' appetites for Richardson while keeping in mind that they still have to read several long novels by other authors. By the end of the second volume, we have lived through Harriet Byron's postmasquerade ordeal and arrived at the point when the phrase "the vile Sir Hargrave Pollexfen" (1: 151) rolls easily off our tongue; we have registered Harriet's metamorphosis from a saucy satirist with a knack for ridiculing other people's self-delusions to a love-sick girl consumed with worry about her imperfections and yet endearingly *"frank"* about her feelings; we have been impressed, humbled, and annoyed by Sir Charles's bravery, endurance, grace, handsomeness, integrity, intellect, popularity, resourcefulness, and self-assurance and by his unwavering beneficence toward horses, servants, tenants, unfaithful stewards, wards, fathers, uncles, sisters, and illegitimate stepbrothers; we have been *"delightfully-scandalized"* by Charlotte's arch remarks and have learned about her and Caroline's cruel treatment at the hands of their *"mistress-keeping"* father; and we have pondered the rhetorical value of italicized words and hyphenated coinages. While the remaining five volumes reinforce these first impressions through a series of compelling vignettes and introduce the controversial topic of a perfect man troublingly in love with two women at once, they do not significantly change what we have learned about the protagonists in the first part. This is why the first 465 pages of the novel could in principle suffice in a course that considers Richardson as only one brilliant novelist in the constellation of talents that we associate with the eighteenth-century novel.

The fifteen-week course that I am describing featured Daniel Defoe's *Moll Flanders*, Henry Fielding's *Tom Jones*, Richardson's *Grandison* (the only novel we did not read in its entirety), Laurence Sterne's *Tristram Shandy*, Frances Burney's *Cecilia*, Ann Radcliffe's *The Italian*, and Jane Austen's *Northanger Abbey*. We met three times a week, and for every class meeting, the students had to read from 80 to 150 pages, averaging 300 pages a week. To ensure that the students stayed on schedule in their reading and remained engaged with the text, I required them to write a series of short papers that called on their knowledge of specific details in the novels. These written assignments, each of them one- to two-pages long, had to be typed and turned in every week (no late or handwritten assignments were accepted). They served as a starting point for our class discussions and—more important—helped the students develop ideas for their longer essays. Instead of grading those assignments, I only marked them with brief comments, occasionally suggesting avenues for further thinking. In the case of *Grandison*, a novel that we read in three weeks, my students wrote short papers on the following topics: female friendships; fallen women; Harriet writes to her Lucy; and, does Harriet change on meeting Sir Charles?

This last was the least successful assignment because, as several students pointed out, the answer was prescripted by the question.

At one point during the semester, I asked my students to fill out an anonymous survey dedicated to *Grandison*, where they reported, among other things, that the practice of writing the short essays enabled them to "get into the novel," which was "important" because they read it "so quickly"; that such exercises were "one of the most rewarding aspects of the text" because they helped students "grapple with the text" and "engage the characters who might seem a little too distant otherwise"; and that the assignments made them "think more about the novel" than they would have if they had "only been reading for pure enjoyment." On a less positive note, one student wrote, "Much as I disliked the book, I liked the writing assignments," especially the one involving impersonating Harriet.

The assignment on Harriet writing to Lucy generated a remarkable series of short essays. It made the students aware of particularities of Richardson's style that they had previously paid little attention to, merely observing that it was "lively" and "funny." I told them to write a letter that Harriet might have sent home after attending the masquerade with Lady Betty and the Reeveses. Because I asked students not to read ahead of the schedule, they did not know that Harriet ends up being abducted by the vile Sir Hargrave Pollexfen. Most of them assumed that the masquerade would be the place where she finally encounters the long-expected hero. Here are several excerpts from their papers:

Letter 23. Miss Byron. To Miss Selby.

My Lucy, in obedience to your injunctions, I will attempt to relate all the particulars of last night's ball. Yet, shall I repeat the compliments without provoking the censure of my uncle? No, I am certain to receive them in his next letter. And how can I give accounts on a new admirer without condemning my sex with those charges of vanity and pride? But do go on, you say. So, I will.

Who do you suppose to be the first person I encountered? That foolish man, Mr. Greville. It seems he thought fit to come so far again into town to ward off his competitors. . . .

. . . All my Lovers (so the Reeveses call them) were to be found at the ball. Yet, Lucy, only one person did I see that I could ever imagine to earn that name from my lips. Oh! His person and his mind, as I well learned from his conversation, seem all too lovely and pure for that Sex. Forgive me, I am too vain to believe only virtuous souls to be found among my sex, am I not? I am. Let my uncle say so. Now however I know virtue is hiding among so many hyenas. But as this letter is long and the particulars of Sir Charles Grandison (for that is his name) are longer, I will break off just here.

(Jaimee Bertram)

My dress . . . just as I had feared, drew the attention of some familiar persons, but not familiar faces. The baronet quickly discovered me under my masque. However, he impressed me with his sprightliness and gentle nature that he possessed while we conversed, which probably was affected by the public. He wore a masque that transformed him into an Ostler, including the speech of that character, which I greatly laughed at.

    . . . Oh how I wished the evening had ended so much sooner on the account of [Mr. Greville's] prying and the several *unagreeable* men that pleaded for my hand.

(Geoffrey G. Young)

The wretched [Sir Hargrave] had carried his ill feelings over a fortnight and made these feelings well known to me at our first possible encounter. What, dear Harriet, did you ever do? you must be asking, my Lucy, and I am obliged to give you the conversation as closely as I will remember it. . . .

    A detail which I must not leave out, dear Lucy, is the costumes of others whom I have related to you in previous letters. Can you even guess what a certain Miss Barnevelt dressed herself as? Yes, she did come in the attire of a *man*, her wishes for one evening becoming true.

(Cecily Galbreath)

Although the students did not anticipate just how frightening Harriet's masquerade adventure would turn out to be, they had registered enough negative vibes in Richardson's account of Harriet's preparation for her Haymarket excursion to know that she would not be able to enjoy it. In fact, one student, Brandon Meier, nicely captured Richardson's didacticism, if not the heroine's actual tone, when he wrote in his letter to Lucy, "My dear Lucy! I have to say the masquerade was as dull as I had previously told you I thought it would be. Of course am I ever wrong about these sorts of things? No, I am Harriet Byron and I am never wrong." Having learned shortly thereafter of Lady Mary Wortley Montagu's sarcastic observation that Harriet might have been carried off by Sir Hargrave in the same manner if she had been going from supper with her Grandmama, my students became attuned to the possibility that Richardson had reimagined several eighteenth-century cultural icons to promote his favorite ideological points. *Grandison's* treatment of masquerade as a place dangerous for virtuous young women thus provided both an ironic sequel to Lady Bellaston's seduction of Tom Jones at a masquerade and a prequel to the ominous skits played out in front of Cecilia during the masked ball at the Harrels.

    Similarly, Richardson's take on dueling provided an important if deeply ambivalent counterpoint to our analysis of the unhappy martial exploits of both Tom Jones and Mortimer Delvile. Sir Charles's refusal to duel when challenged by Sir Hargrave, who is surrounded by his pals, seemed to the class boringly commonsensical until I asked them for a modern equivalent. James Yonts immediately pointed out that we could compare it with the action of a new member of a sport team or a new recruit in the army who refuses to go through some ridiculous, strenuous, or humiliating initiation rite that other members of the team or squad hold sacred and had gone through themselves. Once we envisioned the new guy trying to explain to an increasingly hostile and contemptuous crowd of seasoned athletes or soldiers how unethical, unnecessary, and silly their demands are, the eighteenth-century honor code suddenly came alive in the classroom. We realized that not just anybody would be allowed to turn down the challenge. First, the person refusing to duel would have to prove that he is capable of fighting and not just covering cowardice with noble words about the evils of dueling. Second, it would help if a sterling reputation and a good standing in society preceded the man's refusal and earned him a respectful audience. Third, he would have to be eloquent and self-assured. A person who dares to decry the code of honor thus has to be strong, famous, persuasive, confident, and of the right social class. In other words, that person has to be a Sir Charles Grandison, a realization that subtly undercuts the power of the noble sentiment about the wrongs of dueling. (Just so, Richardson's insistence that only his inimitable Pamela deserved to skyrocket to nobility and that only his nonpareil Clarissa could be forgiven for running away with the rake undercuts the subversive thrust of his previous novels.)

From Richardson's discussion of a perfect hero, we moved on to his view of the perfect heroine. Here we noticed that even if Harriet Byron is "never wrong," as Brandon Meier intuits, Richardson sets careful limits on her agency. To offset the fact that Harriet has potentially more power than even Sir Charles, because her interpretations of events constitute our main source of information, particularly in the first two volumes, Richardson makes sure that Harriet qualifies and indirectly relegates her authorial prerogatives. Hence her frequent interpolations such as, "so my uncle says" (1: 66) or, after she has mimicked the epistolary style of her lesbian acquaintance, Miss Barnevelt, and feels the need to disclaim responsibility for that overenthusiastic parody, "something like this, my Lucy, did Miss Barnevelt once say" (1: 69). In her letter to Lucy, Jaimee Bertram parodied this tendency of Richardson's heroine when she had Harriet interrupt her casual chat with an obligatory qualification: "All my Lovers (so the Reeves call them) were to be found at the ball."

Paradoxically, then, the apparent excess of authorial presence could lead to a radical circumscription of agency. Together we considered the situation of a young man or woman, particularly a woman, coming to the big town for the first time, leaving behind her parents who trust and respect her (as Harriet's surrogate parents do) yet worry about her potential reproductive choices—a scenario that most of my students could immediately relate to. In these circumstances, writing sophisticated and grammatically impeccable letters that report her every move and every thought to the anxious family not only would occupy the time that could otherwise be spent partying but also would evolve into the most effective form of self-chaperoning or self-policing. Sharing those letters later with the devoted sister of her love interest would cement the friendship between the two women and tacitly assure any Charlotte that her future sister-in-law is a "good girl" worthy of the "good man" (note the different meanings of the word *good* when applied to a man and a woman [1: 234, 223]). Our discussion of the epistolary form as a crucial eighteenth-century literary technique was thus informed by the realization that considerations of gender profoundly inform any actual instantiation of this technique. Later in the semester, we returned to this point again, observing Henry Tilney's mock amazement at Catherine Morland's lack of interest in keeping a journal that would allow her "absent cousins to understand the tenour of [her] life in Bath" (Austen, *Northanger Abbey* 24).

The question of who controls the narrative and how the narrative controls the narrator dovetailed with our larger discussion about the author's power over the text (a discussion that we continued later over *Tristram Shandy*). I suggested to my students that Richardson's previous novels had, in a sense, run away from their author. Despite Richardson's efforts to forestall them, *Pamela* generated a series of cynical readings, such as Fielding's *Shamela*. Later, the readers of *Clarissa*, and—most mortifying—the female readers who were Richardson's target audience, actually fell in love with the villainous Lovelace. Early on, I asked my students to pay attention to those moments in *Grandison* that could be understood as Richardson's attempts to prevent any future misinterpretations of his last novel. Having accumulated a list of such moments (for example, the main villain of the novel is about as attractive as a snake) and of the instances in which Richardson failed to keep *Grandison* under his thumb (for example, every topic discussed above), we began to believe that sometimes the novel has to run away from its anxious author. Sometimes the runaway novels kick harder and live longer, however defeated the writer may feel about their unruly tendencies during his or her lifetime.

I have concluded that *The History of Sir Charles Grandison* works extremely well in a course on the eighteenth-century novel because it engages a broad variety of issues that students can both relate to and recognize as constituting the driving energies of other novels of the period. The search for a perfect hero and perfect heroine with all its attendant ironies and ambiguities; the peer pressure and the code of honor; the complexities of female friendships; the relationship between parents and children; the adventures in delayed, relegated, and reasserted narrative authority—all of which *Grandison* deals with in a lively and yet ambivalent manner—render *Grandison* a rewarding choice for the instructor who wants to convey enthusiasm for Richardson to students. We take for granted *Grandison's* status as one of the most influential novels in European literary history, but it is only when our students begin to discuss the connections between Richardson's last work and the novels of Sterne, Burney, Radcliffe, and Austen—and they grasp those connections right away—that we discover the true meaning of that influence.

SURVEY PARTICIPANTS

Janine Barchas, *University of Texas, Austin*
Patricia Brückmann, *Trinity College, University of Toronto*
Helen Deutsch, *University of California, Los Angeles*
Nicky Didicher, *Simon Fraser University*
Teri Ann Doerksen, *Mansfield University of Pennsylvania*
John A. Dussinger, *University of Illinois, Urbana*
Jocelyn Harris, *University of Otago*
David C. Hensley, *McGill University*
Laurie Kaplan, *Goucher College*
Tom Keymer, *Exeter University*
Ann Louise Kibbie, *Bowdoin College*
Elizabeth Kraft, *University of Georgia*
Elizabeth Kubek, *Benedictine University*
Jayne Lewis, *University of California, Irvine*
Oliver Lovesey, *Okanagan University College*
Robert Markley, *University of Illinois, Urbana*
Michael McKeon, *Rutgers University, New Brunswick*
Judith Moore, *University of Alaska, Anchorage*
Mark James Morreale, *Marist College*
Felicity A. Nussbaum, *University of California, Los Angeles*
Ruth Perry, *Massachusetts Institute of Technology*
John Richetti, *University of Pennsylvania*
Albert J. Rivero, *Marquette University*
Peter Sabor, *McGill University*
Kristina Straub, *Carnegie Mellon University*
Cynthia Wall, *University of Virginia*
William B. Warner, *University of California, Santa Barbara*
Jeremy W. Webster, *Ohio University, Athens*
Janet Aikins Yount, *University of New Hampshire*
Lisa Zunshine, *University of Kentucky, Lexington*

NOTES ON CONTRIBUTORS

Janine Barchas is assistant professor of English at the University of Texas, Austin. She is the author of *Graphic Design, Print Culture, and the Eighteenth-Century Novel* (2003), winner of the Book History Prize given by the Society for the History of Authorship, Reading, and Publishing. She is editor of *The Annotations in Lady Bradshaigh's Copy of* Clarissa (1998) as well as the first volume in *Eighteenth-Century British Erotica II* (2004).

Patricia Brückmann is professor emeritus of English at the University of Toronto, Trinity College. She has written *A Manner of Correspondence: A Study of the Scriblerus Club* and articles on Chaucer, More, Pope, Swift, Sterne, Fielding, Richardson, Austen, and Nabokov. She is currently finishing a study of the *Canterbury Tales* and working on recusant authors and on Jacobite drama.

Nicky Didicher is a senior lecturer at Simon Fraser University. She is interested in eighteenth-century fiction, particularly parody, satire, and the relations between maps and texts, and in children's literature, science fiction, and pedagogy. She has published articles on Jonathan Swift, Daniel Defoe, P. L. Travers, Rudyard Kipling and Anne Mc-Caffrey, and pedagogy. Her current work, in the field of scholarship of teaching and learning, concerns blended learning using WebCI in arts classes.

Teri Ann Doerksen is associate professor of English at Mansfield University, where she teaches eighteenth-century literature and the history of the novel. Her publications include "*Sir Charles Grandison*: The Anglican Family and the Admirable Catholic," an essay on the tensions between Anglicanism and Roman Catholicism in Richardson's novel. She is currently working on a book project analyzing political tensions, literature, and national religious identity in eighteenth-century England.

Jocelyn Harris, professor of English at the University of Otago and member of the advisory board of the Cambridge Richardson Project, edited Richardson's *Sir Charles Grandison* (1972), published *Samuel Richardson* (1987) and *Jane Austen's Art of Memory* (1989), and wrote the introduction to volume 1 of Richardson's *Commentary on* Clarissa *1747–65* (1998). She is currently completing a book entitled "Jane Austen's *Persuasion* and the Myth of Limitation."

David C. Hensley is associate professor of English at McGill University. He has published essays on Samuel Richardson's *Clarissa* and the culture of pietism and is writing a book on *Clarissa* as a Behmenist novel that influenced English and German Romanticism. As an editor of The *Clarissa* Project, he is preparing a volume on *Clarissa's* nineteenth-century reception.

Tom Keymer is professor of English at University of Exeter. He is the author of *Richardson's* Clarissa *and the Eighteenth-Century Reader* (1992); *Sterne, the Moderns, and the Novel* (2002); the editor, with Jon Mee, of *The Cambridge Companion to English Literature 1740–1830* (2004); and the general editor, with Peter Sabor, of *The Cambridge Edition of the Works and Correspondence of Samuel Richardson* (forthcoming).

Elizabeth Kraft is professor at the University of Georgia. She is the author of *Character and Consciousness in Eighteenth-Century Comic Fiction* (1992) and *Laurence Sterne Revisited* (1996), the editor of Charlotte Smith's *The Young Philosopher* (1999), the coeditor of two collections of Anna Letitia Barbauld's works (1994 and 2002), and the author of articles on eighteenth-century topics. She is currently working on a book-length study of eighteenth-century women's fiction and the ethics of desire.

Jayne Lewis is professor of English at the University of California, Irvine, where she teaches Restoration and eighteenth-century literature from Milton to Austen. She is the author of *The English Fable: Aesop and Literary Culture in England, 1651–1740* (1996), *Mary Queen of Scots: Romance and Nation* (1999), and *The Trial of Mary Queen of Scots* (1998). She is currently at work on a study of apparitional forms and the invention of atmosphere in England, 1665–1765.

Robert Markley is professor of English at the University of Illinois. He is the author of *Two-Edg'd Weapons: Style and Ideology in the Comedies of Etherege, Wycherley, and Congreve* (1988); *Fallen Languages: Crises of Representation in Newtonian England, 1660-1740* (1993); *Dying Planet: Mars in Science and the Imagination* (2005); and *The Far East and the English Imagination, 1600–1730* (2005). He has written articles in journals such as *Critical Inquiry*, *Genre*, and *Configurations*.

Keith Maslen is an honorary fellow at the English department of the University of Otago. He has coedited *The Bowyer Ledgers: The Printing Accounts of William Bowyer Father and Son* (1991) and *Book and Print in New Zealand: A Guide to Print Culture in Aotearoa* (1997). Other publications include *An Early London Printing House at Work: Studies in the Bowyer Ledgers* (1993) and *Samuel Richardson of London, Printer: A Study of His Printing Based on Ornament Use and Business Accounts* (2001).

Michael McKeon is professor in the English department at Rutgers University, New Brunswick. He has written *Politics and Poetry in Restoration England* (1975), *The Origins of the English Novel, 1600–1740* (1987), and *The Secret History of Domesticity: Public, Private, and the Division of Knowledge* and edited *Theory of the Novel: A Historical Approach* (2000).

Judith Moore is professor of English at the University of Alaska, Anchorage. She is the author of *A Zeal for Responsibility: The Struggle for Professional Nursing in Victorian England, 1868–1883* (1988) and *The Appearance of Truth: The Story of Elizabeth Canning and Eighteenth-Century Narrative* (1994), as well as of several articles on eighteenth-century texts. She is currently working on a study of Samuel Pepys and the contexts of Restoration writing.

Mark James Morreale, lecturer of English and digital library multimedia specialist for the School of Liberal Arts at Marist College, teaches courses in eighteenth-century literature; creative writing; and research methods and hypertext and their scholarly, theoretical, and creative applications. He has contributed to or been a survey participant in two additional volumes to the Approaches to Teaching series.

Felicity A. Nussbaum, professor of English at the University of California, Los Angeles, is the author of *The Limits of the Human: Fictions of Anomaly, Race, and Gender in the Long Eighteenth Century* (2003) and the editor of *The Global Eighteenth Century*

(2003). Her other work includes *The Autobiographical Subject: Gender and Ideology in Eighteenth-Century England* (1989) and *Torrid Zones: Maternity, Sexuality, and Empire* (1995). Her current project is on women in the eighteenth-century theater.

Ruth Perry, past president of the American Society for Eighteenth-Century Studies and founder of the women's studies program at MIT and the Boston Graduate Consortium in Women's Studies, is professor of literature at MIT. She has published on literature and culture in eighteenth-century England. Her most recent book, *Novel Relations: The Transformation of Kinship in England 1748–1818* (2004), owes a great deal to the class described in her essay for this collection.

John Richetti is A. M. Rosenthal Professor of English at the University of Pennsylvania. Among his publications are *Popular Fiction before Richardson: Narrative Patterns 1700–1739* (1969), *Defoe's Narratives: Situations and Structures* (1975), *Philosophical Writing: Locke, Berkeley, Hume* (1983), *The English Novel in History 1700–1789* (1999), and *The Life of Daniel Defoe* (2005). He has edited *The Columbia History of the British Novel* (1994), *The Cambridge Companion of the Eighteenth-Century Novel* (1996), *The Cambridge History of British Literature 1660–1780* (2005), and the Penguin Classics edition of *Robinson Crusoe* (2001).

Peter Sabor is Canada Research Chair in Eighteenth-Century Studies and director of the Burney Centre at McGill University, where he teaches courses on eighteenth-century fiction. His publications include editions of *Pamela*; *Letters and Passages Restored from . . . Clarissa*, and, with Thomas Keymer, *The* Pamela *Controversy*, a six-volume edited collection. Also with Keymer, he is general editor of *The Cambridge Edition of the Works and Correspondence of Samuel Richardson* (forthcoming).

Kristina Straub is professor of literary and cultural studies and associate dean of Humanities and Social Sciences at Carnegie Mellon University, where she teaches eighteenth-century British and gender studies. She is the author of *Divided Fictions*: *Fanny Burney and Feminine Strategy* and *Sexual Suspects: Eighteenth Century Players and Sexual Ideology*. She is the editor of teaching and scholarly editions of eighteenth-century British texts, as well as editor of *Body Guards* with Julia Epstein.

Cynthia Wall is professor of English at the University of Virginia. She is the author of *The Prose of Things: Transformations of Description in the Eighteenth Century* (forthcoming 2006) and *The Literary and Cultural Spaces of Restoration London* (1998) and editor of Pope, Defoe, and Bunyan and of *A Concise Companion to the Restoration and Eighteenth Century, Eighteenth-Century Genre and Culture* (with Dennis Todd [2001]), and *The Bedford Anthology of Eighteenth-Century Literatures in English* (with J. Paul Hunter [forthcoming]).

Jeremy W. Webster is associate professor of English at Ohio University, Athens, where he teaches courses on the history of sexuality, Restoration and eighteenth-century literature, early modern theater, and gay and lesbian literature. He is the author of *Performing Libertinism in Charles II's Court: Politics, Drama, and Sexuality* (2005). He is currently writing on the sexual stereotyping of Jewish men in eighteenth-century British literature.

Janet Aikins Yount is professor and chair of the English department at the University of New Hampshire. She has published on Samuel Richardson, Daniel Defoe, Jonathan

Swift, eighteenth-century drama, and the visual-verbal collaboration between Richardson and the painter and book illustrator Francis Hayman. She is completing a two-volume study of the twentieth-century reception of Richardson's *Clarissa*, to be published as part of The *Clarissa* Project.

Lisa Zunshine is assistant professor of English at the University of Kentucky, Lexington. She is the author of *Bastards and Foundlings: Representations of Illegitimacy in Eighteenth-Century England* (2005) and *Why We Read Fiction: Theory of Mind and the Novel* (2006) and the editor of *Nabokov at the Limits* (1999) and *Philanthropy and Fiction 1698–1818* (2006). Her essays have appeared in *Poetics Today*; *Eighteenth Century: Theory and Interpretation*; *Narrative: Philosophy and Literature*; *Eighteenth-Century Life*; *The Eighteenth-Century Novel*; and *Modern Philology*.

WORKS CITED

Addison, Joseph. *The Guardian*. Ed. John Calhoun Stephens. Lexington: UP of Kentucky, 1982.

———. *The Spectator*. Ed. Donald F. Bond. 5 vols. Oxford: Clarendon, 1965.

Addison, Joseph, and Richard Steele. *The Tatler*. 1709–11. The *Spectator* Project. Ed. Joseph Chaves et al. 20 June 2002. <http://tabula.rutgers.edu/spectator/>. Path: *Tatler* Complete.

Aikins, Janet E. "Pamela's Use of Locke's Words." *Studies in Eighteenth-Century Culture* 25 (1996): 75–97.

———. "Picturing 'Samuel Richardson': Francis Hayman and the Intersections of Word and Image." *Eighteenth-Century Fiction* 14.3–4 (2002): 465–505.

———. "A Plot Discover'd; or, The Uses of *Venice Preserv'd* within *Clarissa*." *University of Toronto Quarterly* 55.3 (1986): 219–34.

———. "Re-presenting the Body in *Pamela II*." *New Historical Literary Study: Essays on Reproducing Texts, Representing History*. Ed. Jeffrey N. Cox and Larry J. Reynolds. Princeton: Princeton UP, 1993. 151–77.

———. "Richardson's 'Speaking Pictures.'" Doody and Sabor 146–66.

Allentuck, Marcia Epstein. "Narration and Illustration: The Problem of Richardson's *Pamela*." *Philological Quarterly* 63 (1972): 874–86.

Altman, Janet Gurkin. *Epistolarity: Approaches to a Form*. Columbus: Ohio State UP, 1982.

Amberg, Anthony, ed. "Appendix 6: The Correspondence of Edward Moore." The Foundling: A Comedy *and* The Gamester: A Tragedy. By Edward Moore. Newark: U of Delaware P, 1991. 394–409.

Amis, Kingsley. *Take a Girl Like You*. London: Gollancz, 1960.

Armstrong, Nancy. *Desire and Domestic Fiction: A Political History of the Novel*. New York: Oxford UP, 1987.

Astell, Mary. *A Serious Proposal to the Ladies for the Advancement of Their True and Greatest Interest*. 1701. New York: Source Book, 1970.

Athenaeus. *The Deipnosophists*. Trans. Charles Burton Gulick. 6 vols. London: Heinemann, 1927.

Austen, Jane. *Northanger Abbey*. New York: Penguin, 1995.

———. *Persuasion*. Ed. Linda Bree. Peterborough, Ont.: Broadview, 1998.

Backscheider, Paula, and John Richetti, eds. *Popular Fiction by Women, 1660–1730: An Anthology*. Oxford: Clarendon, 1999.

Barchas, Janine, ed. [with Gordon Fulton]. *The Annotations in Lady Bradshaigh's Copy of* Clarissa. ELS Monograph Series 76. Victoria, B.C.: U of Victoria, 1998.

————. *Graphic Design, Print Culture, and the Eighteenth-Century Novel*. Cambridge: Cambridge UP, 2003.

Barker-Benfield, G. J. *The Culture of Sensibility: Sex and Society in Eighteenth-Century Britain*. Chicago: U of Chicago P, 1992.

Beebee, Thomas O. Clarissa *on the Continent: Translation and Seduction*. University Park: Pennsylvania State UP, 1990.

Behn, Aphra. *Love-Letters between a Nobleman and His Sister*. 1684, 1685, 1687. Ed. Janet Todd. Harmondsworth: Penguin, 1996.

————. *Oroonoko*. Ed. Catherine Gallagher. Boston: Bedford, 2000.

————. *The Rover. The Works of Aphra Benn*. Ed. Janet Todd. Vol. 5. Columbus: Ohio State UP, 1996. 445–521.

Bellamy, Liz. "Private Virtues, Public Vices: Commercial Morality in the Novels of Samuel Richardson." *Literature and History* 3rd ser. 5.2 (1996): 19–36.

Bender, John. *Imagining the Penitentiary: Fiction and the Architecture of Mind in Eighteenth-Century England*. Chicago: U of Chicago P, 1987.

Blair, Hugh. *Lectures on Rhetoric and Belles Lettres*. Vol. 3. Dublin, 1783. 3 vols.

Blew, James. "Chancery Master's Exhibits—Master Lynch." Class mark C. 105.5, Public Record Office, Kew, United Kingdom.

Blewett, David, ed. *Passion and Virtue: Essays on the Novels of Samuel Richardson*. Toronto: U of Toronto P, 2001.

Boswell, James. *Life of Johnson*. Ed. R. W. Chapman. World's Classics. Oxford: Oxford UP, 1980.

Brissenden, Robert F. *Virtue in Distress: Studies in the Novel of Sentiment from Richardson to Sade*. London: Macmillan, 1974.

Brown, Murray L. "Learning to Read Richardson: *Pamela*, 'Speaking Pictures,' and the 'Visual Hermeneutic.'" *Studies in the Novel* 25 (1993): 129–51.

————, ed. *Refiguring Richardson's* Clarissa. Spec. issue of *Studies in the Literary Imagination* 28.1 (1995): 1–140.

Browne, Alice. *The Eighteenth-Century Feminist Mind*. Brighton: Harvester, 1987.

Brückmann, Patricia C. "Desdemona's Strawberries and Clementina's Ark: Text, Textiles and Scripture in *Sir Charles Grandison*." *Eighteenth-Century Contexts: Historical Inquiries in Honor of Phillip Harth*. Ed. Howard D. Weinbrot, Peter J. Schakel, and Stephen L. Karian. Madison: U of Wisconsin P, 2001. 207–31.

————. "Prisons and Palaces: The Settings of *Pamela*." *Transactions of the Johnson Society of the Northwest* 6 (1973): 1–10.

Bueler, Lois E. Clarissa's *Plots*. Newark: U of Delaware P, 1994.

Buell, Lawrence. "In Pursuit of Ethics." *PMLA* 114 (1999): 7–19.

Bunyan, John. *The Pilgrim's Progress*. Pt. 1. 1678. Ed. N. H. Keeble. Oxford: Oxford UP, 1984.

Burney, Frances. *Cecilia; or, Memoirs of an Heiress*. Ed. Judy Simons. London: Virago, 1986.

————. *Cecilia; or, The Memoirs of an Heiress*. 1782. Ed. Peter Sabor and Margaret Anne Doody. World's Classics. Oxford: Oxford UP, 1988.

―――. *Evelina; or, The History of a Young Lady's Entrance into the World*. 1778. Ed. Edward A. Bloom. Introd. Vivien Jones. World's Classics. Oxford: Oxford UP, 2002.

The Cambridge Companion to the Eighteenth-Century Novel. Ed. John Richetti. Cambridge: Cambridge UP, 1996.

Carroll, John, ed. *Samuel Richardson: A Collection of Critical Essays*. Englewood Cliffs: Prentice-Hall, 1969.

Case, Alison A. *Plotting Women: Gender and Narration in the Eighteenth- and Nineteenth-Century British Novel*. Charlottesville: UP of Virginia, 1999.

Castle, Terry. *Clarissa's Ciphers: Meaning and Disruption in Richardson's* Clarissa. Ithaca: Cornell UP, 1982.

―――. *Masquerade and Civilization: The Carnivalesque in Eighteenth-Century English Culture and Fiction*. Stanford: Stanford UP, 1986.

―――. "P/B: *Pamela* as Sexual Fiction." *SEL* 22 (1982): 469–89.

Centlivre, Susanna. *A Bold Stroke for a Wife*. *The Meridian Anthology of Restoration and Eighteenth-Century Plays by Women*. Ed. Katherine M. Rogers. New York: Meridian, 1994. 185–259.

Chaber, Lois A. "A 'Fatal Attraction'? The BBC and *Clarissa*." *Eighteenth-Century Fiction* 4.3 (1992): 256–63.

―――. "'This Affecting Subject': An 'Interested' Reading of Childbearing in Two Novels by Samuel Richardson." *Eighteenth-Century Fiction* 8.2 (1996): 193–250.

Chambers, Ephraim. *Cyclopedia*. London, 1798–91.

Cheyne, George. *The Letters of Doctor George Cheyne to Samuel Richardson (1733–1743)*. Ed. Charles F. Mullett. Columbia: U of Missouri, 1943.

Chung, Ewha. *Samuel Richardson's New Nation: Paragons of the Domestic Sphere and "Native" Virtue*. New York: Lang, 1998.

Cleland, John. *Fanny Hill; or, Memoirs of a Woman of Pleasure*. London: Penguin, 1985.

―――. *Memoirs of a Woman of Pleasure*. Ed. Peter Sabor. Oxford: Oxford UP, 1985.

Clarissa. By Samuel Richardson. Adapt. David Nokes and Janet Barron. Dir. Robert Bierman. Perf. Sean Bean, Saskia Wickham. 3 episodes. BBC, 27 Nov.–11 Dec. 1991.

Clutton-Brock, A. "Description in Poetry." *Essays and Studies by Members of the English Association*. Vol. 2. Ed. H. C. Beeching. Oxford: Clarendon, 1911. 91–103.

Colley, Linda. *Britons: Forging the Nation, 1707–1837*. New Haven: Yale UP, 1992.

The Compleat Sean Bean. Ed. Winona Kent. 22 Jan. 2001. 18 May 2002 <http://compleatseanbean.com/clari.html>.

Connor, Rebecca H. "'Can You Apply Arithmetick to Every Thing?': *Moll Flanders*, William Petty, and Social Accounting." *Studies in Eighteenth-Century Culture* 27 (1998): 169–94.

Cook, Elizabeth Heckendorn. *Epistolary Bodies: Gender and Genre in the Eighteenth-Century Republic of Letters*. Stanford: Stanford UP, 1996.

Cope, Kevin. "Richardson the Advisor." *New Essays on Samuel Richardson*. Ed. Albert J. Rivero. New York: St. Martin's, 1996. 17–33.

Copeland, Edward. "Remapping London: *Clarissa* and the Woman in the Window." Doody and Sabor 51–69.

Cunningham, Michael. *The Hours*. London: Fourth Estate, 1999.

Damrosch, Leopold, Jr. *God's Plot and Man's Stories: Studies in the Fictional Imagination from Milton to Fielding*. Chicago: U of Chicago P, 1985.

Dangerous Liaisons. Dir. Stephen Frears. Warner, 1988.

Davis, Lennard J. *Factual Fictions: The Origins of the English Novel*. New York: Columbia UP, 1983.

Day, Robert Adams. *Told in Letters: Epistolary Fiction before Richardson*. Ann Arbor: U of Michigan P, 1966.

Defoe, Daniel. *Augusta Triumphans; or, The Way to Make London the Most Flourishing City in the Universe*. London: Roberts, 1728.

———. *Everybody's Business Is Nobody's Business; or, Private Abuses, Public Grievances: Exemplified in the Pride, Insolence, and Exorbitant Wages of Our Women Servants, Footmen, &c*. London: Meadows, 1725.

———. *The Fortunes and Misfortunes of the Famous Moll Flanders*. 1722. Ed. G. A. Starr. World's Classics. Oxford: Oxford UP, 1971.

———. *The Great Law of Subordination Consider'd; or, The Insolence and Unsufferable Behavior of Servants in England Duly Enquir'd Into*. London: Harding, 1724. Rpt. as *The Behaviour of Servants in England Inquired Into*. London: Whittridge, n.d.

———. *Robinson Crusoe*. 1719. Ed. J. Donald Crowley. Oxford: Oxford UP, 1981.

DeMaria, Robert, Jr., ed. *British Literature, 1640–1789: An Anthology*. 2nd ed. Oxford: Blackwell, 2001.

Dennis, John. "Remarks upon Cato." *The Critical Works of John Dennis*. Ed. Edward Niles Hooker. 2 vols. Baltimore: Johns Hopkins UP, 1943. 2: 41–80.

Dodd, William. *An Account of the Rise, Progress, and Present State of the Magdalen Hospital, for the Reception of Penitent Prostitutes. Together with Dr. Dodd's Sermons*. London, 1770.

———. "The Fourth Sermon." Jones 89–93.

Doederlein, Sue Warrick. "*Clarissa* in the Hands of the Critics." *Eighteenth-Century Studies* 16 (1983): 401–15.

Donaldson, Ian. *The Rapes of Lucretia: A Myth and Its Transformations*. Oxford: Oxford UP, 1982.

Doody, Margaret Anne. *A Natural Passion: A Study of the Novels of Samuel Richardson*. Oxford: Clarendon, 1974.

———. "Saying 'No,' Saying 'Yes': The Novels of Samuel Richardson." *Tennessee Studies in Literature* 29 (1985): 67–108.

———. *The True Story of the Novel*. New Brunswick: Rutgers UP, 1996.

Doody, Margaret Anne, and Peter Sabor. Introduction. Doody and Sabor, *Samuel Richardson* 1–8.

———, eds. *Samuel Richardson: Tercentenary Essays*. Cambridge: Cambridge UP, 1989.

Downs, Brian Westerdale. *Richardson*. London: Routledge, 1928.

"Dramatizing *Clarissa*." Clarissa: A Theatre Work. Screenplay by Margaret Anne Doody and Florian Stuber. Videocassette. Stuber-Doody Productions, 1986.

Druick, Douglas W., and Peter Cort Zegers. *Van Gogh and Gauguin: The Studio of the South*. New York: Thames, 2001.

Dryden, John. *Ovid's Epistles, Translated by Several Hands*. 1680. *The Poems of John Dryden*. Ed. James Kinsley. Vol. 1. Oxford: Clarendon, 1958. 4 vols.

Dussinger, John A. "Love and Consanguinity in Richardson's Novels." *Studies in English Literature, 1500–1900* 24.3 (1984): 513–26.

———. "Selected Bibliography: Samuel Richardson." *Eighteenth-Century Resources*. Ed. Jack Lynch. 15 June 2004. 12 July 2004 <www.c18.rutgers.edu/biblio/richardson/html>.

Eagleton, Terry. *The Rape of Clarissa: Writing, Sexuality, and Class Struggle in Samuel Richardson*. Minneapolis: U of Minnesota P, 1982.

Eaves, T. C. Duncan. "Graphic Illustration of the Novels of Samuel Richardson, 1740–1810." *Huntington Library Quarterly* 14 (1950–51): 349–83.

Eaves, T. C. Duncan, and Ben D. Kimpel. "The Composition of *Clarissa* and Its Revision before Publication." *PMLA* 83 (1968): 416–28.

———. "Richardson's Revisions of *Pamela*." *Studies in Bibliography* 20 (1967): 61–88.

———. *Samuel Richardson: A Biography*. Oxford: Clarendon, 1971.

Echlin, Lady Elizabeth. *An Alternative Ending to Richardson's* Clarissa. Ed. Dimiter Daphinoff. Bern: Francke, 1982.

Eckstein, Robert. *XML Pocket Reference*. Beijing: O'Reilly, 1999.

Erickson, Robert A. *Language of the Heart, 1600–1750*. Philadelphia: U of Pennsylvania P, 1997.

———. *Mother Midnight: Birth, Sex, and Fate in Eighteenth-Century Fiction (Defoe, Richardson, and Sterne)*. New York: AMS, 1986.

Ferguson, Frances. "Rape and the Rise of the Novel." *Representations* 20 (1987): 88–112.

Fielding, Henry. *An Apology for the Life of Mrs. Shamela Andrews*. Ed. Sheridan W. Baker. Berkeley: U of California P, 1953.

———. *An Apology for the Life of Mrs. Shamela Andrews*. Keymer and Sabor 1: 49–118.
. *The Jacobite's Journal and Related Writings*. Ed. W. B. Coley. Oxford: Clarendon, 1975.

———. *Joseph Andrews and* Shamela. Ed. Martin C. Battestin. Boston: Houghton, 1961.

———. *Joseph Andrews and* Shamela. Ed. Judith Hawley. London: Penguin, 1999.

———. *Tom Jones*. Ed. John Bender and Simon Stern. World's Classics. Oxford: Oxford UP, 1998.

Fielding, Henry, and Sarah Fielding. *The Correspondence of Henry and Sarah Fielding*. Ed. Martin C. Battestin and Clive T. Probyn. Oxford: Clarendon, 1993.

Fielding, Sarah. *Remarks on* Clarissa. Ed. Peter Sabor. Augustan Rpt. Soc. 231–2. Los Angeles: Clark Lib., 1985.

Filmer, Robert. *Patriarcha and Other Works*. Ed. Johann P. Sommerville. Cambridge: Cambridge UP, 1991.

Finneran, Richard J., ed. *The Literary Text in the Digital Age*. Ann Arbor: U of Michigan P, 1996.

Flint, Christopher. "The Anxiety of Affluence: Family and Class (Dis)order in *Pamela, or, Virtue Rewarded*." *Family Fictions: Narrative and Domestic Relations in Britain, 1688–1798*. Stanford: Stanford UP, 1998. 161–206.

Flynn, Carol Houlihan. Preface. Flynn, *Samuel Richardson* ix–xv.

———. *Samuel Richardson: A Man of Letters*. Princeton: Princeton UP, 1982.

Flynn, Carol Houlihan, and Edward Copeland, eds. *Clarissa and Her Readers: New Essays for The* Clarissa *Project*. New York: AMS, 1999.

Fowles, John. *The French Lieutenant's Woman*. London: Cape, 1969.

Frega, Donnalee. *Speaking in Hunger: Gender, Discourse, and Consumption in* Clarissa. Columbia: U of South Carolina P, 1998.

Galin, Jeffrey R., and Joan Latchaw, eds. *The Dialogic Classroom: Teachers Integrating Computer Technology, Pedagogy, and Research*. Urbana: NCTE, 1998.

Garrick, David. *The Letters of David Garrick*. Ed. David M. Little and George M. Kahrl. 3 vols. London: Oxford UP, 1963.

Genette, Gérard. *Figures of Literary Discourse*. Trans. Alan Sheridan. New York: Columbia UP, 1982.

Gildon, Charles. "The Life and Strange Surprizing Adventures of Mr. D— De F—." 1719. *Robinson Crusoe: An Authoritative Text*. By Daniel DeFoe. Ed. Michael Shinagel. New York: Norton, 1975. 277–81.

Gillis, Christina Marsden. *The Paradox of Privacy: Epistolary Form in* Clarissa. Gainesville: UP of Florida, 1984.

Gray, Thomas, "Some Remarks on the Poems of John Lydgate." *The Works of Thomas Gray in Prose and Verse*. 4 vols. Ed. Edmund Gosse. London: Macmillan, 1884. 1: 392–93.

Goldberg, Rita. *Sex and Enlightenment: Women in Richardson and Diderot*. Cambridge: Cambridge UP, 1984.

Golden, Morris. *Richardson's Characters*. Ann Arbor: U of Michigan P, 1963.

Goody, Jack. *The Development of the Family and Marriage in England*. Cambridge: Cambridge UP, 1983.

Gordon, Scott Paul. *The Power of the Passive Self in English Literature, 1640–1770*. Cambridge: Cambridge UP, 2002.

Greg, W. W. *Dramatic Documents from the Elizabethan Playhouses*. Oxford: Clarendon, 1931.

Grose, Francis. *1811 Dictionary of the Vulgar Tongue*. Fwd. Robert Cromie. Northfield: Digest, 1971.

Guest, Harriet. *Small Change: Women, Learning, Patriotism, 1750–1810*. Chicago: U of Chicago P, 2000.

Guidelines for Electronic Text Encoding and Interchange (TEI P3). 27 June 2005 <http://etext.lib.virginia.edu/standards/tei/teip3/>.

A Guide to Creating Web Sites with HTML, CGI, Java, JavaScript, Graphics. 15 Nov. 2002. <http://www.wdvl.com/Authoring/>.

Gwilliam, Tassie. *Samuel Richardson's Fictions of Gender*. Stanford: Stanford UP, 1993.

"H– J–, for a Rape, 1722." DeMaria 617–18.

Hamon, Philippe. "Rhetorical Status of the Descriptive." Trans. Patricia Baudoin. *Yale French Studies* 61 (1981): 1–26.

Hampton, Christopher. Les liaisons dangereuses, *from the Novel by Choderlos de Laclos: A Play.* London: Faber, 1985.

Hanson, L. W. *Contemporary Printed Sources for British and Irish Economic History, 1701–1750.* Cambridge: Cambridge UP, 1963.

Harold, Elliotte Rusty. *XML Bible.* Foster City: IDG, 1999.

Harris, Jocelyn. "The Influence of Richardson on *Pride and Prejudice*." *Approaches to Teaching Austen's* Pride and Prejudice. Ed. Marcia McClintock Folsom. New York: MLA, 1993. 94–99.

———. Introduction. Richardson, *Samuel Richardson's Published Commentary* 1: vii–xcv.

———. "Protean Lovelace." *Eighteenth-Century Fiction* 2.4 (1990): 327–46. Rpt. in Blewett 92–113.

———."Richardson: Original or Learned Genius?" Doody and Sabor 188–202.

———. *Samuel Richardson.* Cambridge: Cambridge UP, 1987.

Haywood, Eliza. *Anti-Pamela.* London, 1741. Keymer and Sabor, vol. 3.

———. *Fantomina; or, Love in a Maze.* DeMaria 602–16.

———. *A Present for Servants from Their Ministers, Masters, and Other Friends. And a Present for a Servant-Maid.* New York: Garland, 1985.

Heaven Scent. Screenplay by Chuck Jones. Dir. Jones. Voices perf. Mel Blanc. Warner Bros., 1956.

Hecht, J. Jean. *The Domestic Servant Class in Eighteenth-Century England.* London: Routledge, 1956.

Hill, Aaron. Letter to Samuel Richardson. *Forster Ms.* 13.3. Victoria and Albert Museum, London.

———. "Specimen of New Clarissa." Richardson, *Samuel Richardson's Published Commentary* 1: 286–311.

Hill, Bridget. *Servants: English Domestics in the Eighteenth Century.* Oxford: Clarendon, 1996.

Hill, Christopher. "Clarissa Harlowe and Her Times." *Essays in Criticism* 4 (1955): 25–40.

Hinton, Laura. "The Heroine's Subjection: Clarissa, Sadomasochism, and Natural Law." *Eighteenth-Century Studies* 32 (1999): 293–308.

Holy Smoke. Dir. Jane Campion. Miramax, 1999.

Horne, Philip. *Henry James and Revision: The New York Edition.* Oxford: Clarendon, 1990.

Hultgren, Neil. "Taking a Seat with the Best of Men: The Spatial Politeness of Sir Charles Grandison." Unpublished essay, 2001.

Hunt, Margaret R. *The Middling Sort, Commerce, Gender, and the Family in England, 1680–1740.* Berkeley: U of California P, 1996.

Hunter, J. Paul. *Before Novels: The Cultural Contexts of Eighteenth-Century Fiction.* New York: Norton, 1990.

Irigaray, Luce. *An Ethics of Sexual Difference.* Trans. Carolyn Burke and Gillian Gill. Ithaca: Cornell UP, 1993.

James, Henry. "The Art of Fiction." *The Critical Tradition: Classic Texts and Contemporary Trends*. Ed. David Richter. Boston: Bedford, 1998. 436–47.

Johnson, Claudia. *Equivocal Beings: Politics, Gender, and Sentimentality in the 1790s: Wollstonecraft, Radcliffe, Burney, Austen*. Chicago: U of Chicago P, 1995.

Johnson Samuel. *The Letters of Samuel Johnson*. Ed. Bruce Redford. Hyde edition. 5 vols. Princeton: Princeton UP, 1992–94.

———. "Preface to the English Dictionary." *Prose and Poetry*. Ed. Mona Wilson. London: Hart-Davis, 1950. 301–23.

———. *The Rambler*. Ed. W. J. Bate and Albrecht B. Strauss. New Haven: Yale UP, 1969. Vols. 3–5 of *The Yale Edition of the Works of Samuel Johnson*. 17 vols. New Haven: Yale UP, 1958–2004.

Jones, Vivien, ed. *Women in the Eighteenth Century: Constructions of Femininity*. London: Routledge, 1990.

Joyce, Michael. *Of Two Minds: Hypertext, Pedagogy, and Poetics*. Ann Arbor: U of Michigan P, 1995.

Kahn, Madeleine. *Narrative Transvestism: Rhetoric and Gender in the Eighteenth-Century English Novel*. Ithaca: Cornell UP, 1991.

Kaufmann, Linda. *Discourses of Desire: Gender, Genre, and Epistolary Fictions*. Ithaca: Cornell UP, 1986.

Kay, Carol. *Political Constructions: Defoe, Richardson, and Sterne in Relation to Hobbes, Hume, and Burke*. Ithaca: Cornell UP, 1988.

Kelly, John. *Pamela's Conduct in High Life*. Keymer and Sabor, vols. 4 and 5.

Kelsall, Malcolm. *The Great Good Place: The Country House and English Literature*. New York: Columbia UP, 1993.

Kent, Winona. *Clarissa. The Compleat Sean Bean*. 26 Mar. 2003. 8 July 2004 <http://www.compleatseanbean.com/clari.html>.

Keymer, Thomas. Introduction. Richardson, *Pamela* [ed. Keymer and Wakely]. vii–xxxiv.

———. "*Pamela*'s Fables: Aesopian Writing and Political Implication in Samuel Richardson and Sir Roger L'Estrange." *Bulletin de la Société d'Études Anglo-Américaines des XVIIIe Siècles* 41 (1995): 81–101.

———. "Parliamentary Printing, Paper Credit, and Corporate Fraud: A New Episode in Richardson's Early Career." *Eighteenth-Century Fiction* 17.2 (2005): 183–206.

———. *Richardson's* Clarissa *and the Eighteenth-Century Reader*. Cambridge: Cambridge UP, 1992.

Keymer, Thomas, and Peter Sabor, eds. *The* Pamela *Controversy: Criticism and Adaptations of Samuel Richardson's* Pamela, *1740–1750*. 6 vols. London: Pickering, 2001.

Kibbie, Ann Louise. "Sentimental Properties: *Pamela* and *Memoirs of a Woman of Pleasure*." *ELH* 58 (1991): 561–77.

Kilfeather, Siobhan. "The Rise of Richardson Criticism." Doody and Sabor 251–66.

Kinkead-Weekes, Mark. "Clarissa Restored?" *Review of English Studies* ns 10.38 (1959): 156–71.

———. *Samuel Richardson: Dramatic Novelist*. London: Methuen, 1973.

Koehler, Martha. "Epistolary Closure and Triangular Return in Richardson's *Clarissa*." *Journal of Narrative Technique* 24 (1994): 153–72.

Laclos, Choderlos de. *Les liaisons dangereuses*. Amsterdam, 1782.

Lamb, Jonathan. *The Rhetoric of Suffering: Reading the Book of Job in the Eighteenth Century*. Oxford: Clarendon, 1995.

Lambert, Sheila. *Bills and Acts: Legislative Procedure in Eighteenth-Century England*. Cambridge: Cambridge UP, 1971.

———, ed. *House of Commons Sessional Papers of the Eighteenth Century*. Wilmington: SR Scholarly Resources, 1976. 2 vols.

———. "Printing for the House of Commons in the Eighteenth Century." *Library* 23 (1968): 25–46.

Landow, George P. *Hypertext 2.0: The Convergence of Contemporary Critical Theory and Technology*. Baltimore: Johns Hopkins UP, 1997.

———. *Hyper/Text/Theory*. Baltimore: Johns Hopkins UP, 1994.

Lee, Joy Kyunghae. "The Commodification of Virtue: Chastity and the Virginal Body in Richardson's *Clarissa*." *Eighteenth Century: Theory and Interpretation* 36 (1995): 38–54.

Letter to Charles Rivington. 15 Nov. 1740. *Forster Ms*. 16.1. Victoria and Albert Museum, London.

Lewis, Matthew. *The Monk*. 1796. Ed. Howard Anderson. Introd. Emma McEvoy. World's Classics. Oxford: Oxford UP, 1998.

Locke, John. *Some Thoughts concerning Education*. Ed. John W. Yolton and Jean S. Yolton. Oxford: Clarendon, 1989.

———. *Two Treatises on Government*. Ed. Peter Laslett. Cambridge: Cambridge UP, 1991.

London, April. *Women and Property in the Eighteenth-Century English Novel*. Cambridge: Cambridge UP, 1999.

Lovell, Terry. *Consuming Fiction*. London: Verso, 1987. *Literature Online*. <http://lion.chadwyck.com>.

Lowe, Solomon. Letter to Samuel Richardson. 26 June 1748. *Forster Ms*. 15.2. Victoria and Albert Museum, London.

Mancoff, Debra N. *Sunflowers*. Chicago: Art Inst., 2001.

Manley, Delarivier. *The Adventures of Rivella*. London, 1715.

———. *The Memoirs of Europe*. London: Morphew, 1710.

———. *The New Atalantis*. London: Morphew, 1710.

Markley, Robert. "Recent Studies in Restoration and Eighteenth-Century Literature." *Studies in English Literature* 37 (1997): 637–72.

Marks, Sylvia Kasey. *Sir Charles Grandison: The Compleat Conduct Book*. Lewisburg: Bucknell UP, 1986.

Maslen, Keith. *An Early London Printing House at Work: Studies in the Bowyer Ledgers*. New York: Bibliog. Soc. of Amer., 1993.

———. "Samuel Richardson as Printer: Expanding the Canon." *Order and Connexion: Studies in Bibliography and Book History. Selected Papers from the Munby Seminar, Cambridge, July 1994*. Ed. R. C. Alston. Cambridge: Brewer, 1997. 1–16.

————. *Samuel Richardson of London, Printer: A Study of His Printing Based on Ornament Use and Business Accounts*. Dunedin: U of Otago, Dept. of English, 2001. <www.otago.ac.nz>.

————. "Samuel Richardson's Private Acts." *Bibliographical Society of Australia and New Zealand Bulletin* 19 (1995): 3–14.

Maslen, Keith, and John Lancaster, eds. *The Bowyer Ledgers: The Printing Accounts of William Bowyer Father and Son Reproduced on Microfiche, with a Checklist of Bowyer Printing 1699–1777, a Commentary, Indexes, and Appendixes*. London: Bibliog. Soc.; New York: Bibliog. Soc. of Amer., 1991.

McEwan, Ian. *Atonement*. London: Cape, 2001.

McGann, Jerome. *Radiant Textuality: Literature after the World Wide Web*. New York: Palgrave-St. Martin's, 2001.

McKendrick, Neil, John Brewer, and J. H. Plumb. *The Birth of a Consumer Society: The Commercialization of Eighteenth-Century England*. London: Europa, 1982.

McKeon, Michael. "Historicizing Patriarchy: The Emergence of Gender Difference in England, 1660 to 1760." *ECS* 28 (1995): 295–322.

————. *The Origins of the English Novel, 1600–1740*. Baltimore: Johns Hopkins UP, 1987.

McKillop, Alan D. *Samuel Richardson, Printer and Novelist*. Chapel Hill: U of North Carolina P, 1936.

McMaster, Juliet. "Sir Charles Grandison: Richardson on Body and Character." *Eighteenth-Century Fiction* 1 (1989): 83–102.

Memoirs of the Life of Lady H— the Celebrated Pamela. From Her Birth to the Present Time. London, 1741.

Miller, Nancy K. *The Heroine's Text: Readings in the French and English Novel, 1722–1782*. New York: Columbia UP, 1980.

Milton, John. *Paradise Lost. John Milton: The Complete Poems and Major Prose*. Ed. Merritt Y. Hughes, New York: Odyssey, 1957. 206–469.

Moglen, Helene. "*Clarissa* and the Pornographic Imagination." Moglen, *Trauma*. 57–85.

————. *The Trauma of Gender: A Feminist View of the English Novel*. Berkeley: U of California P, 2001.

Moretti, Franco. *Atlas of the European Novel, 1800–1900*. London: Verso, 1998.

Morreale, Mark James. Assignment. "Clarissa Web Project." 2 June 2005 <http://library.marist.edu/faculty-web-pages/morreale/Eighteenth-Century/18c-F02-home.htm>. Path: Clarissa Web Project.

————. Results. "Clarissa Web Project." 2 June 2005 <http://library.marist.edu/faculty-web-pages/morreale/morreale-index.htm>. Path: Student Projects; Clarissa Project.

————, ed. *Samuel Richardson (1689–1761)*. June 2001. James A. Cannavino Lib., Marist Coll. 15 Nov. 2002. <http://library.marist.edu/diglib/english/englishliterature/17th-18thc-authors/richardson-samuel.htm>.

Mullan, John. *Sentiment and Sociability: The Language of Feeling in the Eighteenth Century*. Oxford: Clarendon, 1988.

Murray, Janet H. *Hamlet on the Holodeck: The Future of Narrative in Cyberspace*. New York: Free, 1997.

Myer, Valerie Grosvenor, ed. *Samuel Richardson: Passion and Prudence*. London: Vision, 1986.

Norrman, Ralf, and Jon Haarberg. *Nature and Language: A Semiotic Study of Cucurbits in Literature*. London: Routledge, 1980.

Nussbaum, Felicity. "Polygamy, Pamela, and the Prerogative of Empire." *The Consumption of Culture, 1600–1800: Image, Object, Text*. Ed. Ann Bermingham and John Brewer. New York: Routledge, 1995. 217–36.

Ogden, Daryl. "Richardson's Narrative Space-Off: Freud, Vision, and the (Heterosexual) Problem of Reading *Clarissa*." *Literature and Psychology* 42 (1996): 37–52.

Otway, Thomas. *Venice Preserv'd: or, A Plot Discover'd*. London, 1682. 15 Nov. 2002. <http://www.bibliomania.com/0/6/275/1878/frameset.html>.

Ovid. *Metamorphoses*. Ed. William S. Anderson. Vol. 2. Norman: U of Oklahoma P, 1972.

Partridge, Eric. *A Dictionary of Slang and Unconventional English*. Vol. 1. London: Routledge, 1961.

Pateman, Carole. *The Sexual Contract*. Stanford: Stanford UP, 1988.

Perry, Ruth. "Clarissa's Daughters; or, The History of Innocence Betrayed: How Women Writers Rewrote Richardson." *Women's Writing* 1.1 (1994): 5–24.

———. *Novel Relations: The Transformation of Kinship in English Literature and Culture, 1748–1818*. Cambridge: Cambridge UP, 2004.

Pfaffenberger, Bryan. *Web Publishing with XML in 6 Easy Steps*. Boston: Academic, 1999.

Pierson, Robert Craig. "The Revisions of Richardson's *Sir Charles Grandison*." *Studies in Bibliography* 21 (1968): 163–89.

Pinter, Harold. *The Screenplay of* The French Lieutenant's Woman. London: Cape, 1981.

Plato. *The Symposium*. Trans. Christopher Gill. Harmondsworth: Penguin, 1999.

Pliny. *Natural History*. Trans. W. H. S. Jones. Vol. 6. Cambridge: Harvard UP, 1961.

Plotinus. *The Enneads*. Trans. Stephen MacKenna. 4th ed. Rev. B. S. Page. London: Faber, 1969.

Pope, Alexander. "Eloisa to Abelard." *Alexander Pope: Selected Poetry*. Ed. Douglas Grant. Penguin Poetry Lib. New York: Viking, 1985. 66–77.

———. "Essay on Man." Essay on Man *and Other Poems*. New York: Dover, 1994. 45–79.

———. The Rape of the Lock *and Other Poems*. 3rd ed. London: Methuen, 1962.

Porter, Roy. *English Society in the Eighteenth Century*. London: Penguin, 1990.

Povey, Charles. *The Virgin in Eden; or, The State of Innocency*. London, 1741.

Pretty Woman. Dir. Garry Marshall. Touchstone, 1990.

Quarles, Francis. *Emblemes*. 1635. Introd. A. D. Cousins. Scholars' Facsimiles and Reprints 458. Delmar: Scholars', 1991.

———. *Hieroglyphikes*. 1638. Sel. and ed. John Horden. English Emblem Books 14. Menston, Eng.: Scolar, 1969.

Quinn, Vincent. "Libertines and Libertinism." *Gay Histories and Cultures: An Encyclopedia*. Ed. George Haggerty. New York: Garland, 2000. 540–41.

Radcliffe, Ann. *The Italian; or, The Confessional of the Black Penitents: A Romance.* 1797. Ed. Frederick Garber. World's Classics. Oxford: Oxford UP, 1989.

———. *The Romance of the Forest.* 1791. Ed. Chloe Chard. World's Classics. Oxford: Oxford UP, 1992.

Rain, D. C. "Deconstructing Richardson: Terry Castle and *Clarissa's Ciphers.*" *English Studies* 76 (1995): 520–31.

Raynie, Stephen A. "Hayman and Gravelot's Anti-Pamela Designs for Richardson's Octavo Edition of *Pamela I and II.*" *Eighteenth-Century Life* 23.3 (1999): 77–93.

"Reading *Clarissa* in Real Time." Ed. Ellen Moody and Jim Moody. 23 May 1999. 18 May 2002 <http//www.jimandellen.org/showclarydates.html>.

Rich, Adrienne. "When We Dead Awaken." *Adrienne Rich's Poetry and Prose.* Ed. Barbara Charlesworth Gelpi and Albert Gelpi. New York: Norton, 1975. 166–77.

Richardson, Samuel. *Aesop's Fables.* London, 1740.

———. *The Apprentice's Vade Mecum; or, Young Man's Pocket Companion.* 1734. Introd. Alan Dugald McKillop. Augustan Rpt. Soc. 167–70. Los Angeles: U of California P, 1975.

———. *The Cambridge Edition of the Correspondence of Samuel Richardson.* Ed. Thomas Keymer and Peter Sabor. Cambridge: Cambridge UP, forthcoming.

———. *Clarissa; or, The History of a Young Lady.* 1st ed. 7 vols. London, 1748.

———. *Clarissa; or, The History of a Young Lady: Comprehending the Most Important Concerns of Private Life.* 1748. Based on English Short Title Catalogue. *Eighteenth-Century Collections Online.* InfoTrac. <http://galenet.galegroup.com/servlet/ECCO>.

———. *Clarissa.* 1st ed. 1747–48. *Literature Online.* <http://lion.chadwyck.com>.

———. *Clarissa; or, The History of a Young Lady.* 3rd ed. 8 vols. London, 1751.

———. *Clarissa.* 3rd ed. 1751. *Literature Online.* <http://lion.chadwyck.com>.

———. *Clarissa; or, The History of a Young Lady.* Ed. George Sherburn. Abr. ed. Boston: Houghton, 1962.

———. *Clarissa; or, The History of a Young Lady.* Ed. Angus Ross. London: Penguin, 1985.

———. *Clarissa; or, The History of a Young Lady.* 1751. 3rd ed. Introd. Florian Stuber. The *Clarissa* Project. 8 vols. New York: AMS, 1990.

———. *The Correspondence of Samuel Richardson.* Ed. Anna Laetitia Barbauld. 6 vols. 1804. New York: AMS, 1966.

———. *Familiar Letters on Important Occasions.* 1741. Ed Brian Downs. London: Routledge, 1928.

———. *The History of Pamela; or, Virtue Rewarded. Abridged from the Works of Samuel Richardson, Esq.* London: Newbery, 1769, 1790.

———. *The History of Sir Charles Grandison.* Ed. Jocelyn Harris. London: Oxford UP, 1972. Rpt 1986. Otago, 2001. 3 parts.

———. *Pamela; or, Virtue Rewarded.* 6th ed. 4 vols. London, 1742. Corr. ed. *Literature Online.* <http://lion.chadwyck.com>.

———. *Pamela; or, Virtue Rewarded.* Ed. William M. Sale, Jr. New York: Norton, 1958.

———. *Pamela; or, Virtue Rewarded.* Ed. T. C. Duncan Eaves and Ben Kimpel. Riverside Edition. Boston: Houghton, 1971.

———. *Pamela. Pamela* [and] *Shamela.* Ed. S. Field. New York: New Amer. Lib., 1980.

———. *Pamela; or, Virtue Rewarded.* Ed. Peter Sabor. Introd. Margaret Anne Doody. Harmondsworth: Penguin, 1980.

———. *Pamela; or, Virtue Rewarded. 1740.* Ed. Thomas Keymer and Alice Wakely. World's Classics. Oxford: Oxford UP, 2001.

———. *Pamela's Conduct in High Life.* [*Pamela II*]. London: Ward, 1741.

———. *The Richardson-Stinstra Correspondence and Stinstra's Prefaces to* Clarissa. Ed. William C. Slattery. Carbondale: Southern Illinois UP, 1969.

———. *Samuel Richardson's Published Commentary on* Clarissa *1747–65.* Gen. ed. Florian Stuber. Assoc. ed. Margaret Doody. Textual coord. Jim Springer Borck. Vol. 1. *Prefaces, Postscripts, and Related Writings.* Ed. Thomas Keymer. Introd. Jocelyn Harris. Vol. 2. *Letters and Passages Restored from the Original Manuscripts of Clarissa.* 1751. Introd. Peter Sabor. Bibliog. essay O. M. Brack. Vol. 3. *A Collection of the Moral and Instructive Sentiments, Maxims, Cautions, and Reflections, Contained in the Histories of* Pamela, Clarissa, *and* Sir Charles Grandison. 1755. Introd. John A. Dussinger. Afterword Ann Jessie Van Sant. London: Pickering, 1998. 3 vols.

———. *A Seasonable Examination of the Pleas and Pretensions of the Proprietors of, and Subscribers to, the Play-houses.* London: Cooper, 1735.

———. *Selected Letters of Samuel Richardson.* Ed. John Carroll. Oxford: Clarendon, 1964.

Richetti, John. *The English Novel in History, 1700–1780.* London: Routledge, 1998.

———. "Richardson's Dramatic Art in *Clarissa.*" *British Theatre and the Other Arts, 1660–1800.* Ed. Shirley Strum Kenny. Washington: Folger Shakespeare Lib.; London: Assoc. Univ. P, 1984. 288–308.

Rivero, Albert J. "The Place of Sally Godfrey in Richardson's *Pamela.*" *Eighteenth-Century Fiction* 6.1 (1993): 29–46.

———. Preface. *New Essays on Samuel Richardson.* Ed. Rivero. New York: St. Martin's, 1996. vii–viii.

Rogers, Pat. "Lines of Cultural Force in the Age of Richardson." Doody and Sabor 203–22.

Ross, Angus. Introduction. Richardson, *Clarissa* [ed. Ross] 15–26.

Rothstein, Eric. "The Framework of *Shamela.*" *ELH* 35 (1968): 381–402.

Sabor, Peter. "The Cooke-Everyman Edition of *Pamela.*" *Library* 32 (1977): 360–66.

———. Introduction. Richardson, *Samuel Richardson's Published Commentary* 2: vii–xxxviii.

———. "Note on the Text." Richardson, *Pamela* [ed. Sabor] 25–26.

———. "Richardson's Continuation of *Pamela*: A Chronology of the Early Editions." *Notes and Queries* ns 26.6 (1979): 31–32.

Saintsbury, George. "The Four Wheels of the Novel Wain." *The English Novel.* London: Dent, 1913. 8 Dec. 2005 <http://www.gutenberg.org/files/14469/14469-h/14469-h.htm>.

Sale, William Merritt, Jr. *Samuel Richardson: A Bibliographical Record of His Literary Career with Historical Notes*. New Haven: Yale UP, 1936.

———. *Samuel Richardson: Master Printer*. Ithaca: Cornell UP, 1950.

Schellenberg, Betty A. "Enclosing the Immovable: Structuring Social Authority in *Pamela 2*." *Eighteenth-Century Fiction* 4. 1(1991): 27–42.

Schor, Hilary. "Notes of a Libertine Daughter: *Clarissa*, Feminism and the Rise of the Novel." *Critical History: The Career of Ian Watt*. Ed. Bruce Thompson, Ryan Johnson, and Laura McGrane. Spec. issue of *Stanford Humanities Review* 8.1 (2000): 94–117.

Scott, Sarah. *Millenium Hall*. 1762. Ed. Gary Kelly. Peterborough, Ont.: Broadview, 1995.

Sherburn, George. Introduction. Richardson, *Clarissa* [ed. Sherburn] i–xxi.

Shesgreen, Sean, ed. *Engravings by Hogarth: 101 Prints*. New York: Dover, 1973.

Simpson, Anthony E. "'The Blackmail Myth' and the Prosecution of Rape and Its Attempt in 18th-Century London: The Creation of a Legal Tradition." *Journal of Criminal Law and Criminology* 77 (1986): 101–50.

Sinclair, Upton. *Another Pamela; or, Virtue Still Rewarded*. New York: Viking, 1950.

Smith, Alexander. "Madam Clark, Mistress to the Earl of Rochester." 1716. *Rochesteriana*. Ed. Johannes Prinz. Leipzig: n. pub., 1926. 17–21.

Smith, Charlotte. *Emmeline, the Orphan of the Castle*. 1788. London: Oxford UP, 1971.

Snitow, Ann. "Mass Market Romance: Pornography for Women Is Different." *Radical History Review* 20 (1979): 141–61.

Spacks, Patricia Meyer. *Desire and Truth: Functions of Plot in Eighteenth-Century English Novels*. Chicago: U of Chicago P, 1990.

Staves, Susan. "Fielding and the Comedy of Attempted Rape." *History, Gender, and Eighteenth-Century Literature*. Ed. Beth Fowkes Tobin. Athens: U of Georgia P, 1994. 86–112.

Stephanson, Raymond. "Richardson's 'Nerves': The Physiology of Sensibility in *Clarissa*." *Journal of the History of Ideas* 49 (1988): 267–85.

Stephen, Leslie. "Richardson's Novels." *Hours in a Library*. Vol. 1. London: Smith, 1892. 46–93. 3 vols.

Stillinger, Jack. *Coleridge and Textual Instability: The Multiple Versions of the Major Poems*. New York: Oxford UP, 1994.

Straub, Kristina. "Reconstructing the Gaze: Voyeurism in Richardson's *Pamela*." *Studies in Eighteenth-Century Culture* 18 (1988): 419–31.

Stretzer, Thomas. *A New Description of Merryland*. London, 1740.

Stuber, Florian. "Clarissa and Her World: Form and Content in Richardson's *Clarissa*." Diss. Columbia U, 1980.

———. "Teaching *Pamela*." Doody and Sabor 8–22.

Sussman, Charlotte. "'I Wonder Whether Poor Miss Sally Godfrey Be Living or Dead': The Married Woman and the Rise of the Novel." *Diacritics* 20.1 (1990): 88–102.

Sutherland, Kathryn, ed. *Electronic Text: Investigations in Method and Theory*. Oxford: Clarendon, 1997.

Swift, Jonathan. *The Battle of the Books. Writings of Jonathan Swift*. Ed. William Piper and Robert A. Greenberg. New York: Norton, 1973.

———. *Directions to Servants in General*. London: Dodsley, 1745.

Take a Girl Like You. Dir. Jonathan Miller. Videocasette. Albion, 1970.

Take a Girl Like You. Dir. Nick Hurran. BBC. WGBH, Boston. 2000.

Taylor, Jeremy. *The Rule and Exercises of Holy Dying*. London, 1651.

Thompson, James. *Models of Value: Eighteenth-Century Political Economy and the Novel*. Durham: Duke UP, 1996.

Tom Jones. By Henry Fielding. Dir. Metin Hüseyin. A & E Home Video. BBC, 1998.

Traugott, John. "*Clarissa's* Richardson: An Essay to Find the Reader." *English Literature and the Age of Disguise*. Ed. Maximillian E. Novak. Berkeley: U of California P, 1977. 157–203.

Turner, James Grantham. "The Properties of Libertinism." *Eighteenth-Century Life* 9 (1985): 75–87.

Vane, Frances. "The Memoirs of a Lady of Quality." *The Adventures of Peregrine Pickle*. 1751. By Tobias Smollett. Ed. James L. Clifford and Paul-Gabriel Boucé. Oxford: Oxford UP, 1983. 432–539.

Van Ghent, Dorothy. *The English Novel: Form and Function*. New York: Holt, 1953.

Van Marter, Shirley. "Richardson's Revisions of *Clarissa* in the Second Edition." *Studies in Bibliography* 26 (1973): 107–32.

———. "Richardson's Revisions of *Clarissa* in the Third and Fourth Editions." *Studies in Bibliography* 28 (1975): 119–52.

Van Sant, Ann Jessie. *Eighteenth-Century Sensibility and the Novel: The Senses in Social Context*. Cambridge: Cambridge UP, 1993.

Vermillion, Mary. "*Clarissa* and the Marriage Act." *Eighteenth-Century Fiction* 10 (1997): 395–412.

W—., J—, esq. *Pamela; or, The Fair Impostor. A Poem in Five Cantas*. Dublin, 1743. Keymer and Sabor 1: 256–57.

Wagner, Peter. "Introduction: Ekphrasis, Icontexts, and Intermediality—the State(s) of the Art(s)." *Icons-Texts-Iconotexts: Essays on Ekphrasis and Intermediality*. Ed. Wagner. Berlin: De Gruyter, 1966. 1–40.

Wall, Cynthia. "The Spaces of *Clarissa* in Text and Film." *The Eighteenth Century in Film*. Ed. Robert Mayer. Cambridge: Cambridge UP, 2002. 106–22.

Warner, William Beatty. *Licensing Entertainment: The Elevation of Novel Reading in Britain, 1684–1750*. Berkeley: U of California P, 1998.

———. *Reading* Clarissa: *The Struggles of Interpretation*. New Haven: Yale UP, 1979.

Watt, Ian. *The Rise of the Novel*. Berkeley: U of California P, 1957.

Webb, R. K. *Modern England from the Eighteenth Century to the Present*. New York: Harper, 1980.

Wilkes, Wetenhall. *A Letter of Genteel and Moral Advice to a Young Lady*. 1740. Jones 29–35.

Williams, Gordon. *A Dictionary of Sexual Language and Imagery in Shakespearean and Stuart Literature*. 3 vols. London: Athlone, 1994.

Wilt, Judith. "He Could Go No Farther: A Modest Proposal about Lovelace and Clarissa." *PMLA* 92 (1977): 19–32.

Wither, George. *A Collection of Emblemes.* 1635. Sel. and ed. John Horden. English Emblem Books 12. Menston, Eng.: Scolar, 1968.

———. *A Collection of Emblemes.* 1635. Introd. Michael Bath. Aldershot, Eng.: Scolar, c.1989.

Wolff, Cynthia Griffin. *Samuel Richardson and the Eighteenth-Century Puritan Character.* Hamden: Archon, 1972.

Wollstonecraft, Mary. *A Vindication of the Rights of Women.* 1792. Ed. Carol H. Poston. New York: Norton, 1988.

Woolf, Virginia. *Mrs. Dalloway.* Harmondsworth: Penguin, 1964.

———. *A Room of One's Own.* London: Triad, 1984.

Woolley, Hannah. *The Gentlewomans Companion; or, A Guide to the Female Sex.* London, 1673.

World Wide Web Consortium (W3C). 15 Nov. 2002 <http://www.w3.org/>.

Young, Edward. *The Correspondence of Edward Young.* Ed. Henry Pettit. Oxford: Clarendon, 1971.

Young, Michael J. *Step by Step XML.* Redmond: Microsoft, 2000.

Yount, Janet Aikins. Home page. 23 June 2004. 14 July 2004 <http://www.unh.edu/english/faculty/Yount/pamela_illustrations.html>.

Zimmerman, Everett. *The Boundaries of Fiction: History and the Eighteenth-Century British Novel.* Ithaca: Cornell UP, 1996.

Zomchick, John P. *Family and the Law in Eighteenth-Century Fiction: The Public Conscience in the Private Sphere.* Cambridge: Cambridge UP, 1993.

INDEX

Modern Language Association of America

Approaches to Teaching World Literature

Joseph Gibaldi, series editor

Dramas of Euripides. Ed. Robin Mitchell-Boyask. 2002.

Faulkner's The Sound and the Fury. Ed. Stephen Hahn and Arthur F. Kinney. 1996.

Flaubert's Madame Bovary. Ed. Laurence M. Porter and Eugene F. Gray. 1995.

García Márquez's One Hundred Years of Solitude. Ed. María Elena de Valdés and Mario J. Valdés. 1990.

Gilman's "The Yellow Wall-Paper" and Herland. Ed. Denise D. Knight and Cynthia J. Davis. 2003.

Goethe's Faust. Ed. Douglas J. McMillan. 1987.

Gothic Fiction: The British and American Traditions. Ed. Diane Long Hoeveler and Tamar Heller. 2003.

Hebrew Bible as Literature in Translation. Ed. Barry N. Olshen and Yael S. Feldman. 1989.

Homer's Iliad *and* Odyssey. Ed. Kostas Myrsiades. 1987.

Ibsen's A Doll House. Ed. Yvonne Shafer. 1985.

Henry James's Daisy Miller *and* The Turn of the Screw. Ed. Kimberly C. Reed and Peter G. Beidler. 2005.

Works of Samuel Johnson. Ed. David R. Anderson and Gwin J. Kolb. 1993.

Joyce's Ulysses. Ed. Kathleen McCormick and Erwin R. Steinberg. 1993.

Kafka's Short Fiction. Ed. Richard T. Gray. 1995.

Keats's Poetry. Ed. Walter H. Evert and Jack W. Rhodes. 1991.

Kingston's The Woman Warrior. Ed. Shirley Geok-lin Lim. 1991.

Lafayette's The Princess of Clèves. Ed. Faith E. Beasley and Katharine Ann Jensen. 1998.

Works of D. H. Lawrence. Ed. M. Elizabeth Sargent and Garry Watson. 2001.

Lessing's The Golden Notebook. Ed. Carey Kaplan and Ellen Cronan Rose. 1989.

Mann's Death in Venice *and Other Short Fiction*. Ed. Jeffrey B. Berlin. 1992.

Medieval English Drama. Ed. Richard K. Emmerson. 1990.

Melville's Moby-Dick. Ed. Martin Bickman. 1985.

Metaphysical Poets. Ed. Sidney Gottlieb. 1990.

Miller's Death of a Salesman. Ed. Matthew C. Roudané. 1995.

Milton's Paradise Lost. Ed. Galbraith M. Crump. 1986.

Molière's Tartuffe *and Other Plays*. Ed. James F. Gaines and Michael S. Koppisch. 1995.

Momaday's The Way to Rainy Mountain. Ed. Kenneth M. Roemer. 1988.

Montaigne's Essays. Ed. Patrick Henry. 1994.

Novels of Toni Morrison. Ed. Nellie Y. McKay and Kathryn Earle. 1997.

Murasaki Shikibu's The Tale of Genji. Ed. Edward Kamens. 1993.

Pope's Poetry. Ed. Wallace Jackson and R. Paul Yoder. 1993.

Proust's Fiction and Criticism. Ed. Elyane Dezon-Jones and Inge Crosman Wimmers. 2003.

Novels of Samuel Richardson. Ed. Lisa Zunshine and Jocelyn Harris. 2006.

Rousseau's Confessions *and* Reveries of the Solitary Walker. Ed. John C. O'Neal and Ourida Mostefai. 2003.

Shakespeare's Hamlet. Ed. Bernice W. Kliman. 2001.

Shakespeare's King Lear. Ed. Robert H. Ray. 1986.

Shakespeare's Othello. Ed. Peter Erickson and Maurice Hunt. 2005.

Shakespeare's Romeo and Juliet. Ed. Maurice Hunt. 2000.

Shakespeare's The Tempest *and Other Late Romances.* Ed. Maurice Hunt. 1992.

Shelley's Frankenstein. Ed. Stephen C. Behrendt. 1990.

Shelley's Poetry. Ed. Spencer Hall. 1990.

Sir Gawain and the Green Knight. Ed. Miriam Youngerman Miller and Jane Chance. 1986.

Spenser's Faerie Queene. Ed. David Lee Miller and Alexander Dunlop. 1994.

Stendhal's The Red and the Black. Ed. Dean de la Motte and Stirling Haig. 1999.

Sterne's Tristram Shandy. Ed. Melvyn New. 1989.

Stowe's Uncle Tom's Cabin. Ed. Elizabeth Ammons and Susan Belasco. 2000.

Swift's Gulliver's Travels. Ed. Edward J. Rielly. 1988.

Thoreau's Walden *and Other Works.* Ed. Richard J. Schneider. 1996.

Tolstoy's Anna Karenina. Ed. Liza Knapp and Amy Mandelker. 2003.

Vergil's Aeneid. Ed. William S. Anderson and Lorina N. Quartarone. 2002.

Voltaire's Candide. Ed. Renée Waldinger. 1987.

Whitman's Leaves of Grass. Ed. Donald D. Kummings. 1990.

Woolf's To the Lighthouse. Ed. Beth Rigel Daugherty and Mary Beth Pringle. 2001.

Wordsworth's Poetry. Ed. Spencer Hall, with Jonathan Ramsey. 1986.

Wright's Native Son. Ed. James A. Miller. 1997.